SOCIAL THEORY IN POPULAR CULTURE

This book is dedicated to Grace

Social Theory in Popular Culture

Lee Barron

Published by
PALGRAVE MACMILLAN

Palgrave Macmillan in the UK is an imprint of Macmillan Publishers Limited, registered in England, company number 785998, of Houndmills, Basingstoke, Hampshire RG21 6XS.

Palgrave Macmillan in the US is a division of St Martin's Press LLC, 175 Fifth Avenue, New York, NY 10010.

Palgrave Macmillan is the global academic imprint of the above companies and has companies and representatives throughout the world.

Palgrave® and Macmillan® are registered trademarks in the United States, the United Kingdom, Europe and other countries

ISBN 978–0–230–28498–2 hardback
ISBN 978–0–230–28499–9 paperback

This book is printed on paper suitable for recycling and made from fully managed and sustained forest sources. Logging, pulping and manufacturing processes are expected to conform to the environmental regulations of the country of origin.

A catalogue record for this book is available from the British Library.

10   9   8   7   6   5   4   3   2   1
22 21 20 19 18 17 16 15 14 13

Printed and bound in Great Britain by
CPI Antony Rowe, Chippenham and Eastbourne

Contents

Preface

As the title of this book suggests, its theme is not popular culture and social theory, but social theory *in* popular culture. As such, the book is neither simply an introductory text to the major figures and theories that comprise what has now been dubbed 'cultural studies' nor is at an introductory approach to classical sociological theorists and theories. Rather, it is a book that combines these areas in an active manner and which reiterates the spirit of C. Wright Mills' conception of the sociological imagination. Although the book does arguably introduce a range of ideas and is not predicated upon the reader having any prior knowledge of Marx, Weber, Durkheim, Simmel, Adorno, Gilman, Barthes, or the principles underpinning neoliberalism, it is intended to do more than this.

Social Theory in Popular Culture aligns classic theorists and ideas with examples drawn from popular culture in order to identify and explain the major points associated with them, but then demonstrates the ways in which these ideas can be located within a range of contemporary cultural forms, from hip- hop music, teen cinema, fashion and celebrity, to television, sport, tattoo designs and the capitalism-revering fiction of Ayn Rand. The motivation for this approach is to illustrate the major precepts of each theorist/theory/approach and to exhibit the currency of these ideas, most of which form the foundations of sociology or can be considered to be 'classic'. As such, the book encourages readers simultaneously to understand and apply classic sociology, and, crucially, to begin to engage in this process themselves in relation to other theorists and ideas and alternative examples – the essence of Mills' framework for developing intellectual craftsmanship and cultivating a sociological imagination.

The examples drawn from popular culture are of my choosing, as are the theorists and bodies of thought discussed. Thus I make no claims to being exhaustive, nor did I intend to be. The examples cover the major figures associated with early sociological thought and address many of the salient issues that underpin sociological inquiry, and if readers can think of omissions and further examples then the book has done its job. I want readers to locate further examples of their own and subsequently deepen their understanding of theory.

Social theory should not be a set of ideas to be understood by students as only a core part of the general course of a sociological education, but rather, it is a potent and rich set of social blueprints that must be grappled with, criticized and applied to the world around us, be it with regard to political events or those that come to us during our consumption of popular culture. That is the spirit which infuses this book and the motivation for its production.

LEE BARRON

Acknowledgements

I would like to thank students on the 'Understanding Through Media' module at Northumbria University who gave supportive feedback to many of the ideas subsequently developed in the book, and to the Arts and Social Sciences students who kindly discussed the symbolic meaning of their tattoo designs with me in a series of interviews.

I would also like to thank Dr John Armitage for his encouragement and advice from the beginning of the project. I must also thank Anna Reeve and Esther Croom from Palgrave Macmillan for their continual support and patience throughout the preparation and writing of the book, and Keith Povey for his invaluable editorial guidance.

LEE BARRON

Introduction

Every student of sociology rapidly becomes familiar with a litany of names, a roll call of classic theorists that invariably begins with Karl Marx, Émile Durkheim and Max Weber, then extends to Herbert Spencer, Georg Simmel, George Herbert Mead, Talcott Parsons, Herbert Blumer, C. Wright Mills, or Charlotte Perkins Gilman. With each name comes a theoretical approach that is distinctive and which makes each name unique in the progressive development of social theories: those blueprints that offer explanations of why things are as they are (and how they might be changed). Furthermore, with each name comes a collection of key texts students must grapple with to discern what these blueprints are, such as *Capital*, *The Division of Labour in Society*, *The Protestant Ethic and the Spirit of Capitalism*, *The Sociological Imagination*, and *Women and Economics*. But, although such texts have formed the bedrock of sociology and sociological enquiry, they are also considered classics because they were written many years ago and in some instances are well over a century old. So, why continue to read them? Why give these now long-dead thinkers such primacy? Should we not simply pass quickly over them, acknowledge their legacy but move on to Anthony Giddens, Michel Foucault, Jean-François Lyotard, Jacques Derrida, Jürgen Habermas, Zygmunt Bauman, Jean Baudrillard, Dorothy Smith, Richard Sennett, Pierre Bourdieu, Judith Butler, Manuel Castells, Donna Haraway, Ulrich Beck, or Harrison White? After all, these are theorists who have analysed (and in some instances continue to analyse) core aspects of society that remain readily observable, such as the impact of globalization on politics and economics, and the social effects of technology and media.

In his book, *Social Theory: A Historical Introduction*, Alex Callinicos points to two challenges facing his enterprise of returning to the foundations of sociology: first, that social theory, especially classic social theory, is considered an outdated or old-fashioned subject; and second, social theory has been an increasingly marginalized subject in the wake of the popularity of cultural studies. However, the relationship between classic sociological theory and cultural studies need not be problematic. Quite the reverse: they go together in a dynamic fashion when related to the subject of much cultural analysis – popular culture. The issue of what culture is, and by extension what popular culture is, is a central factor within the academic analysis of the subject and typically includes discussions of the following ideas:

- the apparent division between high and low culture;
- popular culture as that which remains once the properties of high or 'elite' culture are defined (art, ballet, opera, classical/symphonic music, etc);
- popular culture as the result of the development of a mass media or mass communication system and set of institutions;
- popular culture as just that, i.e. populist culture, ways of living that emerge from folk culture;
- popular culture as the result of negotiations between the 'people' and the forces of authority;
- popular culture as the result of a complex fusion of economic, technological, political, social and cultural transformations. (Storey, 2009; Strinati, 1995; Guins and Cruz, 2005)

But popular culture is also (by way of Raymond Williams' classic conception) related to the products of intellectual and especially artistic activity, and it is these cultural 'texts', be they soap operas, pop music bands or comic books (Storey, 1997), that are the focus of this book – the 'stuff' of popular culture and the ways in which they can be used critically to explore key ideas within classic social theory. So, returning to the perennial questions that many social sciences students ask on first approaching classical social theory, such as 'What is the point of this in the twenty-first century?' or 'What do the thoughts of men and women who have been dead for a century or more have to say about the contemporary world?', the answer is simple: they have *much* to say. The central issues that underpin classic social thought – class, conflict, sexual oppression, gender, power, consumerism, social relations and stability, ethnicity, the body, economic systems and social status – are all factors that can be readily discerned within the modern global world and everyday cultural life. Yet all of these factors can also be located in a range of popular cultural texts from the worlds of popular music, cinema, celebrity, fashion, sport, television, body modification and literature/popular fiction. Furthermore, the key themes of classic sociological texts can also be illuminated through the 'stuff' of our culture. And that is exactly what this book seeks to do: it selects examples from popular culture that can be used to critically illustrate the essence of a particular social theorist/theory, and demonstrates the ways in which contemporary popular culture can acutely reflect classic social ideas and enhance understanding.

The linking of social theory (or social ideas) and cultural texts is not surprising, given that social ideas infuse popular culture. For me, this process occurred long before my formal understanding of sociological theory in my introduction to the fiction of Ayn Rand (the subject of Chapter 8) in the mid-1980s. At the time I knew nothing about the libertarian economic and philosophical nature of her work, but as an aficionado of the Canadian rock band Rush, and especially their Ayn Rand-inspired concept album, *2112*, I researched Rand to understand the ways in which songs such as the *2112 suite*, but also *Anthem* and *Freewill* were directly inspired by her writings and philosophical outlook. The issue was that in amongst the virtuoso musicianship and sci-fi themes was an articulation of an economic ideology that was already gaining global momentum in the 1980s. But it was a different issue when (now fully furnished with a sociological mode of thinking), I made a conceptual link between semiotics and tattooing through watching the lives and work of tattoo artists who were the subject of the TV series *Miami Ink*. Acquainted with the works of Ferdinand de Saussure and Roland Barthes, as I watched the series I began to think about the ways in which the various customers utilized their bodies as a signifying 'text', as evidenced by the stories and rationales many of those who came to be tattooed told about their choice of design: that they were not merely for decorative purposes, but that they communicated precise 'stories' through specific symbols that *semiotically* communicated aspects of their identities. Furthermore, the connection between Karl Marx and hip hop/rap music emerged from an enthusiasm for the music of the US group, Public Enemy, which then developed (on the informed recommendation of another hip hop enthusiast) to seeking out further examples of radical political expression within the genre, such as the music of Immortal Technique. All these examples will be explored in this book.

The connections were made through an awareness of theory (as a sociology undergraduate, then a university lecturer in sociological and cultural theory), but also as a consumer and, in many cases, a fan. Moreover, this approach would become central within my own writing as an academic. For instance, in writing about the French sociologist Pierre Bourdieu (1930–2002) and his now classic concept of habitus (articulated in his 1984 text, *Distinction*), I related the concept, which explains how social order is maintained and is based upon culturally inscribed bodily techniques, modes of presentation, gendered patterns of dress and personal lifestyles, to fashion. However, rather than consider habitus and fashion in a broad sense, I examined Bourdieu's theoretical approach with reference to the career of the British actress and model Elizabeth Hurley, with a particular focus on her emergence as a beachwear fashion designer. The study's central concern was the consistent marketing and media focus on her image and body as an 'aspirational' cultural role model – as a representative of a distinctive habitus (Barron, 2007). In other work I have critically analysed post-colonial theories through a discussion of the charitable work undertaken by the Hollywood actress, Angelina Jolie, on behalf of the UN High Commissioner for Refugees (Barron, 2009). I have also charted the development of Western feminist thought via an analysis of the female companion character in the long-running British science fiction series, *Doctor Who* (1963–89, then re-commissioned in 2005), using the series as a longitudinal text illustrating changes in female representation on television (Barron, 2010).

This approach, therefore, informs the strategy of this book, looking, as it does, to the ways in which classic social theory can be identified, explored and understood through unlikely sources. In essence, this approach resonates with C. Wright Mills' proposition in his seminal book, *The Sociological Imagination* (1959). In the section entitled 'On Intellectual Craftsmanship', Mills offers instruction to fledgling sociologists as to how original sociological ideas can be generated. But, while consultation with literature is one part of the educational process, the other is to develop a reflective attitude to life; to be attuned to and use life experience, from overheard conversations to the content of dreams, and to translate this into academic work. Now, while this may involve monitoring the political issues of the day, it can also be extended to the products of the popular culture that dominates our leisure time. Thus, when listening to music, reading about celebrity, watching Oscar-winning films, assessing the fashion strategies of Madonna, Kylie Minogue, Beyoncé or Lady Gaga, reading the fiction of Ayn Rand (or listening to Rush), leafing through a tattoo magazine (or planning a tattoo design), and perusing tabloid coverage of the latest sport star's wife or girlfriend, you can be stimulating the sociological imagination and, as I will illustrate in this book, reflexively and critically thinking about the thought of Marx, Durkheim, Weber, Simmel, Adorno, Gilman, Barthes, de Saussure and Milton Friedman.

In terms of approach, *Social Theory In Popular Culture* links each theorist/approach with an example drawn from popular culture and the media that illustrates the nature of the ideas, demonstrates their continuing cultural validity and explores the ways in which sociological theory, culture, and media can come together. Each chapter, therefore, synthesizes a sociological approach to an illustrative cultural example: case studies that have been deliberately chosen for their contemporary and enduring qualities and status, and that are accessible and culturally identifiable to students. Structurally, the chapters will be divided into three sections:

- The theory or theorist.
- The media example and how they illustrate the theoretical ideas.
- A critical appraisal of the theory/theorist.

Chapter 1 relates Marxism to music, examining the Marxist concepts of class, ideology and exploitation in detail through an analysis of popular music and rap and hip hop music, and critically engaging with key weaknesses of the Marxist approach to social inequality. With a strong seam of political characteristics and lyrical positioning, there are artists who clearly articulate critical political stances, for example, Public Enemy, and explicitly Marxist messages, notably The Coup and Immortal Technique, whose Marxist influences are apparent in album titles such as *Revolutionary Vol. 1* and *Revolutionary Vol. 2*. The chapter will demonstrate how Marx's critical ideas are identifiable within a popular musical idiom. However, for all of the manifestly Marxist expressions in such music, the primacy of class is a critical issue, as is the centrality of ethnicity. At one level, segments of the hip hop recording 'community' seemingly collude with commodity fetishism and capitalist ideology in their apparent devotion to materialism. Yet critical rap is often caught in a dilemma between the primacy of class or racial inequality and expressions of revolution or social critique are expressed in ways that seemingly preclude any common 'proletarian' collective consciousness. In this way, such differing expressions of inequality serve to problematize the 'Marxist message' and, with regard to gender and ethnicity, some inequalities are silenced altogether, with class inequality eclipsing all others, a source of long-standing feminist critique of Marx.

Chapter 2 examines the sociology of Max Weber in relation to film and develops the discussion of class in Chapter 1 in relation to Weber's analysis of social class and the dynamics of class formation. Although retaining connections with Marx (the link between class and economic differences and inequalities between social groups), Weber extends class analysis to incorporate the idea of class positioning being linked to the individual's relation to markets. However, a crucial aspect of Weber's approach is the inclusion of the idea of status as an aspect of class identity and class positioning. In this respect, economic power might not be easily converted into class mobility due to an individual's status. This aspect of Weber's analysis of social and cultural class will be critically explored and illustrated through reference to *Mean Girls*, *The Devil Wears Prada*, and especially, Danny Boyle's multi-Oscar Award-winning film *Slumdog Millionaire*.

Chapter 3 examines the sociological analysis of social solidarity as articulated by Émile Durkheim, using contemporary celebrity culture as the illustrative example. In this chapter the key aspects of Durkheim's sociology relating to solidarity and the function of religious or 'sacred' ritual will be explored. However, in addition to examining Durkheim's examples illustrating the ways in which societies hold together, the chapter will focus on the contemporary cultural and public interest in 'celebrity' to stress the applicability of his sociology to twenty-first-century modern societies. Hence, in addition to the division of labour, the hallmark of organic solidarity, shared celebrity discourse (arguably) becomes a common form of cultural and social 'glue' that can connect potentially 'anomic' individuals via consumption, 'fandom', gossip, or even mutual dislike.

Chapter 4 concerns the often unsung fourth 'founding father' of classic social thought, Georg Simmel, and examines his work in relation to fashion as worn by singers and marketed within contemporary pop music. The chapter will focus on Simmel's conception of the Metropolis and fashion, which linked consumption to new ways of social life that were emerging in the large cities of late nineteenth- and early twentieth-century Europe. Such heavily populated urban environments, argued Simmel, placed pressure on social actors to seek out 'an appearance of individuality', to 'cultivate a blasé attitude' and a form of individualism 'through the pursuit of signs of status, fashion or marks of individual eccentricity'. A key factor in this process was the role of fashion as a visible means of either marking oneself out from other social actors via dress and style, or acting as a trend-setter and potential inspiration for imitation. The chapter will critically revisit Simmel's approach in relation to pop celebrities such as Madonna, Kylie Minogue, Lady Gaga, Rihanna and others who are associated with a series of fashion-created 'looks' which have become key aspects of their cultural identities. So, the chapter suggest that such figures employ fashion strategically to 'stand out' in a competitive musical market in a manner akin to Simmel's metropolitan individual.

Chapter 5 focuses on a later theorist, Theodor Adorno, and his critiques of mass culture in consumer capitalism, analysing his work on the television industry of the 1950s and its ideological function and conservative nature. To extend the analysis of Adorno, I will look at more contemporary trends within popular television, most notably talent and reality TV programmes such as *American Idol* and *The X Factor* (both syndicated globally). A crucial aspect of these programmes is the role and nature of the audience, in that it is they, via telephone voting, who are the apparent deciders as to which contestant progresses through the shows, and which contestant will be the ultimate winner and gain a recording contract. Moreover, it is a sizeable portion of the audience who will ultimately become the consumers of the recorded product and the 'fans' of the winning performer. In this sense, *The X Factor*, *American Idol* and international versions of such shows (with regard to *The X Factor*, this includes Russian, Arabian, Australian and Indian versions) have established significant directions in contemporary popular music, directions that resonate with debates concerning 'authentic' and 'synthetic' forms of music and the 'disposable' pop product (the winner's first officially released song is invariably a cover version). However, the use of these television examples enables a critical evaluation of Adorno's mass culture approach because, while the nature, marketing and consumption of programmes such as *The X Factor* do ostensibly appear to validate the 'critical theory' view, they also arguably constitute a refutation that the 'mass audience' is a powerless agent due to the intrinsically participatory role the audience plays.

Having focused upon a series of individuals, Chapter 6 takes a broader view with the analysis of feminism and masculinity in relation to sport. However, the analysis still draws attention to a particular thinker in its examination of the classic feminism of Charlotte Perkins Gilman and her book, *Women and Economics*, first published in 1898. Gilman argued that there is a marked economic condition affecting the human race, that humans are the only animal species in which the sex relation is also an economic relation. For Gilman, within human society, an entire sex lives in a relation of economic dependence upon the other sex, and the economic status of the human race is governed mainly by the activities of the male, with the female obtaining 'her share only through him' (Gilman, 1998: 9). The chapter will discuss Gilman's thought and the influence of her legacy on subsequent waves of feminist thought that arose to resist such a relation; however it will also critically apply her ideas in a contemporary cultural context in relation to sport, using examples of the 'WAG', a tabloid media cultural concept which initially referred to the England 2006 World Cup football team's Wives And Girlfriends, a designation that has endured in media discourse ever since. The chapter will suggest that the WAG can be read as a category that forms a continuum with Gilman's analysis of women. However, this is not merely in terms of financial or lifestyle material issues, but 'symbolically' – that media attention will only continue with attachment to a male footballer. Consequently, the chapter will draw on popular magazines and tabloid accounts of the WAG and relate this to the development of post-feminism in which fashion and consumption can be read as empowering factors. However, the chapter will also consider the importance of conceptions of masculinity in sport, principally the ways in which football has seen changes from 'tough' sporting masculinities to displays of 'metrosexuality' and more fashion-conscious representations of masculinity based upon conspicuous consumption (David Beckham, for example). The chapter will also stress the development of American football stars such as Tom Brady who have dominated the game, entered celebrity culture and represent a specific image of masculinity. The linking of feminism and masculinity will allow for a crucial analysis of the ways in which gender debates have developed and can critically come together in the area of sport.

Chapter 7 examines semiotics: the study of signs and how signs communicate meaning. The chapter will discuss theorists such as Ferdinand de Saussure, Roland Barthes, and Umberto Eco. However, the analysis goes beyond the habitual applications of semiotic analysis (cinema, art, advertising, etc.) in its focus on the practice of tattooing. As such, it will illustrate this semiotic process at the level of popular culture through a discussion of the Russian prison tattoo culture, whereby inmates communicate their life histories through tattoo designs, histories which can be deciphered and read by those who understand the symbols; reference to the plethora of documentary and reality television programmes devoted to tattooing (*Miami Ink, LA Ink, London Ink, NY Ink*); and the popularity and visibility of tattoo magazines (*Tattoo, Tattoo Life, Total Tattoo, Skin Deep*, to name but a few). In this way, the discussion uses the subject of body modification to identify critical issues in relation to semiotics but also critical reactions to semiotic denotations in which interpretations and readings of signs may be beyond the control of authors and open to multiple 'deconstructions'.

Finally, Chapter 8 examines aspects of neoliberalism in relation to fiction. Discussing a wide-ranging and historically well established set of ideas, this final chapter will discuss the principles of Adam Smith, Friedrich von Hayek, Ludwig von Mises and Milton Friedman which, although differing in intensity, broadly argued that the ideal society should be one that is economically organized in line with markets that are (aside from the issue of establishing security and defence) free from governmental and state intervention, propositions arguably initiated in the US by Ronald Reagan and in the UK by Margaret Thatcher. However, to fully explore and evaluate the nature of neoliberalist thought, the chapter will look at it through the prism of the fictional work of the émigré novelist, Ayn Rand (1905–82). Rand's work, written in response to her early life in post-revolutionary Russia and her embrace of America and American capitalism (which she argued was the world's ideal social system), represents an extreme (and controversial) celebration of capitalistic enterprise and free markets. Together with a credo that argued that humans are rational, self-interested, and pledged to individualism, Rand's work, as expressed in her key novels *Anthem, The Fountainhead* and *Atlas Shrugged*, contains a mode of liberal and libertarian thought that both reflected and influenced emergent neoliberalism. Indeed, in the wake of acute Western economic crises, sales of *Atlas Shrugged* have soared, buoyed by the opinion that the root of the economic problems was not that capitalism is a flawed system; that it is still not 'pure' enough and still over-fettered by state intervention; and that it should accord with Rand's vision, an ethos foundational to the American Republican off-shoot political group, the Tea Party. Subsequently, the chapter will pose critical questions concerning neoliberalism and its cultural expression in fiction and wider economic culture, taking the book full circle back to Chapter 1 and Marx with a theoretical and economic system fundamentally opposed to Marxism, and popularized by works of fiction that castigate Marx and venerate capitalism as the ideal social system.

Marx and music

The alignment of the social theory of Karl Marx with hip-hop music may seem to be an unlikely combination, but it is a form of popular music that is of considerable use when considering Marx's thoughts on the nature of class and class conflict, capitalism and ideology, and this is exactly the focus of this first chapter. In terms of his enduring status as one of the primary 'founding fathers' of sociology, Karl Marx (1818–83) is a good starting point in the relation of classic social theory with popular culture. There is a long-standing relationship between Marx, Marxism and art (Socialist Realism), cinema (Luis Buñuel, Jean Renoir, Bernardo Bertolucci, Pier Paolo Pasolini) and literature (Jack London, Bertolt Brecht, Upton Sinclair, China Miéville). However, with regard to popular music, the extent to which it can be considered 'oppositional' is invariably tempered by the ways in which it is commercially marketed and positioned by a capitalistic, profit-oriented music industry. In Negus' (1999) analysis, musical genres are not simply collectives of musical styles, but invariably they are the result of narrow marketing forms consciously targeted at specific markets. In effect, popular music is a commodity, a status ably encapsulated by Attali, who, examining the political economy of the music business, succinctly concluded that: 'wherever there is music, there is money' (1977: 3).

However, popular music has alternatively expressed distinctive and distinctly subversive messages and stances: from art school musicians such as John Lennon, global music-based resistance against the Soviet regime in Eastern Europe and Chinese student movements in post-Tiananmen Square China, to the socio-political fusion of pop/rock music and fund/consciousness-raising associated with Live Aid in 1985 (Bennett, 2000) and the subsequent anti-Third World debt Live 8 concerts in 2005. Popular music has also been decisively linked with youth cultures, or youth 'subcultures', the formation of youth groups formalized around issues of image, clothing and music: from Teddy Boys and Mods to Punks and Goths (Hall and Jefferson, 1976; Hebdige, 1979;

Hodkinson, 2002). The foundations of youth subcultural research stemmed from the Birmingham Centre for Contemporary Cultural Studies' (CCCS) work in the 1970s and 1980s, studies that used Marxist theory (and the work of the neo-Marxist, Antonio Gramsci) to argue that subcultures represented resistances to a transforming working-class world (the loss of traditional 'working-class' communities) and thus constituted (however 'imaginary' and ineffective) a challenge to the dominant capitalist socio-economic system. While a major critique of the CCCS tradition was the very means by which youth subcultures expressed their resistance through the consumption of the products of capitalism and the mass consumer system, including items of dress style and popular music (Bennett, 1999), the association between Marx and music is significant.

Aside from possible political activities occurring in music-based subcultures, popular music has long played a significant role in the cultural articulation of 'oppositional' practices and political criticism. For instance, the protest songs of the 1960s, particularly the music of Bob Dylan, but with roots going back to earlier American folk singers, such as Woody Guthrie, emerged from a folk consciousness that was explicitly influenced by the works of Karl Marx, and which frequently expressed communist sentiments. Of the nature and political perception of protest music, Denisoff and Peterson state: 'songs have been composed to teach, convert, seduce, pacify, and arouse. Diverse persecuted groups have galvanized around music; and both political and church authorities, fearing its powers, have tried to repress the joyful noise' (1972: 1). As Eyerman and Jamison (1998) argue, the 1960s would witness the fusion of protest-led folk music with a series of political social groups centred upon civil rights, anti-war and student movements. Furthermore, with the onus on civil rights and ethnicity, music such as gospel and blues has played a critical role in the experience of African Americans, and although the swaggering and belligerent soul and funk sound of James Brown would musically convey the forthright activism of groups such as the Black Panthers, rap music, developing in the late 1970s, was 'an electrified folk poetry of the streets...a way for young blacks to speak their minds' (1998: 105).

Consequently, if folk music was influenced by the critical theory of Marx, this would later be expressed, to differing degrees, in the 'heir' to this tradition, rap music, from the general social critique of Public Enemy and Arrested Development, to the explicitly Marx-influenced sound of The Coup and Immortal Technique. This connection will be outlined and explored in this chapter, with a focus on how hip-hop performers such as The Coup, Immortal Technique and others express Marxist ideas through music and can be used to illustrate key aspects of Marx's theory. But first, what are the fundamental aspects of Marx's thought that these performers draw upon and seek to communicate?

MARX: CAPITALISM, CLASS CONFLICT AND IDEOLOGY

Karl Marx's thought was produced against rapid and substantial mid-nineteenth-century social change across a Europe that, in addition to wars and tumultuous revolutions, witnessed the establishment of industry and industrial sources of production proliferate, resulting in distinctive new social classes and class relations, and an oppressive relationship by the class that owned these forms of production towards the class that worked for them. Marx gained a keen insight into the nature of these transformations working as a journalist for the *New York Tribune*, in which he reported European trade with China, French and British economic and financial developments, the American slave trade, and British imperial rule in India (Marx, 2007). In essence, at an early professional age Marx became well acquainted with social economics and oppression in an international context.

Initially influenced by the German idealist philosophy of Georg Hegel (1770–1831), which, in texts such as *The Phenomenology of Spirit*, broadly appealed to the concept of truth as a means with which to initiate social trans-formation, Marx would turn away from Hegel's idealism and the notion that history could be explained in terms of ideas and that the history of humanity is 'the history of the abstract spirit of humanity' (Marx, 1990: 72). Marx would ultimately take a different view, one that would centrally define his thought and characterize it as an 'activist' philosophy. Thus, Marx rejected idealist or abstract philosophy, arguing that, 'the philosophers have only *interpreted* the world in different ways; the point is to change it' (Marx, 1990: 84). As Marx outlined in *The German Ideology*, for Hegel and Hegelians, social and historical change was solely understandable as the product of human consciousness, but they were mistaken, in that they were not combating conditions in the real world. Consequently, Marx countered the idealist conception of history and historical change with what would become one of the central Marxist concepts, the *materialist* conception of history, and linked to what he called the *first premise* of all human history, which is the existence of living human individuals. This means that in order to shape the world, humans must secure the means by which to survive, such as eating, drinking, housing and clothing. As Marx states:

> The first historical act is thus the production of the means to satisfy these needs, the production of material life itself. And indeed this is an historical act, a fundamental condition of all history, which today, as thousands of years ago, must be daily and hourly fulfilled merely in order to sustain human life. (1998: 47)

It is this process of acquiring their basic subsistence that not only enables humans to survive, but which would also become the driving engine of history. Marx argued that at one level, humans differentiate themselves from animals by the manner in which they obtain subsistence and the means of life from nature, but, in the course of doing so, humans do something far more profound, because, 'by producing their means of subsistence [humans] are directly produc-ing their material life' (Marx, 1998: 37). This is so because the securing of initial basic needs ultimately leads to new needs, the satisfaction of which necessitates systems of production and the development of distinctive divisions of labour.

Thus, the creation of new needs is the first historical act, and when viewed retrospectively, human societies have been organized in a series of specific production systems to achieve the satisfaction of needs. The first of these took the form of *tribal property*, a generally undeveloped stage of production dominated by hunting and fishing, cattle raising and early agriculture. The second form of productive system arose from this simple stage, and was dubbed by Marx the *ancient communal* or *primitive communism* stage. This period developed due to the unification of numerous tribes into early city-states, primarily via military conquests, and saw, crucially, the development of private property in the form of slaves furnished by territorial invasions and combat, and typified by ancient Rome. However, the decline of Rome and its ultimate conquest by European 'barbarians' saw the decline of the agricultural and market trade that it had established, paving the way for the third economic stage, the *feudal* or *estate property* structure. In place of a slave class, the feudal period saw the emergence of a new subordinate class, the enserfed peasantry governed by the authority of the feudal noble and landed property owner, to which the peasantry gave up a proportion of their produce. In the developing urban trade centres, this hierarchical division was mirrored in the relationship between individual craftsmen and their apprentices, and was the ultimate site of the fourth and most crucial stage of production, the *capitalist* system. This principally developed in sixteenth-century Europe but became a dominant economic force in the eighteenth century, characterized by its societal value of free competition and the emergence of a new and distinctive class structure.

In terms of the nature of the classes in the capitalist mode of production, in *Capital: Volume 3* (1991), Marx outlined the existence of three classes: the owners of mere labour-power, the owners of capital and the landowners. However, the conventional analysis of class relations in this epoch reduces these to two: the bourgeoisie and the proletariat, engaged in a relationship that is unequal and exploitative, and which is characterized by conflict, as were the preceding modes of production. As Marx (with Friedrich Engels) famously states in *The Communist Manifesto*:

> The history of all hitherto existing society is the history of class struggle. Freeman and slave, patrician and plebeian, lord and serf ... in a word, oppressor and oppressed, stood in constant opposition to one another, carried on an uninterrupted, now hidden, now open fight, a fight that each time ended, either in a revolutionary reconstitution of society at large, or in the common ruin of the contending classes. (1985: 79)

Marx contends that class conflict is the prime mover of social change, and that the modern bourgeois society that developed from the 'ruins' of feudal society inherited its class antagonisms, simply in a new form. The capitalist epoch has, in addition to creating a new economic productive system, also established new classes, new conditions of oppression and new forms of struggle in place of the old ones. Hence, the epoch of the bourgeoisie possesses a distinctive feature in that it has simplified the class antagonisms into two principle classes that directly face each other: the bourgeoisie and proletariat. According to Marx's analysis, since the establishment of the capitalist industrial system and the creation of a world market, the bourgeoisie has seized command of the state to create only one true form of freedom: that of free trade. However, in the process of creating this system they constructed an economic system predicated upon the principle of 'naked, shameless, direct, brutal exploitation' (1985: 82). Therefore, the labouring class, who must sell themselves to the capitalists, are also nothing more than commodities, and, owing to the extensive use of machinery and a strict division of labour, the work of the proletariat has lost all individual character as workers are 'daily and hourly enslaved by the machine, by the overlooker, and, above all, by the individual bourgeoisie manufacturer himself' (1985: 87–8).

A question that may occur to us here is that if the nature of capitalism is so unpleasant, and the proletariat's status no more than that of a modern-day slave, why is it tolerated by the industrial working class? Why does the proletariat seemingly collude with this state of affairs? The answer is that the ways in which members of the proletariat perceive their class position and economic status is distorted or masked by the process dubbed 'ideology'. Devised in the late eighteenth century by the French philosopher Destutt de Tracey to describe 'the science of ideas' (Williams, 1977: 56), ideology is used by Marx to refer to the existence of illusory ideas and the manner in which they contribute to the creation of a 'false consciousness' in the proletariat. The concept of ideology points to a key feature of Marx's analysis of the social system and its interrelated constituent parts, typically referred to as the *base* and *superstructure* of society. As Marx states in *A Contribution to the Critique of Political Economy*, written in 1859 and expressing one of the most fundamental aspects of his thought:

> In the social production of their existence, men inevitably enter into definite relations, which are independent of their will, namely relations of production appropriate to a given stage in the development of their material forces of production. The totality of these relations of production constitutes the economic structure of society, the real foundation, on which arises a legal and political superstructure and to which correspond definite forms of social consciousness. The mode of production of material life conditions the general process of social, political and intellectual life. It is not the consciousness of men that determines their existence, but their social existence that determines their consciousness. (1903: 11–12)

In Marx's analysis, the propertied class can translate their economic power into control over political, cultural and social institutions such as the state, education, law or religion, and use the institutions of the superstructure to legitimize and naturalize the nature of the economic 'base' of society. In this sense, bourgeois ideology acts to systematically misrepresent the reality of bourgeois society, and acts to deliberately mould the consciousness of the proletariat. Hence, there is a potent sense of synergy between economics and values in capitalist society, and a further layer of control because, as Marx states in *The German Ideology*:

> The ideas of the ruling class are in every epoch the ruling ideas, i.e., the class which is the ruling *material* force of society is at the same time its ruling *intellectual* force. The class which has the means of material production at its disposal, consequently also controls the means of mental production, so that the ideas of those who lack the means of mental production are on the whole subject to it. (1998: 67)

Accordingly, these ideas both represent the ideas of the dominant social class and express its domination. But what does the bourgeoisie have to hide? If they control the means of production, why does that have to be naturalized and legitimated to the point of instilling illusory ideas in the proletariat? The answer, from Marx's perspective, rests on the entire capitalist enterprise, and its central purpose: to generate profit. It is for this reason that Marx states, in *Capital: Volume 1*, that the means with which to analyse the nature of capitalism lies within its central product: the commodity. A commodity, Marx explains, is 'in the first place, an object outside us, a thing that by its properties satisfies human wants of some sort or another' (1974: 43). Furthermore, commodities possess a number of forms of 'value', such as the exchange value when sold, and, more importantly, a use value, reflecting the manner in which commodities only truly become commodities, become an actual reality, through the act of consumption. However, the commodity also contains the human labour time that was expended in producing it, time that can be measured in terms of weeks, days or hours. This is the direct reflection of the relationship between the labourer and the bourgeois owner of the means of production; it constitutes a meeting point in the market in which the bourgeoisie act as the 'buyer' of the sole property the labourer possesses: their ability to labour, which they must 'sell' to the capitalist, thus effectively selling his/her 'living self' (1974: 165). In return for this act of selling, the labourer receives a 'living wage' that enables him/her to exist and it also guarantees the maintenance of the proletariat. As the energies of the worker are expended in the act of labour (a definite quantity of human muscle, nerve and brain), these must be restored at the close of the labour process to enable the labourer to begin anew the next day. This is covered by the average income obtained by the labourer from the bourgeoisie, and in terms of perception, this arrangement between the bourgeois owner of the means of production and the labour-selling member of the proletariat appears transparent and equitable, as it is codified in the form of a contract based upon the premise of 'a fair day's wage for a fair day's work' (Hall *et al.*, 1978: 198). However, this is not in fact the case because the apparent openness of the deal between the classes hides the fundamental factor of capitalism: the acquisition of profit. Consequently, the rightful nature of the capitalist and labourer relationship is this:

The one with an air of importance, smirking, intent on business; the other, timid and holding back, like one who is bringing his own hide to market and has nothing to expect but – a hiding. (Marx, 1974: 172)

The 'smirking' and 'self-satisfied' response of the capitalist arises from what the apparently unambiguous contractual agreement deliberately hides: exploitation in the form of the production of surplus value. Marx contended that the value of a commodity is determined by the quantity of labour expended in producing it, and the working time needed to carry out the production process. However, while the value of subsistence required by the worker may be earned in half a day's labour, the work continues for the remaining portion of the day. As such, the subsistence need of the labourer only costs the capitalist half a day's labour, and once this subsistence wage is earned, the labourer works on, producing additional value that is accrued by the capitalist employer, a consequence fully foreseen by the capitalist. So, the capitalist production system is not only founded on the production of commodities, but it is also defined by the production of surplus value.

Consequently, labourers do not produce for themselves, but directly for capital as surplus value is appropriated by the owners of production. The process of hidden acquisition represents the foundation of the capitalist system, a reality successfully obscured through ideological means. *Capital*, then, acts as a means by which the obscuring ideological sheen cast by capitalism over its true workings and intentions, and its ruthlessly exploitative economic mode of production, can be revealed and acted upon, because the capitalist system is not the final stage of history.

Marx argues that just as capitalism was the product of a series of revolutions that occurred within the feudal period (the rise of a manufacturing middle class and expanding world markets produced as the result of voyages of discovery and better sea navigation techniques), to the extent that they caused the downfall of the stage, so it will be for capitalism. The transformative zeal of the new class of the bourgeoisie revolutionized feudal society and ushered in a new economic system and a new set of social classes. And this process will repeat itself in capitalism. Marx predicted that with the progressive development of industry (and the instabilities of capitalism due to its tendency to over-produce and experience economic recession and crisis), the proletariat would steadily become concentrated in ever greater masses, its strength growing as a political force: a strength that results in conflict as workers begin to organize in collective forms (such as trade unions) to stand against the bourgeoisie. This is so because, 'of all the classes that stand face to face with the bourgeoisie, the proletariat alone is a really revolutionary class' (1985: 91).

As a result, a new social formation will emerge: communism. This will be achieved through the overthrow of the capitalist class by a politicized and revolutionary proletariat, and will result in the abolition of bourgeois property and of the principle of private property, a form of ownership founded on class antagonism and upon the 'exploitation of the many by the few' (1985: 96).

Subsequently, the minimum wage and subsistence existence of the proletariat will be overturned and labour restored to its true nature: as an enriching aspect of human existence that is predicated upon the free development of all individuals. Thus, in Marx's analysis, revolution is both necessary and inevitable because the bourgeoisie cannot be overthrown by any other means: it is the driving force of history.

TWENTY-FIRST-CENTURY MARX: THE HIP-HOP MARXIST MESSAGE

In the view of the neo-Marxist thinker, Alex Callinicos (2003), Marx's thought was (and remains) a means by which to imagine other worlds: social structures free from the exploitative and hierarchical nature of capitalism and its antagonistic class relations. It is an approach that has had an extensive presence in art and cultural products, and also popular culture in the form of popular music. As observed at the beginning of the chapter, strands of folk music took a decisive political form, some of which was expressly influenced by Marx's thought. However, from the late 1970s, a popular musical form would develop that would similarly reflect such a political influence and express to a contemporary audience the thought and political nature of Karl Marx and this was hip-hop music (although it has been argued that rap and hip-hop refer respectively to the music and the styles that surround it (Shuker, 1998), hip-hop is commonly used to describe the sound, and I will refer to the music as such). It is to this form that I now turn to illustrate the ways in which music can be utilized to demonstrate Marx's contemporary currency in popular culture, and to use hip-hop to illustrate aspects of Marx's theoretical approach.

Although multi-faceted in expression, hip-hop is defined by Melville as a musical form which 'marries the production techniques of scratching and sampling, to spoken word rapping' (2004: 30). It is this latter 'rapping' component that designates hip-hop's extensive musical heritage and this is traceable to the griots of Nigeria and the Gambia, the scats of Cab Calloway, the 'street talk boasts' of Bo Diddley, children's skipping-rope rhymes, the 'jive' of Muhammad Ali and the narrative poems or 'toasts' of prison and army rhyming stories (Toop, 1984). While it was not until October 1979 that rap and hip-hop music officially gained cultural visibility, with the chart success of The Sugarhill Gang's 'Rapper's Delight' (Miyakawa, 2005), rap/hip-hop music had been developing in African American and Latino neighbourhoods since the early 1970s. In the wake of 'Rapper's Delight', hip-hop would commercially develop throughout the 1980s through performers such as Flash and the Furious Five, Run-D.M.C., Afrika Bambaataa and KRS-One, artists who not only developed a fresh mode of music, but incorporated new forms of political expression into the sound.

In terms of cultural visibility, hip-hop was discernible particularly in New York (Sullivan, 2003); hence, it was a musical form that emerged 'from the streets of inner-city neighborhoods as a genuine reflection of hopes, concerns, and aspirations of urban Black youth' (Tabb Powell, 1991: 245). Although persistently embroiled in 'moral panics' and social anxieties concerning lyrical content and image, particularly with regard to sexist representations of women and violence (Toop, 1991; Baker, Jr, 1993; Springhall, 1998; Armstrong, 2001; Abu-Jamal, 2006), several notable hip-hop performers, such as N.W.A., Public Enemy, Ice-T and Ice-Cube, potently articulated 'experiences and conditions of black Americans living in violent ghetto conditions' (Kellner, 1995: 176), reflecting the stark nature of a 'hardcore urban reality' (Forman, 2002: 3). Consequently, rap and hip-hop music is a 'blend of reality and fiction' and much of it was a 'contemporary response to conditions of joblessness, poverty, and disempowerment' (Smitherman, 1997: 5). Kellner cites Public Enemy's song, 'Fight the Power', as a key example of how hip-hop music incarnates what the Marx-inspired Herbert Marcuse described as 'the great refusal', a social refusal to submit to domination and oppression. As Phillips *et al.* state, hip-hop frequently represents 'the voices of the culturally, politically, and economically marginal and disenfranchised [and] remains an oppositional and potentially liberatory project' (2005: 254). However, although a general critical and radical stance is readily discernible in many instances of the sound, there are further examples of hip-hop performers who express their protests in ways that are explicitly radical and which consciously articulate the ideas of Karl Marx, and I will examine two examples, The Coup and Immortal Technique, in this regard.

Although also influenced by the works of Franz Fanon and the Black Panther Party's theories of class struggle (Ogbar, 1999), The Coup, based in Oakland, California, also consistently express the revolutionary thought of Karl Marx in their hip-hop music. Formed in 1992, and consisting of Raymond 'Boots' Riley, E-Roc and Pam The Funktress, The Coup have released a number of albums, such as: *Kill My Landlord* (1993), *Genocide and Juice* (1994), *Steal This Album* (1998), *Party Music* (2001) and *Pick A Bigger Weapon* (2006), all of which contain a substantive radical political ethos. The music produced by The Coup (as the band's name suggests) deals with the social reality and economic conditions of lower or 'underclass' America in ways that express oppressive economic exploitation and inequality, compounded by racism and police brutality. However, while a pervasive tone of political opposition and critique is discernible in hip-hop music, The Coup express this in an overtly Marxist manner, actively drawing upon the language of Marx's writing and the major political thrust of his work.

Consequently, The Coup's music, lyrics, album imagery and videos consistently cite key Marxist ideas: the oppressive existence of the wealthy ruling capitalist bourgeois elite, the need for a redistribution of wealth throughout society, and the necessity of social change in the form of a revolution that will result in the proletariat seizing the means of production. Thus, for The Coup, the conditions of class exploitation and conflict present in Marx's nineteenth century remain, and must be confronted. Such political confrontation and agitation has been controversially represented by the band. For instance, the cover of their *Party Music* album consists of an image of the World Trade Center's twin towers in flames (due to the 11 September terrorist attack), symbolizing the 'smashing of the capitalist system' (Riley, 2001).

There are numerous examples of Marxist expression in specific songs. For instance, 'The Shipment' lyrically exposes the machinations of an exploitative state and makes clear references to the existence of an oppressive 'ruling class' and the deliberate macro-economic blocks to social freedom and the exploitative profit-making that this class represents. Similarly, 'Dig It' begins with the statement that Riley has read *The Communist Manifesto* and considers it to still constitute the manual for the overthrow of an economic system that represents four hundred years of exploitation. This has been cloaked in an 'ideological anaesthesia' transmitted by television stations (in the form of mass entertainment TV) that dulls collective class consciousness and political activism. Furthermore, the band's eponymous song, 'The Coup', articulates the major thrust of Marx's thought, with its lyrical refrain that the only way in which oppressive social and economic forces can be overcome is through revolution, and specifically, a *communist* revolution. Indeed, as Boots Riley unambiguously states of his political position, expressed via his music:

> I am a communist. I have been a communist/socialist since I was 14 years old. I think that people should have democratic control over the profits that they produce. It is not real democracy until you have that. And the plain and simple definition of communism is the people having democratic control over the profits that they create. When you first have a revolution, you are heading into socialism. (Riley, 2001, lyricstime.com)

The Coup are engaged in the process of producing hip-hop communist manifestos and transmitting a Marxist message via hip-hop music. And they are not alone in this political endeavour, which brings me to my second example of Marxist ideas finding expression in hip-hop music: that of the New York rap artist, Immortal Technique (aka Felipe Andres Coronel). The critical consciousness of Immortal Technique's music, with its distinctive Afro-Peruvian slant, is most apparent in the titles of his 2001 and 2003 albums, *Revolutionary Vol. 1* and *Revolutionary Vol. 2*, – 'the Truth in the form of Hip-hop' – which represent his avowed attack upon 'the hypocritical economic aristocracy' (Vol. 3 is promised in the near future). In terms of style, Immortal Technique is an 'underground' rapper, essentially self-releasing his earlier work without any major record company assistance. The album titles themselves make reference to a distinctive Marxist influence, as does the use of a sickle and microphone (a stylistic play on the Soviet Communist hammer and sickle icon), and like The Coup, many of the tracks on these albums have an explicit political tone that unequivocally reflects Marx's concepts. For example, the song 'Freedom of Speech' conveys an anti-corporate stance, while 'The Message and the Money' casts rap artists as members of an exploited proletariat, representing nothing more than parts of the 'machine' of the profit-hungry record industry. In this sense, Immortal Technique extends the scope of what constitutes the contemporary mode of production, in this instance, the modern music industry as an exploitative facet of Western capitalism. Consequently, Immortal Technique, like The Coup, employs specific Marxist concepts in a manner that reflects the essence of Marx's critique of capitalism: that it is founded upon the exploitation of a larger but oppressed and brutally exploited working class. Furthermore, the song 'The 4th Branch' (from *Revolutionary Vol. 2*) deals explicitly with the concept of ideology, and articulates its function in the contemporary superstructure of capitalist society. As the inner sleeve commentary of the album states:

> The news media has the potential to be the voice of the people and provide the public with useful information and a historical reality of the actions of our nation in order to better our democracy. Instead they have become the rubber stamp of the military and the government. They are now the most useful propaganda machine that the system has…They are no longer the voice of the people; they are corporate controlled entities who put profit margins before truth, they are people who write puff pieces on government and business interests instead of vocalizing the criticisms of millions. They are the 4th branch of the government.

Here, journalism and the news media can no longer be seen in their traditional role as a 'watchdog' (Tumber, 2001) acting against governments on behalf of the people, nor do they act as a critical component of the public sphere, but rather, as an ideological part of the superstructure striving to legitimate the economic base and the unequal class status quo through its biased news provision. Indeed, contemporary critics identify the media system itself as a further bastion of the economic ruling class, effectively constituting a new 'information-based bourgeoisie' in the form of media conglomerates such as Rupert Murdoch's News Corporation (Straubhaar and LaRose, 2006). Although the workings of the media as an ideological conservative force are associated with the approach of later neo-Marxists – principally Herbert Marcuse (1964), Louis Althusser (1971) and Ralph Miliband (1973) – and the issue of the mass media's role in the manufacturing of public consent has been extensively debated (Herman and Chomsky, 2002), Immortal Technique presents a Marxist analysis of his own. In 'The 4th Branch' the media are read as possessing a key ideological role, one that serves to contemporaneously legitimate the capitalist system and obscure its 'true' exploitative nature, the antithesis of the founding principles of journalism. And extending this specific critical vein, the song 'Industrial Revolution' deals not only with the nature of capitalism, but the ways in which the media and business collude to control social perceptions of the nature of capitalism.

With regard to the production of radical 'manifestos', the song 'The Poverty of Philosophy' (the title drawn from Marx's book of the same name) is a clear example of the influence of Marx, and the performer's familiarity with his works. 'The Poverty of Philosophy' is not a conventional rap, in that it is not structured in terms of lyrics or rhymes, rather, it is a detailed spoken word proposal that addresses the material conditions of the contemporary 'proletariat': their need to survive through obtaining the means of daily material subsistence; the consequent inability of the majority of people in society to philosophize about freedom and socialist democracy. This is further compounded by a superstructure that now has a pervasive media system as one of its key institutions, and thus they do not recognize their subordinate status. Consequently, they are unable to coalesce into, and act as, a 'class for themselves'. Yet, echoing the activist nature of Marx's thought, this state of 'ignorance' can be overcome. Here, Immortal Technique moves away from a consistent focus on racial oppression, a factor that is present in alternative examples of rap and hip-hop music (Public Enemy, for instance), and is more concerned with class oppression and economic exploitation. As Immortal Technique states in 'The Poverty of Philosophy', his enemy is not white people as a monolithic ethnic group, but the specific white people that are not immediately visible: politicians and the corporate monopoly owners, the owners of the means of production that force the majority into a state of subservience rather than self-control, and a condition of paralysis due to the degree to which we are in thrall to petty material things in our lives – the direct 'fetishistic' products of capitalism. Thus, to overcome this social and economic state, classism is the crucial issue, as 'The Poverty of Philosophy' states: there is an imperative for social solidarity that must be free of any ethnic divisions, because such partitions will undermine the ultimate goal of the proletariat. This is potently expressed in the defiant final cry of the song: 'VIVA LA REVOLUCIÓN!' and it is an exclamation that mirrors Marx's and Engels' proclamation at the conclusion of *The Communist Manifesto*:

> Let the ruling classes tremble at a Communistic revolution. The proletarians have nothing to lose but their chains. They have a world to win: Working men of all countries, unite! (1985: 121)

However, the revolution will, according to Immortal Technique in the title track of the 2008-released album *The 3rd World,* be initiated in a global rather than national context, emanating from the South, not the West – the Third World – and will truly be an international revolutionary movement.

With reference to hip-hop music, oppositional discourses are powerfully articulated and deeply political; however, with regard to confrontational performers such as The Coup and Immortal Technique, hip-hop culture is one of the prime cultural zones in which Marx's thought and revolutionary aspirations, written in the mid-nineteenth century, are being contemporaneously articulated and communicated within a popular cultural form. Furthermore, the references to Marx are not simply thematic, but are central to the music and the message. Boots Riley's overt communist political affiliations *are* inspired by Marx, as are Immortal Technique's. What is more, with regard to the latter performer, his albums are positioned not simply as music, but also as political pamphlets, with political messages, statements and commentaries on the songs that express their subject matter and revolutionary content provided in album sleeve notes.

Although I have focused on two examples to illustrate how the fundamental theoretical ideas of Marx can be illustrated via popular music, it is significant to note that The Coup and Immortal Technique are not the only examples of Marxist-inflected hip-hop bands. For further discussion and illustration, the American hip-hop duo Dead Prez combine African American political statements with clear socialist underpinnings, as does the rap performer Talib Kweli. Furthermore, The Coup's Boots Riley has teamed up with Tom Morello from the politically informed rock/rap band Rage Against The Machine to form the band Street Sweeper Social Club, a rap/rock crossover project. Their eponymous album (released in 2009) is characterized by songs such as 'Fight! Smash! Win!', which unambiguously communicates an oppositional message that reflects both The Coup's communist and socially emancipatory political stance, and Rage Against The Machine's anarchist principles. Therefore, Marxist-inspired critical hip-hop that communicates a demand for structural social and cultural change retains vitality and expression.

While it cannot be overlooked that political hip-hop represents gritty, urban milieus that are highly marketable, that 'street culture has always been a good sales pitch for pushing vicarious thrills on the mass market' (Toop, 1991: 22); or that 'ghetto' Gangsta Rap is heavily consumed by white suburban teenagers drawn by its extremism and 'parental advisory' labels (Wilson, 2008), hip-hop music represents a powerful pop cultural expression of radical political messages. However, it also highlights some of the critical reactions to Marx, and arguably shares them.

The issue of class analysis and economic resistance is a critical factor that is pertinent within Marx's thought and the hip-hop music that espouses a Marxist message. In this regard, economic oppression and inequality is the dominant force in society, and class conflict the driving force of history. As such, class and its expression in terms of ownership or non-ownership of production is the salient focus in much of Marx's thought and the primary form of inequality that must be abolished. The issue of gender, for example, is secondary. As Marx and Engels state in *The Communist Manifesto*, issues of gender have no 'distinctive social validity for the working class. All are instruments of labour' (1985: 88). Such an evaluation would ultimately result in critical feminist reactions to Marx (Radical and Marxist Feminism, for example), and perhaps most notably that of Shulamith Firestone's work, and her seminal text, *The Dialectic of Sex* (1971), which reformulated Marx's and Engels' approach to history and its emphasis on class conflict into a manifesto for a gendered revolution (to free women from dependency on males due to childbirth and child-rearing). In Firestone's analysis, because of its inability to account for the 'invisible' issue of sex class, gender inequality would not be abolished with the removal of capitalism and the development of socialism. And so it arguably is with Marxist-inspired hip-hop: class remains the dominant force and the primary component within calls for revolutionary change. Indeed, as Phillips *et al.* (2005) argue, although women played a vital role in the development of the genre (for example, ShaRock, Lady B, Queen Lisa Lee, Lady Tee, Salt-n-Pepa, Sister Soulja, Queen Latifah and Missy

Elliott), hip-hop music is predominantly a masculine discourse, with the exclusion of women a common trait. However, while agreeing with this assessment, Gupta-Carlson (2010) argues that there are contemporary examples of an alignment between hip-hop music and female empowerment (the Planet B-Girl network, for instance) that utilizes the sound as an empowering political feminist force and allies it with class to call for social change.

A further critical issue that has been raised in relation to Marx and the nature of his social analysis is its ignorance of ethnicity and ethnic inequality. The primary social category in Marx's work is that of class, with all other categories (gender and ethnicity, but we could also cite sexuality, age and disability) rendered secondary. Class and class conflict is the driving engine of history, and it is the ultimate conflict between the ruling class and the proletariat that will result in the 'end of history', and the coming of the final epoch of socialism. Later work with regard to Marx and ethnicity has pointed to the ways in which racism has served as a force with which to further stratify a potential revolutionary class, sub-dividing it in terms of differing status positions and subverting a shared sense of class consciousness. As such, politically conscious rap and hip-hop music recognizes the status of ethnicity, but attempts to link it with a class-based analysis. While some expressions of oppositional protest within rap appear to be focused on the issue of ethnicity and white power (Public Enemy and their references to the 'Nation of Islam', for instance), both The Coup and Immortal Technique, while emphasizing the differential experiences ethnic groups face in a capitalist world, nevertheless turn to Marx and his theory based upon class oppression, and thus class remains the dominant force in their musical discourse.

Arguably, hip-hop forms a continuum with folk protest music, but, with regard to the key examples discussed in this chapter, the social theory of Karl Marx, and his key ideas of class, class conflict, exploitation and ideology, is contemporaneously expressed and illustrated with reference to this musical form. Hence, it is perhaps not surprising that, in an international context, the growth of rap and hip-hop music in Cuba since the early 1990s (represented by performers such as Orishas) is predominantly based on the principles of the Cuban revolution and, in the form of government-funded hip-hop festivals, seeks to 'project a revolutionary message from Cuba, a commitment to the cause of the downtrodden in the world' (Baker, 2005: 368).

Although the issue of how authentic 'street music' or the 'sound of the underground' can ever be present in a music industry that is just that, an industry (Thornton, 1995; Rief, 2009), the classical theory of Marx and his revolutionary ideals, as argued in this chapter, nevertheless finds expression in a distinctive form of popular music and popular culture, because in political activism and Marx-inspired social resistance, culture is an essential force. As Boots Riley of The Coup asserts: 'culture is expression, how we communicate and get across. It fills the soil and gets people ready' (www.workers.org). Regardless of the history or status of societies that ostensibly have historically embraced the Marxist/socialist social vision (Soviet Russia, Cuba or North

Korea), the underpinnings and message of Marx's social theory, written in the mid-nineteenth century, are being communicated through popular culture, at its most popular, to a hip-hop beat.

QUESTIONS TO CONSIDER

1. How does Marx define class?
2. What is ideology? And what is ideology designed, according to Marx, to obscure?
3. Why are rap and hip-hop music frequently characterized as representing an 'oppositional' political stance?

FURTHER READING

Key works by Marx for further reading should include *The Communist Manifesto* and Chapter 1 of *The German Ideology* for his (and Engels') analysis of ideology. Also, the preface to *A Contribution To The Critique of Political Economy* is useful for a succinct explanation of the nature of the base and superstructure organization of capitalist society. For an expansive discussion of Marx and his theory, David McLellan's *The Thought of Karl Marx* remains an authoritative text. Readers should also see George Ciccariello Maher's article, 'Brechtian Hip-Hop: Didactics and Self-Production in Post-Gangsta Political Mixtapes' (*Journal of Black Studies*, Vol. 36, No. 1, pp. 129–60) for a further example of Marxist/radical-influenced hip-hop music, especially that of Dead Prez (their *Hip-Hop* and its promotional video is particularly relevant and illustrative).

Weber and film

2

In this chapter we stay with the classic founding theorists of sociology, in this instance, Max Weber (1864–1920). The sociology of Weber, born in Germany in the last quarter of the nineteenth century, was predominantly concerned with social change in relation to the effects of industrialization, nationalism, and the increasingly bureaucratized nature of European societies and culture (and the dominating effects of bureaucracy). However, Weber is frequently compared to Karl Marx due to their shared focus on the issues of class and especially capitalism. For example, Weber's major text, *The Protestant Ethic and the Spirit of Capitalism*, published in English in 1930, is a study which provided a very different explanation for the development of capitalism from that of Marx. Citing not merely economic factors or class conflict, Weber reasoned that the rise of capitalism (in specific Western geographical locations) was based on the interrelationship between economic thought and wisdom (represented by adages such as: 'Remember, that time is money'; 'Money can beget money'; and 'Remember, that credit is money'), and a religious mode of thought and activity, specifically that of the Ascetic branch of Calvinist 'Puritan' Protestantism. The relevance of this particular form of Christianity was that it actively discouraged the enjoyment of wealth (judging it to be ethically bad), but venerated work (an individual's 'calling'), a combination that led to the generation of further wealth due to the saving of accumulated economic assets, a process that resulted in the development of 'a rational bourgeois economic man' (Weber, 2000: 174) and the foundation of the later capitalist class.

However, Weber's work was wide-ranging in its scope, to the point that, Schroeder observes, aside from his writings on the Protestant Ethic and his analysis of the nature of bureaucracy, there is no body of systematic thought that can be dubbed 'Weberian' (1992: 1). Weber's work also included economic history, politics, rationality, the nature of charisma and social authority, structures of power, and comparative examinations of world religions such as Catholicism, Hinduism, Buddhism, Confucianism, Islam and Judaism. Additionally, Weber also advocated a distinctly individualized methodological approach to the social world that recognized the central role that individuals play in social structures and institutions. In terms of personal outlook, far from advocating social revolution, as Marx did, Weber described himself as a free market liberal, a 'class conscious bourgeois' (Allen, 2004: 15), and did not see any possibility for the revolutionary removal of capitalism. But, although Weber differed markedly from Marx, they did share a focus on the nature and development of capitalism and on the nature of social class, with the major point of distinction between the classic theorists being that, in broad terms, Marx's position on class division ran along the lines of the ownership or non-ownership of private property. Weber did not disagree with this, but it did not address the issue of multiple levels of distinction and separation in the property-less class, along the lines of education, occupation or religion. In consequence, whereas a social majority may be connected via the fact that they must sell their labour to a more powerful class, that majority is fragmented into a myriad of differing status groups, many of which do not see any grounds or scope for class solidarity, a state that became the basis of now classic works of British sociological analysis such as Lockwood's (1966) study of the ways in which white-collar employees could see no sense of common class consciousness or position with manual workers.

The focus of this chapter, however, is not to re-iterate Weber in terms of his approach and sociological legacy, but to illustrate his thought in the context of popular culture; and in this instance, the source of popular cultural texts will be drawn from film. While Weber's work has been applied to culture at large, such as the bureaucratic and 'rational' nature of the Holocaust and the Nazi death camps in World War II (Bauman, 1989), the organizational culture of the McDonald's fast-food restaurant chain (Ritzer, 1996), and the work 'ethic' of computer hackers (Himanen, 2001), it has also found its way into discussions of popular culture. Two notable examples that spring to mind are the application of his concept of charisma to the nature of fame and celebrity (Alberoni, 1972; Bowden, 2010), and the use of his idea of 'disenchantment' to explain the 're-enchanting' appeal of fantasy literature such J.R.R. Tolkien's *Lord of the Rings* novels (Curry, 1997), read as a means of escape from a rational, modern culture. However, Weber's analysis of class and status can also be identified in popular film in ways that allow for the nuances of his theoretical work to be critically elaborated upon and illustrated. Thus, this chapter will discuss Weber's theoretical articulation of the concept of class, but more specifically that of status, and then illustrate it in relation to three film case studies, all of which (in differing ways) centrally deal with the nature of status and social stratification: *Mean Girls*, *The Devil Wears Prada*, and *Slumdog Millionaire*. But first, what exactly does Weber mean by status, and how does it differ from class?

WEBER, CLASS AND STATUS

In a short (and unfinished) essay entitled 'Class, Status, Party', Weber set out an alternative view on the nature of class from that of Marx, in which he accounted for the ways in which certain societies were socially stratified in multiple forms, stressing the nature of the relationship between class situation and market situation, with the former determined by the latter. In Weber's view, a class could be said to exist when a substantial number of people have in common a particular causal aspect of their life chances to the extent that these are represented entirely by economic interests in terms of the ownership of goods and opportunities for income in relation to labour markets. These aspects of class identity and class conditions establish an individual's class situation, a situation that will set the boundaries for types of goods, income, living conditions, the gaining of a position in life, and even finding what Weber calls 'inner satisfactions', a 'probability which derives from the relative control over goods and skills and from their income-producing uses within a given economic order' (Weber, 1978: 302). Consequently, Weber argues that 'the term "class" refers to any group of people that is found in the same class situation' (cited in Gerth and Mills, 1961: 181). But class and status are frequently connected, as class is a key force in the formation of status groups. This is because 'class situation is by far the predominant factor for the possibility of a style of life expected by members of a status group' (Weber, cited in Gerth and Mills, 1961: 190) and it is invariably economically conditioned. Nevertheless, Weber did acknowledge that access to goods, income and lifestyles was not equal, and the meeting of individuals in a competitive market creates distinctive and differing life chances. Thus far, Weber's analysis of class is not that dissimilar to Marx's. The arena of exchange upon which life chances will be set is not an equal one, and the key distinguishing factor is the ownership and non-ownership of property. Consequently, in terms of acquiring highly valued goods, Weber states that the market favours the owners of production and gives them a monopoly in the procurement of goods. Hence, '"property" and "lack of property" are the basic categories of all class situations' (Weber, cited in Gerth and Mills, 1961: 182). Nevertheless, the ways in which individuals live and act within classes is not uniform. This is so because the market is typified by the need for differing services, and individuals possess differing skills and services to offer the market. As such, even though there may be a common class identity among those who own no property, they do not necessarily see themselves as a monolithic or unified class because Weber's approach allows for a process of social mobility and class fluidity. This is a key difference between Weber and Marx in their analysis of class, that social classes are (or can be) extensively sub-divided within themselves and not strictly along the lines of property, but due to the differential possession of 'status'. As Weber states:

> Those [individuals] whose fate is not determined by the chance of using goods or services for themselves on the market, e.g. slaves, are not ... a 'class'

in the technical sense of the term. They are, rather, a 'status group'. (cited in Gerth and Mills, 1961: 183)

Explaining the nature of status and status groups, Weber argues that it is typically founded on a style of life which could be expressed in terms of levels of formal education, training or instruction, heredity, wealth or occupational prestige. As a result, power, influence or equality is more multi-varied than Marx's model may express, and it is certainly, in Weber's view, more complex. As he states of the relationship between class and status:

> Status may rest on class position of a distinct or an ambiguous kind. However, it is not solely determined by it; money and an entrepreneurial position are not in themselves status qualifications, although they may lead to them; and a lack of property is not in itself a status disqualification, although this may be a reason for it. Conversely, status may influence, if not completely determine, a class position without being identical with it. The class position of an officer, a civil servant or a student may vary greatly according to their wealth and yet not lead to a different status since upbringing and education create a common style of life. (Weber, 1978: 306)

The key issue that emerges from Weber's concept of the status group is that it reflects a sense of social plurality. Hence, within a larger group which may be a class group, there can be differing levels of status and social prestige. In this regard, the possession of wealth can be overridden and rendered invalid by a status position that is empowered by some form of socially sanctioned esteem. To illustrate, this means that financially impoverished members of the aristocracy can still command greater levels of social esteem due to their hereditary background than wealthy and self-made members of a 'nouveau riche' or 'bourgeois' type, simply because they possess a specific and socially/culturally recognized degree of honour. So, in certain circumstances, economic income can be treated with indifference and be outweighed by the possession of a specific and culturally valued form of status.

Therefore, Weber argues that status groups resemble 'communities' that possess a distinctive style of life that is exhibited by all who desire to belong to specific status circles. However, and this is an important point, while status groups can be created by propertied classes, they can also be self-styled, that is, established from within occupational and educational groups, to the extent that barriers are erected to close off access to social goods and privileges to other groups or individuals deemed to possess lower status. Indeed, status groups can be generally characterized by the restrictive practices that they engage in and the ways in which they act as closed and exclusive 'castes'. To illustrate this process, Allen (2004) cites the example of teachers who reinforce their possession of specific educational qualifications and credentials to underscore the view that fellow, but less qualified, educational workers such as classroom assistants cannot engage in teaching activities. In a similar vein, we could also cite the example of lawyers and paralegals. So, although individuals may share the same class position (with regard to property ownership), there can be, and are, clear lines of division between them that have nothing to do with class, but everything to do with status. Even if there are similarities between the concepts of class and status, they are distinctive. As Weber explains:

> With some over-simplification, one might thus say that 'classes' are stratified according to their relations to the production and acquisition of goods; whereas 'status groups' are stratified according to the principles of their consumption of goods as represented by special 'styles of life'. (Cited in Gerth and Mills, 1961: 193)

This idea of 'styles of life' is key to Weber's analysis of status, and it is one that can be explored and illustrated in the popular culture of today, and in this instance, film. It is through the medium of film that we shall further contemporize Weber culturally, exploring the concept of status, both in terms of representations of its nature and also the practices by which status group boundaries are erected and enforced.

WEBER, STATUS AND FILM

In Chapter 1 I cited expressions of Marxist thought in hip hop music that represent deliberate articulations of Marx's political theory, and his thought has also found considerable expression in cinema. Although, as Kleinhans (2000) points out, Marx never went to the cinema, Marxist theory would find expression in the work of politically motivated directors such as Sergei Eisenstein in Soviet Russia, Hollywood's Douglas Sirk, and France's Jean-Luc Godard. Additionally, the emergent disciple of film studies would read Marxist and neo-Marxist themes in a number of films. As an example, and to provide a populist instance, Kendrick (1999) identifies a consistent 'Marxist' thematic thread running throughout key films directed by the mega-budget Hollywood film-maker, James Cameron. Citing *Aliens* (1986), *The Abyss* (1989) and *Titanic* (1997), Kendrick argues that these films represent a sustained critique of class divisions and, with reference to the science fiction texts, exploitative global capitalist expansion (and such an analysis could be readily applied to Cameron's 2009 3-D sci-fi epic, *Avatar*, with its narrative based on corporate greed, the acquisition of natural resources and neo-imperialism).

While Weber presumably did go to the movies, it is not readily apparent that film directors have sought to consciously present his ideas in their films in any similar cognisant manner; nor is there any specific 'Weberian' school of film criticism akin to that inspired by Marx. Yet, the issue of status as a specific social phenomenon can be 'read' in a number of films due to the ways in which they push the concept to the foreground of their narratives and plots, whether they deal with groups that self-define their status criteria, or those 'life chances' which are imposed at a societal level. In terms of illustration, I have selected three key case studies, all very different, but linked by their consistent emphasis and representation of status as Weber has formulated it. The first example to be discussed is *Mean Girls* (Mark Waters, 2004).

In terms of genre or film type, *Mean Girls* is ostensibly a 'teen movie' as its plot concerns the central character, 16-year-old Cady Heron (Lindsay Lohan) in the wake of her return to the United States following years spent in Africa with her zoologist parents, and her entry to high school. So, it is through Cady's eyes, from her point of view, that the internal structure and socializing forces of high school society are revealed, and it is through Cady's re-integration into American life that the concept of status is both presented and explored. How the film expresses this is through the numerous social groups that Cady encounters, to the extent that there is no collective 'student body', but rather a number of distinctive groups, or 'cliques' that are utterly segregated from each other. These groups range from the 'Asian Nerds', the 'Cool Asians', the 'Unfriendly Black Hotties' and the 'Desperate Wannabes', to the 'Burnouts', the 'Art Freaks' and the 'Mathletes'. However, the 'A' clique is represented by the 'Plastics', the 'teen royalty' of the school society that is constituted by Gretchen Wieners (Lacey Chabert), Karen Smith (Amanda Seyfried) and the 'Queen Bee', Regina George (Rachel McAdams). The film explores the nature of teen status groups and the rules and conventions that govern them, as Cady joins the Plastics and adheres to their strict rules (which include strictures such as dressing in pink on Wednesdays, the wearing of jeans and a ponytail only once a week, and forbidding the donning of a tank top two days in a row). Consequently, regardless of the fact that the characters are ostensibly 'middle-class' and affluent (significantly, Gretchen is actually a member of the 'bourgeoisie' due to her father's industrial ownership and millionaire economic status), class is secondary in relation to status. Indeed, it is a redundant factor as the film is centrally concerned with status as related to distinctive styles of life that accord with Weber's notion of social closure: the active and defensive policing of status group entry. As Parkin notes:

> By social closure [Weber] means the process by which various groups attempt to improve their lot by restricting access to rewards and privileges to a limited circle. In order to do this they single out certain social and physical attributes that they themselves possess and define these as the criteria of eligibility. (2002: 100)

Although *Mean Girls* conveys this idea of social closure based on status in a highly exaggerated, stylized and unrealistic manner, nevertheless, the activities of the Plastics do serve to reflect Weber's conception of the social practice. The Plastics represent a school 'aristocracy' that is based entirely on fashion, comportment and style and not educational attainment or prowess (Karen is represented as lacking intellect to comedic levels). Alternatively, access to the group is by invitation and strict adherence to the social rules and conventions demanded by the clique (however arbitrary they may seem). However, despite being a fictional representation of teenage status group behaviour, the innumerable societies based on specific status attributes represented in *Mean Girls* is identifiable within school cultures. For instance, Adler and Adler's (1995) social psychological research into the dynamics of inclusion and exclusion in pre-adolescent school cliques (defined as friendship circles) found them to be rigidly hierarchical in structure, to employ processes of membership screening, and to be typically dominated by a leader figure. Furthermore, high-school cliques are exclusive to the extent that not all who desire membership are accepted. Thus, school groups are centrally defined by the principles of status and power, and are marked by keen structures and processes of status stratification and movement, principally of those with the closest ties to the leader of the clique – factors which are present and illustrated in the narrative of *Mean Girls*. Consequently, while the issue of class and class identity is obliquely alluded to in the film, the dominant factor is that of exclusivity based upon status and, crucially, self-defined entrance criteria. As a result of Cady's machinations, Regina ultimately loses her status as the leader (by gaining weight due to eating a sports bar that Cady falsely assures her is guaranteed to help shed weight). Accordingly, as Regina's fashionable and clique-ordained svelte and stylish figure fades, she is replaced by Cady as the new 'Queen Bee' and is progressively ostracized by the fellow members of the Plastics group. Therefore, reflecting a social milieu that is strictly stratified in terms of specific status attributes, *Mean Girls* presents a cogent view of a micro-cosmic society that is governed by what Weber argued was central to all status societies: 'conventions which regulate the style of life' (1978: 307), and by a specific system of status honour 'expected by all those who wish to belong to the circle' (1961: 187).

If *Mean Girls* offers examples through which to visually explore processes of micro-social status stratification and social closure (and I argue that it does), the second film example I have selected, *The Devil Wears Prada* (David Frankel, 2006), combines a micro-view of status and status closure with a distinctive and socially powerful macro-social view. The plot concerns a young journalism graduate, Andrea 'Andy' Sachs (Anne Hathaway) taking a job as an assistant to the editor-in-chief of *Runway*, a top New York fashion magazine, as a stopgap until she can establish herself as a journalist, but expressions of status, status symbols and status ranking and closure are central to the narrative. The crux of the film revolves around the demanding nature and fearsome persona of editor-in-chief Miranda Priestly (Meryl Streep) and the degree to which she runs the magazine to almost impossibly exacting standards. More importantly, her authority as an arbiter of fashion is one of the primary ways in which the film presents an examination of status in a way that separates it from the issue of class.

At one level, Miranda's dominant professional status and the authority it grants her over her employees and in the wider fashion industry is the most obvious example to identify. Here, status equals absolute power. What Miranda (the 'devil' of the film's title) demands, she gets, with no resistance offered. However, it is the character of Andy that presents the more interesting articulation of status. As a highly educated woman (we learn that she rejected Stanford

Law School to pursue journalism), Andy effectively 'deigns' to work as Miranda's assistant. However, her educational status counts for nothing in the world of *Runway* or with Miranda due to her lack of fashion-consciousness and knowledge. Indeed, the opening credit sequence of the film visually establishes this with scenes of several young women dressing in the morning in fashionable, labelled 'in vogue' underwear, clothing, shoes and cosmetics while the first images of Andy show her as having no conception of fashion at all with her 'sensible' but dour, non-designer clothing, and her unkempt hairstyle. Consequently, Andy's dress sense is starkly juxtaposed with the central setting of the film, the chic and stylized metropolis of New York, and the fashion world in which Andy is suddenly immersed. But while none of this is subtle, nor terribly realistic, the narrative becomes that of Andy's eventual personal transformation, connected as it is with processes of closure and status mobility.

It is primarily through the occupational culture Andy enters that the film expresses this idea. On her first day of employment at *Runway*, Andy is informed by her fellow assistant, Emily Charlton (Emily Blunt), that she is the 'second assistant', and is consequently lower down the office hierarchy chain. In the face of Miranda's apathetic treatment of Emily (her first act upon entering her office is to unceremoniously, if not contemptuously, drop her coat onto Emily's desk), Emily's response is to establish for herself a superior status position in terms of the two key aspects of her role: taking The Book (the proofs of the new *Runway* edition) to Miranda's residence, and attending Paris Fashion Week. Consequently, Andy is tasked merely with the mundane roles befitting her junior status, such as collecting coffee and taking Miranda's telephone calls. These scenes present incisive examples of Weber's idea of occupational groups erecting barriers to close off access to privileges to those others deemed to possess lower status. Even though Andy and Emily share the same powerless occupational position, a status barrier is nevertheless constructed by Emily, based initially on her caustic assessment that Andy possesses no style or sense of fashion.

So, *The Devil Wears Prada* is not concerned with educational or occupational divisions, but instead status is related to fashion and the recognition of what is or is not fashionable (codes effectively enforced, as Miranda states in a memorable monologue, by her and others like her). As a result, it is ironic that Emily's attempt at closure based upon her rival's lack of style ultimately fails because Miranda initiates Andy into the ways of fashion by granting her access to the wealth of designer clothes stored at the magazine, and instructing Nigel (Stanley Tucci), *Runway*'s Art Director, to 'teach' her how to wear them. As regards the cultural importance of dress, clothing has long been read as an integral aspect of symbolic communication, as Cunningham and Voso Lab state: clothing plays an important role in daily life because 'it is often through its meaning that we substantiate our sense of self and our place in society' (1991: 1). In Craik's (1994) view, fashion performs the functions of a 'mask' disguising the 'true' nature of the body or person, while dress acts as a means by which individuals translate 'fashion into everyday practice' (Entwhistle, 2000: 237).

Accordingly, through dress and her instruction in the ways of fashionable clothing, Andy effectively 'translates fashion into everyday practice' and ultimately emulates the women she was juxtaposed with in the opening credits. As her fashion expertise develops, enabling her to independently put together dress ensembles, as well as becoming increasingly effective in the face of Miranda's often seemingly impossible demands (such as requiring Andy to procure a copy of an as yet unpublished *Harry Potter* novel manuscript for her children, a charge Andy successfully achieves) so does her status in the office, her ultimate eclipse of Emily signified by her invitation to be the assistant who goes to Paris.

Although the film makes some nominal nods to sexism in the workplace (at one stage Miranda comments that her 'sadistic' and 'impossible' work ethic would not be questioned if she were a man) and concludes with a moralistic rejection of sorts of the ways in which fashion is merely superficial (Andy rejects Miranda's world of high fashion and her own transformation into a shallow 'Glamazon' to take a job with a small but socially aware newspaper), the film contains many incisive comments and representations of status. It demonstrates how it can be established as a stratified system of closure within a micro-social environment (that of Miranda's outer office) and as a means of precluding occupational solidarity; and the ways in which the knowledge of fashion acts as a status indicator and as means of social and cultural demarcation. With regard to the competitive nature of Emily, the film visually presents a potent example of Weber's argument that status groups emerge within social classes. Emily and Andy share the same beleaguered occupational position, yet are divided by an arbitrary status line set up by Emily to protect her (illusory) perception of office seniority and higher hierarchical status, a standing that Miranda does not recognize, and indeed, constantly undermines due to the exercise of her own powerful status.

Mean Girls and *The Devil Wears Prada* both arguably present cogent examples of status that accord with Weber's analysis of the concept. The two films marginalize the issue of class and (albeit in differing ways) are predicated on the concept of status as a social and cultural phenomenon that is directly related to lifestyles and occupational positions. Furthermore, both films deal with micro-social instances of status stratification and group closure. However, they also flag some of the key criticisms of Weber and the process of social closure driven by differing status groups and positions. Weber suggested that closure practices related to differential forms of status can be based on virtually any social or cultural category, as the films examined in this chapter illustrate. Here, status closure is based on factors such as a lack of fashion sense, knowledge or attitude. These are processes which clearly occur in society (as noted, the clique mentality expressed in *Mean Girls* is readily identifiable inside educational institutions). However, in a wider social and cultural sense, as Parkin (2002) points out, closure practices are frequently both related to external social power agencies and instigated by the state because exclusionary status practices based on ethnicity, gender or religion are not arbitrary, nor are they habitually established at an internal social and cultural level. Furthermore, Weber's conception of the nature of status proliferated in later sociological studies, from the analysis of occupational groups, the nature of the 'power elite', and race and gender, to the exalted social status of contemporary celebrities (Kurzman *et al.*, 2007); so, whether mistakenly applied to modern societies and social groups or not, Weber's conception of status has endured and has been widely applied.

The issue of status stratification and closure in relation to social power, culture and wider social forces brings me to my third and final film example, *Slumdog Millionaire* (Danny Boyle, 2008), a film that deals with status and status closure in numerous ways that do not neglect the forces of religion, culture and economics that work to determine life chances, market positions and social and cultural status. Grossing $377 million worldwide at the box office and winning eight Academy Awards, the British-made *Slumdog Millionaire* is a globally successful film in which the central character, Jamal Malik (Dev Patel), wins 20 million rupees on the Indian version of the Western quiz show, *Who Wants To Be A Millionaire*.

> The story concerns the narrative of a young man from the slums who knows the answers to the quiz questions because each refer to something he has experienced in his life, rather than knowledge he gained through education. (Branston and Stafford, 2010: 163)

As this synopsis suggests, the film is centrally concerned with the issue of 'life chances' and articulates social and cultural attitudes to status in contemporary India in significant ways, including critical readings and reactions to the film that were not celebratory. While the film garnered considerable critical plaudits, writers such as Arundhati Roy and Salman Rushdie levelled the claims that the film's setting in the slums of Mumbai were romanticized to the extent that they constituted 'exploitative poverty porn that exoticised and packaged Indian slum life for the consumption of voyeuristic Western audiences' (Mendes, 2010: 473). In essence, their arguments pointed to the ways in which the film ignored India's emerging economic superpower ranking to reinforce and perpetuate its poverty-stricken global image, and buttress Western perceptions of this national status.

But the film's narrative also emphasizes the centrality of status and provides instances of status closure in a setting that serves to further illustrate Weber's ideas. In his analysis of Hinduism and the caste system, for instance, he defined it as a social structure that organizes ethnically segregated groups into a vertical system of subordination (Weber, 1978). Castes, he argued, represent closed status groups that are set apart due to the strict social and cultural blockades that exist to enforce a lack of movement or mobility between differing castes and their socially prescribed characteristics. In terms of the social effects of caste and status, Weber states that marriages between members of different castes cannot take place, and that various forms of 'social intercourse' and contact are strictly forbidden. Thus, 'castes combine religious beliefs with rigid observance of status differences' (Bendix, 1966: 143). Weber further argues of the historically based Indian system that:

> Such a caste situation is part of the phenomenon of 'pariah' peoples and is found all over the world. These people form communities, acquire specific occupational traditions of handicrafts or of other arts, and cultivate a belief in their ethnic community. They live in a 'diaspora' strictly segregated from all personal intercourse, except that of an unavoidable sort. (Cited in Gerth and Mills, 1961: 189)

Even though *Slumdog Millionaire* does not deal with a formalized or religiously based notion of caste (religious status groups are present, though), it nevertheless reflects Weber's statement keenly, representing, as it does, a contemporary pariah class, the 'slumdogs' – the denizens of the Mumbai slum districts – and consistently presents examples of the ways in which this 'diasporic' group is shunned and socially oppressed. In terms of narrative structure, the film begins with scenes of Jamal being physically assaulted, tortured and questioned by the police. The rationale for this brutal treatment is linked with Jamal's class and status position in Indian society, a status that means that Jamal (who is only one question away from winning the 20 million rupees) is assumed to be a cheat because he is an 'uneducated 18-year-old boy from the slums of Mumbai' – a 'slumdog' – and as such socially incapable of legitimately possessing the knowledge that has enabled him to reach this stage. As the police inspector (Irrfan Khan) states, contestants including university professors, lawyers and doctors – the possessors of esteemed educational and occupational status – have not been able to reach the point at which Jamal has arrived. So it is the issue of status that has placed Jamal in the police station, accused of illegality. However, the narrative conceit of the film is that it is precisely Jamal's status and life chances that are the key to his success on the quiz show. In the face of an interrogation that involves the inspector playing a taped edition of the show, Jamal's responses are represented in a series of flashbacks to his childhood and subsequent life events, all of which have provided him with the answers to the various questions he is asked on the show. Thus, it is only because he is a 'slumdog' who has grown up with a specific lifestyle within a socially defined status group that he is poised to become a millionaire.

The first flashback to his early childhood depicts Jamal and his brother, Salim, at play with a group of other street children, pursued by the police through streets strewn with refuse and houses bearing rusted corrugated metal roofs. In addition to their economic status (signified by the urban space in which they live) Jamal and Salim possess a further status signifier, that of their Muslim ethnic identity, poignantly revealed in another flashback triggered by the quiz question: 'What is Rama holding in his right hand?' Jamal knows the answer because he saw a small boy dressed in the guise of Rama (and holding a bow in his right hand) who was part of a Hindu group that attacked his Muslim community, a religiously/ethnically-motivated assault in which his mother was killed and which precipitated the brothers' subsequent orphaned and nomadic street life. As a result, Jamal is not only a 'slumdog', but as an Indian Muslim, he experiences further persecution due to his religious and ethnic status. In this sense, an economic assessment of Jamal's social position is too limiting, and the film visually works to represent the sub-divisions and multiple levels of stratification that exist in Jamal's world.

The scenes that depict Jamal's interaction with the quiz show's host, Prem Kapur (Anil Kapoor), provide specific illustrations of status and status closure, and constitute a recurring reinforcement of Jamal's slumdog status, and his 'low' occupational grade, that of *chi-wallah* (tea boy) in a Mumbai call centre. The interplay between Kapur and Jamal is 'mock-friendly' and designed to subtly humiliate Jamal before the live studio audience with sustained references to his status, job and financial prospects. For example, following the asking of the question: 'Which statesman's portrait is on a $100 bill?', Kapur sarcastically adds: 'Jamal, get a lot of $100 bills in your line of work?' Similarly, Kapur implies (in relation to a question concerning Alexandre Dumas' novel, *The Three Musketeers*) that Jamal may be illiterate (he is not), and urges Jamal to repeatedly take the money at various levels with (off-camera) remarks that he will never be able to answer the next question. But aside from any socially ingrained prejudice against Jamal's pariah status, the film posits that Kapur's scorn is based on an attempt at mobility closure. During a filming break, Kapur says to Jamal, in the men's washroom, 'A guy from the slums becomes a millionaire overnight. Do you know the only other person who's done that? Me.' On leaving, Kapur writes the letter B on the steamed mirror – the apparent answer to the next question – in an act of seeming 'slumdog solidarity', an offer Jamal rejects as he chooses option D – which is the correct answer. In this scene, Kapur is engaging in an act of status closure, trying to ensure that his mobility will not be emulated by another, and refusing to recognize any class or status connection with Jamal. Indeed, it is Kapur who reports Jamal to the police, denouncing him as a cheat, citing his 'slumdog' status as the 'proof', because if Jamal wins, he wins not only a vast financial prize, but also access to a new life, and, crucially, an undreamed-of status beyond the slums and the call centre. However, as Weber states, a reaction endemic to many status groups is frequently that of defensive action against incursion from 'outsiders' and non-status group members, even if aspiring members acquire considerable economic means:

> If mere economic acquisition and naked economic power still bearing the stigma of its extra-status origin could bestow upon anyone who has won it the same honor as those who are interested in status by virtue of style of life claim for themselves, the status would be threatened at its very root ... Therefore all groups having interests in the status order react with special sharpness precisely against the pretensions of purely economic acquisition. In most cases they react the more vigorously the more they feel themselves threatened. (Cited in Gerth and Mills, 1961: 192)

From a Weberian perspective, Kapur's actions are patent: Mumbai has space for only one 'slumdog millionaire', and he has no desire to allow Jamal to share his status position. As such, this sequence of the film serves as a potent reflection of Weber's conception of the closed nature of status groups and the ways in which possession of economic wealth is not always sufficient to overcome closed boundaries. So, even though the climax of the film sees Jamal triumphant, having answered the final question correctly and set to become a millionaire, he is also finally reunited with his childhood friend and subsequent true love, Latika (Frieda Pinto). The closing sequence pays homage to India's 'Bollywood' cinema heritage, emulating the group dance numbers that are a signature feature of many Indian films. The end scene implies that Jamal and Latika will live 'happily ever after', and leaves unsaid the possibility that, as Weber's analysis suggests, Jamal's wealth may never enable him to shake off his 'slumdog' status entirely, and that he may face future acts of social closure. This is so because, regardless of economic means:

> The 'parvenu' is never accepted, personally and without reservation, by the privileged status groups, no matter how completely his style of life has been adjusted to theirs. They will only accept his descendents who have been educated in the conventions of their status group. (Cited in Gerth and Mills, 1961: 192)

Jamal is the perfect example of the 'parvenu', an individual who is a newcomer to a specific socio-economic class. According to Weber's analysis, Jamal's and Latika's children are the ones who would be fully accepted in the new strata to which his wealth takes him, and, due to the power of a system that is traceable back to the social conventions of courtly knights, Jamal, the possessor of 20 million rupees notwithstanding, will perhaps always be the 'slumdog millionaire'.

Weber's ideas concerning class and status have been extensively applied in subsequent social theory, but linking these concepts, especially that of status, with examples drawn from popular film enables us to visualize and illustrate them in comprehensible ways. The three films discussed in this chapter are all popular films that share one common theme: they are based on representations of clearly demarcated status differences and exclusionary practices. These range from the micro-social environment and individual status-defined world of the American high school, through the arbitrary hierarchies of office politics reinforced by the societal and cultural codes and conventions of the fashion system, to status positions enforced by external social forces that see class and status explicitly linked with poverty, life chances and religious *and* economic persecution.

The juxtaposition of 'light' films such as *Mean Girls* and *The Devil Wears Prada* with a film that represents the limitations and human costs of socially enforced life chances is a deliberate one. Status takes numerous forms, as do the ways in which status closure is enacted, and as such, it is observable in the world around us, be it the schoolyard, the classroom, the workplace or a global perspective of cultures and societies. Consequently, the sociological ideas Weber formulated almost a century ago can be located on the cinema screen and explored in ways that not only illuminate his thought, but also demonstrate the currency his ideas retain in relation to the surrounding social world. Class remains a central force in the world, but the divisions and stratifications within it are also significant and perceptible. But while these can be discerned from academic texts or newspapers, they can also be explored and critically analysed in scenes from *Mean Girls*, *The Devil Wears Prada* and *Slumdog Millionaire*. It may not be deliberate, but Weber is there.

QUESTIONS TO CONSIDER

1. What are the key differences and contrasts between Marx's conception of class and Weber's idea of status?
2. What are the major ways in which *Mean Girls* and *The Devil Wears Prada* can be argued to represent the micro-social expression of status and status closure?
3. What are the major differences in terms of the articulation of status between *Slumdog Millionaire,* and *Mean Girls* and *The Devil Wears Prada*?

FURTHER READING

For further detail concerning Weber's theory of class and status, readers should consult H.H. Gerth and C. Wright Mills' *From Max Weber: Essays in Sociology,* and Weber's short discussion of the subjects in *Economy and Class Vol. 1*. For good critical discussions of Weber's work, readers should see Kieran Allen's *Max Weber: A Critical Introduction* and Frank Parkin's *Max Weber*. In terms of contemporary discussions and applications of Weber's concept of status, Charles Kurzman's 'Celebrity Status' (in *Sociological Theory*, Vol. 25, No. 4, pp. 347–67) summarizes the concept succinctly and explores it in relation to a historical and contemporary analysis of celebrity and fame.

Durkheim and celebrity

3

Having discussed the approaches of Marx and Weber in the previous two chapters, it is only fitting that we now turn to the third of the so-called 'fathers of sociology', the French thinker, Émile Durkheim (1858–1917). Like Marx, Durkheim was a crucial thinker in the creation of classical sociology because 'he located social forces "outside" the individual actor' (Alexander, 2005: 136). But, unlike Marx, Durkheim was concerned not with any radical project to transform society, but rather with the 'functions' of key society and their influences on the individuals who comprised it. As such, Durkheim is frequently regarded as the more 'conservative' of the classic founders of sociology (Giddens, 1971; Lukes, 1973; Lemert, 2006). Durkheim's work has much to say about the ways in which societies operate as societies – indeed, how they constitute a society at all, rather than being made up of atomized and disconnected individuals. It also finds a particularly significant expression in relation to a specific social group that has come to dominate media discourse in recent years: celebrity, that class of individuals from the worlds of cinema, television, fashion, popular music and sport who, as a result of extensive media coverage, command a considerable degree of public attention, if not (as some commentators suggest) emotions akin to religious worship. But even beyond more extreme reactions to the lives of celebrities, on a day-to-day basis celebrity, whether loved or loathed, provides a common cultural ground, a subject that is widely recognized and thereby capable of uniting social actors into shared ways of seeing the world, and thus experiencing distinctive moments of popular culture-inspired 'solidarity'. In other instances, the deaths of celebrity figures (Princess Diana and Michael Jackson, for example) have produced widespread public expressions of grief that have served to create social collectives. So, celebrity is the example of popular culture to be examined in this chapter in relation to classic sociology. But first, who was Émile Durkheim, and what was the subject of his sociology?

DURKHEIM'S SOCIOLOGY

Born in Épinal, France, Émile Durkheim was pivotal in establishing sociology as a key component of the humanities. Influenced by industrial and cultural change in France, Durkheim not only produced the seminal works that would establish sociology as a major discipline, but he was, on his appointment to a chair in sociology in 1913, one of the first professional sociologists in the field. Durkheim argued that the subject was a scientific discipline; consequently he became a key figure in what would become known as the Positivist perspective (the foundation of the quantitative methodological approach). Throughout his key works, *The Division of Labour in Society* (1893), *The Rules of Sociological Method* (1896), *Suicide* (1897) and *The Elementary Forms of Religious Life* (1912), Durkheim articulated the ways in which social institutions played a fundamental shaping role in societies. He set out models of how societies are knitted together, the power of social structures and events to directly affect human behaviour (to the extent that even the drive to commit suicide was a social imperative, not a psychological one), and devised the specific methodological rules required to understand these interconnected institutions and their social influences.

Durkheim's approach was directly influenced by the work of his fellow French theorist, Auguste Comte (1798–1857). It was Comte who, in his extensive book, *Course of Positive Philosophy* (1830–42), had set out the basic principles of Positivism, and who actually created the term 'sociology'. In Comte's view, social science had to strive to mirror the approaches of natural science and to be able to produce 'positive' knowledge based on the empirical methodology that was the product of the European Enlightenment movement. The Enlightenment represented an extended moment in human history in which the Greco-Roman and Christian traditions of social thought were challenged: 'a new science of society stemming from great scientific breakthroughs from the fifteenth to the seventeenth centuries ... of Copernicus, Kepler, Galileo and Newton' (Hamilton, 1992: 21). Consequently, the previously dominant cosmological view of a perfectly ordered, divinely created universe was questioned in the wake of a scientific revolution that alternatively regarded the universe as a complex mechanical system that obeyed natural, not divine, laws. As such, the collective ultimately dubbed the 'Enlightenment' rejected modes of understanding based exclusively on religious or philosophical grounds in favour of forms of knowledge that had to submit themselves to the principles of the scientific method, especially that of empiricism: 'the idea that all thought and knowledge about the natural and social world is based upon empirical facts, things that all human beings can apprehend through their sense organs' (ibid.). Comte attempted to apply this empirical approach to understanding the social world and the actions of humans within social organizations. As with the natural scientist, so the social scientist must seek to understand social phenomena through direct observation and adherence to objective 'facts'. In this manner, Comte argued that sociology could produce 'positive knowledge' every bit as certain as the knowledge produced by the primary natural sciences (physics, chemistry, biology), but with distinctive characteristics of its own.

Durkheim's conception of the nature of society in relation to the individuals comprising it (and consequently how it should be studied by the sociologist) is unambiguously set forth in *The Rules of Sociological Method*. As he states at the outset of the book:

> There is in every society a certain group of phenomena which may be differentiated from those studied by the other natural sciences. When I fulfil my obligations as brother, husband, or citizen, when I execute my contracts, I perform duties which are defined, externally to myself and my acts, in law and in custom. (1964: 1)

Durkheim's point here is to illustrate the absolute influence of society over the individual. So, attitudes, sentiments, beliefs and values that may be felt to be intrinsically subjective and internal to individual consciousness are, in fact, objectively instilled from social institutions. To illustrate, Durkheim cites the example of religious belief and practice. A social actor may perceive that their religious values are central to their behaviour, indeed, central to their identity. However, the precepts and values that make up a particular (and typical) religious belief existed before the particular follower came to be part of it. As such, a church member's beliefs and practices are ready made at birth, existing before and operating outside of his or her physical existence. Furthermore, an institution such as the Church is not merely external to the individual, but it possesses coercive powers which can be imposed upon the individual. So, in Durkheim's context, religious belief may be socially enforced and may have nothing to do with personal, individual choice of values. Religion constitutes a primary example of what Durkheim called a 'social fact', a key institution that interacts 'functionally' with its fellow institutions.

At this stage we may argue in the wake of the long-standing 'secularization' process, a general decline in the influence of religion that many (but not all) societies have experienced across the world (Saliba, 1995; Wilson, 1999; Brown, 2009), that religion is a limited example. However, the coercive force of social facts extends beyond that of religious belief and attendant modes of behaviour. Morality, argues Durkheim, is enforced through official modes of punishment (the criminal justice system), and the education system is a primary institution to 'imprint' the values and mores of a given society upon the individual from the earliest age. As Durkheim explains:

> Education is a continuous effort to impose on the child ways of seeing, feeling, and acting which he could not have arrived at spontaneously. From the very first hours of his life, we compel him to eat, drink, and sleep at regular hours; we constrain him to cleanliness, calmness, and obedience; later we exert pressure upon him in order that he may learn proper consideration for others, respect for customs and conventions, the need for work, etc. If, in

time, this constraint ceases to be felt, it is because it gradually gives rise to habits and to internal tendencies that render constraint unnecessary; but nevertheless it is not abolished, for it is still the source from which these habits were derived. (1964: 6)

This process constitutes a prime example of the manner in which the socialization of individuals into the values of a given society or large-scale social grouping is effected. Here, the education system does not simply provide knowledge about the world, but it is a central institution instrumental in the instilling of key social values and ways of being; it is within this context that social actors are effectively 'constituted' by society, which consists of a series of interrelated and mutually supporting 'social facts', which Durkheim exhorted readers to accept as 'things' that expressed and inculcated collective values. Thus:

A social fact is every way of acting, fixed or not, capable of exercising on the individual an external constraint; or again, every way of acting which is general throughout a given society, while at the same time existing in its own right independent of its individual manifestations. (1964: 13)

For Durkheim, incidences of social behaviour, emotions or behavioural tendencies are *not* the result of individual quirks of consciousness; they are the result of the social conditions in which a number of individuals find themselves. It is society that influences individual action, not internal psychology, to the extent that even suicide, the act of conscious self-destruction, is ultimately explicable by recourse to social causes, not innate drives or emotion. In this view, suicide is related to social forces and values, especially that inspired by the condition known as anomie, 'the state of mental confusion caused by the absence of workable norms for the conduct of daily life' (Lemert, 2006: 11); this is evidenced by social factors such as divorce, morality and structural social upheaval (war, economic crashes, bankruptcy, and so on) and its attendant effect on predictable social values and 'norms'. Since the level of analysis is at the level of the social, traces of these social facts as concrete 'things' exist in the form of statistics and statistical patterns (marriage or suicide rates, for instance). Consequently, according to Durkheim:

All that is given, all that is subject to observation, has thereby the character of a thing. To treat phenomena as things is to treat them as data, and these constitute the point of departure of science. (1964: 27)

Furthermore, Durkheim, in producing *The Rules of Sociological Method*, set out the sociologists' manual, to be followed precisely in accordance with the central principles of the scientific method. Subsequently, if seeking to ascertain the nature of social facts as social things, the sociologist needed to set aside all subjective preconceptions and reject sensation in favour of objectivity – just as the physicist would use precise instruments (thermometer or electrometer) to measure temperature and electricity, rather than simply relying on feelings of sensation. Only through such an approach, rooted in the scientific method, could the sociologist produce certain, or 'positive' knowledge about the nature of society.

A further issue of significance in the work of Durkheim, and one to be illustrated and contemporized later in this chapter, is how societies, especially large-scale societies, maintain a 'harmonious' structure. In a broad sense, the Durkheimian view does not look to the dominance of power groups as, albeit in differing ways, Marx and Weber would. The coercive nature of Marx's model of society, a literal form of class-based coercion and overt ideological control, is not to be readily found in Durkheim. Instead, the collective nature of society, Durkheim's quintessential articulation of social structure, stems from his extensive study of the concept of solidarity.

DURKHEIM AND SOLIDARITY

Durkheim sets out his conception of how societies, from simple and small-scale to more complex and industrial operate, in *The Division of Labour in Society*, arguing that the division of labour is a necessary condition for both the intellectual and material development of societies, indeed, it is the very source of civilization itself. Although there are clear and necessary economic outcomes from the existence and operation of a social division of labour, any economic service is secondary to its true function: 'to create between two or more people a feeling of solidarity' (1984: 17). Therefore, the division of labour is a key source of the 'social glue' that binds individuals together to form a functional and integrated society, and as such, an essential component of the social structure, performing a crucial role whereby:

> Individuals are linked to one another who would otherwise be independent; instead of developing separately, they concert their efforts. They are solidly tied to one another and the links between them function not only in the brief moments when they engage in an exchange of services, but extend considerably beyond. (1984: 21)

However, the division of labour applies to only one of Durkheim's conceptions of solidarity, *organic*, but there is a primary form, and one that tends to explain the ways in which integrative social 'networks' have been established in smaller-scale societies, a form of solidarity called *mechanical* solidarity. In basic terms, mechanical solidarity is illustrated by what Durkheim refers to as 'solidarity by similarities' and manifests itself in the form of feelings and mores shared by the majority of a social group, for example, etiquette, ritual, and ceremonial or religious practices, what Durkheim calls the collective, common or the 'conscious collective': 'the set of beliefs and sentiments common to the average members of a single society [which] forms a determinate system that has its own life' (cited in Lukes, 1973: 4). That it has a 'life of its own' is explained in terms of its detachment from specific social conditions and specific individuals because it outlives them, it persists as generations come and go. Consequently, it represents something quite different from the consciousness of individuals, existing above and beyond them as a common social consciousness that influences the morality and social behaviour of individuals to instil social cohesion. This sense of a collective, shared conscious, or way of acting, set of beliefs, etc., is spread throughout an entire society.

But how is this achieved? How can an external consciousness collectively influence a group of individuals into a coherent sense of solidarity? Social laws, rules sanctioned by punishments for transgressing the conscious collective are one means (we have already seen examples of this, such as the education system), but religion is another. And it is religion and religious practices and rituals that are an essential component in the creation and maintenance of social cohesiveness, or social solidarity. In *The Elementary Forms of Religious Life*, Durkheim argued that:

> A religion is a unified system of beliefs and practices relative to sacred things, that is to say, things set apart and forbidden – beliefs and practices which unite into one single moral community called a Church, all those who adhere to them. (1976: 47)

Within his study of religion, Durkheim did not see it (as Marx did) as a social force that necessarily functioned as a means of maintaining social power and legitimating class inequality, but examined its function as a key source of mechanical solidarity. *The Elementary Forms of Religious Life* was based on the analysis of 'elementary', 'primitive' or 'humble' religious and ceremonial practices, specifically those practised by Australian Aboriginal tribal societies in relation to 'totemic' religious rituals. A totem object typically took the form of either a plant/vegetable or an animal (although there were instances of inanimate objects being chosen, such as rocks, clouds, rain, hail, frost, the moon and the sun), and had exclusive, emblematic significance for a particular clan, representing 'collective ideals that have fixed themselves on material objects' (cited in Lukes, 1973: 25). It is a sacred object, regarded with veneration and surrounded by various ritual activities. Totemic objects are endowed with the value of being *sacred* to the group, and they are segregated from alternative *profane* plants, vegetables, animals, or objects. The latter serve as food, while it is prohibited to eat those objects which have been sanctified as sacred. In Durkheim's view, the totem becomes a symbol of the clan/tribe, and in the course of collective ceremonies and feasts that surround the totemic object, the social group is bound together. Thus, religion upholds and reaffirms collective sentiments and collective ideas, reinforcing unity and cementing mechanical solidarity. However, what of larger social forms, ones that are not defined by ceremonial religious practices, but characterized by increasing individual differentiation, not similarity? Durkheim's answer returns us to the division of labour, and the second form of solidarity: organic.

Organic solidarity is the unifying force of the secular world. Where everything social was religious, the power of religion is a diminishing force in industrialized societies, argues Durkheim. In the place of religious functions, political, economic and scientific functions have established themselves as powerful social forces to the extent that 'God, from being at first present in every human relationship, has progressively withdrawn' (1984: 119). So, if the power of sacred objects or the institution of the Church and its integrative values has ebbed, how does society continue to exist? How does it function in terms of instilling a common consciousness into a large number of individuals? The answer lies in difference, or differentiation. The structural nature of an 'organic' society is entirely different from a 'mechanical' one, and is why it is called 'organic'. Instead of homogeneous values, organic solidarity is characterized by a system of difference, of different 'organs' which act, as organs do within a living body, in a co-ordinated fashion, each possessing a specialized function. Each 'organ' is different, but vitally interrelated to the 'body' as a whole. As Durkheim states:

> This social type relies upon principles so utterly different from the preceding type that it can only develop to the extent that the latter has vanished. Indeed individuals are distributed within it in groups that are no longer formed in terms of any ancestral relationship, but according to the special activity to which they devote themselves. (1984: 132)

So, within increasingly urban and industrial societies, social groupings that are not bound by close-knit blood relations, or specific sacred practices, the socially solidifying forces come from specialized, but differing, employment roles – what Durkheim calls 'the division of labour'. Consequently, in densely populated spaces, urban centres that necessitate constant social contact, individuals, despite their numerousness and lack of emotional or familial connections, form a society through industrial interdependence and co-operation. Hence, the differing roles serve to knit industrial societies together. Within a condition of organic solidarity, social actors have what Durkheim dubs 'a sphere of action', a specific role or form of employment that is entirely specific to them. The same is true for other social actors in the given society, who, while physically atomized, come together through their interdependence. Thus, some individuals may produce food, others clothing, while others still perform manufacturing roles or service provision. Durkheim's vision of society is that of an interconnected web of social dependencies coming together to form a cohesive social whole: a harmonious collective.

Although individuals meet each other in terms of their differing jobs, the outcome is far more significant, argues Durkheim. What is actually occurring is a process whereby individuals meet as differing 'social functions'; as such, 'society has an interest in the interplay of these functions: depending on whether they co-operate regularly or not, society will be healthy or sick' (1984: 338). Consequently, Durkheim's approach to the issue of labour, or work, in highly populated and industrial societies is not especially concerned with the economic impact or nature of the collective division of labour. This is because the economic provisions of the division of labour are secondary when compared with the 'moral' consequence that it generates, because the actual function of the division of labour, as with religious or sacred practices before it, 'is to create between two or more people a feeling of solidarity' (1984: 17).

SOLIDARITY THROUGH CELEBRITY?

Unsurprisingly, Durkheim's sociology, like that of Marx and Weber, would transcend his lifetime and influence later social thought. For instance, Durkheim's concept of anomie would be applied to the study of crime – most notably that produced by Robert K. Merton in the 1930s. Anomie would also constitute a key explanatory factor in the persistence and proliferation of religious groups and beliefs that flourished from the mid-twentieth century, from New Ageism and Scientology to spiritualism and astrology, in the face of the fragmentary and 'anomic' nature of industrial and urban modernization throughout the Western world (Saliba, 1995; Nelson, 1969; Tiryakian, 1972). However, Durkheim has also found his way into studies concerned with contemporary popular culture such as sport. For example, Carter and Carter (2007) apply the typically structural manifestation of anomie to the psychological level, with its apparent manifestation in the form of criminal activities and anti-social behaviours exhibited by NFL football players in the wake of rapidly changing lifestyles (wealth, social acclaim and cultural status). Turning to British football and the issue of solidarity, King's (1997) analysis of the structural transformations that occurred in the sport in the 1990s (such as television deals that financially changed the nature of the game in terms of suitability of broadcasts (mid-week in addition to the long-standing Saturday afternoon fixtures) and the re-design of stadiums into all-seat environments) similarly turns to Durkheim to explain the ways in which long-standing Manchester United supporters affirmed their loyalty to the club, clinging to traditional supporter values in the face of an influx of 'new fans'. However, there is a further example that can be drawn from popular culture that can be used to demonstrate the continuing saliency of Durkheim's sociology, and that example is celebrity.

Reflecting on the characteristics of celebrity in the mid-1990s, the writer J.G. Ballard stated that, because society had shifted its focus and adulation away from historical figures such as John F. Kennedy to television personalities, models and actors, celebrity was something of an exhausted concept; indeed, Ballard went so far as to state that it was possible that popular culture was 'nearing the end of celebrity' (cited in Vale and Ryan, 2004: 80). However, Ballard was mistaken. Far from witnessing the end of celebrity, the latter part of the twentieth century and the beginning of the twenty-first was characterized by an intensification of interest in celebrity, and a pantheon of individuals who possess famous names and famous faces, from actors such as Brad Pitt, Tom Cruise, James Pattison, Shah Rukh Khan and Angelina Jolie, and pop stars such as Madonna, Britney

Spears, Katy Perry or Justin Bieber, to sports stars of the stature of David Beckham, Tom Brady and Yao Ming. Even politicians such as Barrack Obama and Sarah Palin have transcended the world of politics to become celebrity figures. Although the study of stardom is not new, recent years have seen not only the media-led intensification in the reporting of a distinctive social group dubbed 'celebrities', but also an attendant growth in the sociological study of celebrity as a social phenomenon.

In terms of definitions, as Rojek states, the Latin root of the word celebrity is *celebren*, which is associated with 'fame' and being 'thronged', while the French word *célèbre,* meaning 'well known in public' evokes a similar association, all of which have become central to the contemporary conception of celebrity (2001: 9). In this regard, Evans (2004: 17) points to the key issues that are conventionally associated with individuals who have attained, or been granted, the status of celebrity, that of the possession of some form of charismatic appeal (where Weber has been especially useful) and the perception that they possess extraordinary merits, hence the designator 'star', whereby select individuals are perceived to 'emanate a bright and powerful light'. However, there are a number of key social prerequisites for the existence of celebrity status, such as: economic development above a subsistence level, a degree of social mobility, a structured social system, a clear separation between the spheres of work and leisure, the existence of a mass society and mass culture, and most significantly, the development and entrenchment of mass communication technologies (Alberoni, 1972; Dyer, 1982; Marshall, 1997). Thus, Giles provides a pertinent definition of the nature of current celebrity when he states that the 'ultimate modern celebrity is the member of the public who becomes famous solely through media involvement' (2000: 25). This is a valid designation for societies awash with tabloid tales of celebrity exploits, print media buttressed by the existence of specialist glossy celebrity magazines such as *Hello!* and *OK!,* joined by cable/satellite TV broadcast correlates such as *E!* and online blog spaces typified by Perezhilton.com, a site devoted exclusively to celebrity gossip. It is also a definition that captures the ways in which mass communication technology creates celebrity figures, ranging from traditional means (cinema, television, sport and music) through to what Turner (2004) refers to as the 'fabricated' celebrities created by webcams, and more significantly, the television genre known as 'reality TV', typified by the globally syndicated game show, *Big Brother,* which precipitated a conspicuous increase in the number of 'ordinary' people able to appear on television (Holmes, 2004). Convergent self-broadcast channels, most significantly YouTube, have also served to intensify this process. An illustrative example in this regard is the case of 'internet celebrity' Chris Crocker's now infamous tearful self-broadcast 'Leave Britney Alone!' weblog defence of the pop singer Britney Spears' critically derided MTV Music Video Awards performance in 2007. The broadcast that was viewed by over four million people in two days and made Crocker internationally known, albeit the renown was invariably coloured by mockery and disdain, perfectly epitomizes Giles' conception of celebrity.

But the history of fame predates these structural and technological factors, illuminating the fact that the desire for celebrity, the motivation to stand out from the social 'mass', is a long-standing one in human civilization. As Garland (2010) notes, the first recorded act of gratuitous (and pathological) fame-seeking is arguably that of Herostratus who, in 348 BCE, set fire to the temple at Ephesus, driven by an insatiable appetite for fame. However, Leo Braudy (1986) states in his book, *The Frenzy of Renown*, that the search for fame as modern societies understand it effectively begins with the Macedonian king and 'conqueror of the world', Alexander the Great, born in 356 BCE. Braudy goes beyond Alexander's salient fame, his military prowess and achievements, to focus on his active desire to control his own image and ensure his fame within his own lifetime, and beyond it throughout history. Alexander's mission was to establish his descent from the Homeric hero, Achilles, and thus weave an image that reinforced his superhuman abilities, and he achieved this through the active stage management of his image, and the employment of Callisthenes, his official historian, on his military campaign against Persia. Consequently, argues Braudy, Alexander sought cultural and imaginative domination in addition to military pacification and the glories bestowed by war. Callisthenes therefore ranks as one of history's first public relations operatives, an individual charged with positively manipulating his employer's public image, with an emphasis on confirming Alexander's divine nature (he claimed ancestry to Dionysus, Perseus and Hercules) for his subjects back in Macedonia (to which Alexander never returned). Even more presciently, Alexander realized that later generations would have to know what he looked like, so he also commissioned artists to capture his likeness, and had his image stamped on coins (an image-transmitting strategy continued by later ancient rulers such as the Roman emperor, Augustus), which served to perpetuate his name and his legend due to the 'continued circulation of coins with his markings for years after his death' (Braudy, 1986: 104).

But, as Giles states, from such auspicious beginnings, the quest for personal fame was not significant in Western society, due largely to the absolute authority of the Church. However, this began to change with a number of technological developments that enabled the mass transmission of names and images, most notably the invention of the printing press, the increased use of engraving, and the development of portraiture that depicted humans faces and figures in non-religious contexts. At the level of social structure, massive population growth and industrialization necessitated the rise of urbanization. For Inglis (2010), it is in the major eighteenth-century Western urban spaces that celebrity develops as a distinctive status and definitive social category. It was within the cultural life of 1760s London that the celebrity system so pervasive in contemporary culture was formed. To illustrate, he cites the development of the theatre under the direction of David Garrick, the 'first' late eighteenth-century celebrity figure and the actor, producer and theatre owner who established a clear spatial divide between the theatrical player and the audience – an audience hungry for tales of the actors' 'scandalous' private lives. Inglis places such developments in the context of the processes of the 'industrialisation of leisure', and the growth of public spaces such as concert halls and promenading gardens. These areas, which existed beyond working life, were intimately connected with developing consumerism and individual visibility, and acted as forums for the display of those who possessed famous faces. These factors were further developed in relation to Paris and New York of the late nineteenth and early twentieth centuries, principally the rise of the department store, arcades and café culture in Paris. Such spaces were the social and cultural rendezvous sites of the anonymous and the famous, and the ostentatiously displayed trappings of luxury flaunted by New York's industrial classes were extensively reported by emergent journalistic genres predicated extensively upon gossip, scandal and muckraking about the lives of the famous – a process intensified by developments in the 'new media' technology of radio, cinema and television, creating globally recognized icons such as Cary Grant, John Wayne and Marilyn Monroe, through to Bob Dylan, The Beatles, Jim Morrison, Tom Cruise, Princess Diana and Tiger Woods. However, Inglis argues that in contemporary popular culture, celebrity is firmly established and now difficult to map because it is now 'disorientingly large: from Aung San Suu Kyi to the individuals who appear on Reality TV and celebrity chefs' (2010: 17).

So, celebrity as we recognize it from popular media today has a history of some 250 years, and most significantly, it is the product of social transformation – more cogently the product of urbanization and the development of large-scale social organizations. In other words, exactly the type of society Durkheim analysed with regard to his concept of organic solidarity. And yet, celebrity points to the ways in which the shift from mechanical to organic was perhaps never total – there has always been a degree of slippage between them. On the one hand, the various discussions of new religious movements that developed from the second half of the twentieth century have already pointed to this slippage. The case for the need for some form of spirituality in the face of an anomic world characterized by upheaval (of which urbanization and industrialization were prime examples) has been convincingly made. On the other hand, however, celebrity has increasingly been seen to represent something akin to a new religious movement, albeit a secular one. Therefore, given the levels of worship and adoration bestowed upon celebrities, it therefore arguably fulfils the mechanical role that Durkheim argued totemic practices were based on.

In *The Elementary Forms of the Religious Life*, Durkheim stated that of the myriad forms of religious practices examined, there exist rituals and rites which are performed without recourse to specific gods or god-like figures:

> All religious powers do not emanate from divine personalities, and there are relations of cult which have other objects than uniting man to a deity. Religion is more than the idea of gods or spirits, and consequently cannot be defined exclusively in relation to these latter. (1976: 35)

For many commentators, celebrity can be read as functioning in this manner, whereby celebrities are perceived to be figures worthy of worship, and, although offering no salvation (Rojek, 2001), are nevertheless approached in a religious manner. At one level, this can be by association, or even the endorsement of particular religious belief systems, such as Tom Cruise and Scientology, or Madonna and Kabbalah. However, celebrity as a 'social fact', a distinctive social force, has numerous similarities with religious practice and religious worship.

Rojek identifies a number of conspicuous parallels between religious belief and approaches to celebrity which clearly point to the amalgamation of religion and celebrity in numerous contemporary societies. One example is the construction of 'reliquaries of celebrity culture', a secular version of the church reliquary, or receptacle for holy relics. From the standpoint of celebrity, 'totemic' relics range from personalized autographs to 'film stars' soap, chewed pieces of gum, lipstick tissues and even a blade of grass from a star's lawn' (2001: 58), but they take on a particularly 'sacred' quality. Defining celebrity as a form of 'neopaganism', Marche argues that the owners of Esther's Haircutting, the salon in which Britney Spears notoriously shaved herself bald in 2006, 'knew immediately that the relics of her breakdown were sacred. The sweepings from their floor along with a blue lighter and the half can of Red Bull the star left behind went on auction a few days later with a reserve of a million dollars' (2010: 10). A further example of the disproportionate value placed on mundane items discarded by celebrities is the selling on the electronic auction site eBay, for $6,600, of the Hollywood actress Scarlett Johansson's used handkerchief.

A further dimension of celebrity religiosity is the degree to which film and popular music fans engage in 'pilgrimages' to sites associated with a celebrity's life, such as Graceland, Elvis Presley's Tennessee home, or locations of their remains after death. Consequently, cemeteries that have the bodies of celebrity figures interred within them have become much-frequented tourist locations, such as Père Lachaise in Paris, where Balzac, Isadora Duncan, Edith Piaf, Oscar Wilde and Jim Morrison are buried. Similarly, Levitt (2010) cites sources that estimate that in the twenty-first century some 350 people visit the Los Angles-located grave of Marilyn Monroe every day, while the actor Heath Ledger's apartment became the site of numerous objects of commemoration left by fans, as did Apple stores in the wake of Steve Jobs' death in 2011.

The effect that celebrity deaths have on the public is due, argues Levitt, to the unremitting stream of information concerning celebrity lives provided by the media, a flow that establishes a strong sense of familiarity and identification, even though any kind of immediate or personal connection is absent, which, for most members of the public, is the norm in relation to celebrities. It is this second-hand, media-created proximity (frequently dubbed the 'parasocial relation') that is put forward to account for the often highly emotional reaction that can accompany news of the death of a particular celebrity. Thus, while celebrity elicits practices analogous to religious worship, the deaths of some celebrity figures have produced extraordinary moments of social and cultural cohesion. In effect: incidents of social solidarity.

The social significance and power of celebrity death was illustrated as early as 1926 in the case of the silent film era actor, Rudolf Valentino, when 100,000 people came to the funeral home to view his body and thousands watched his funeral procession. But the most telling example of the social influence of a celebrity in the wake of their death was that of Diana, Princess of Wales. Following her death on 31 August 1997 as the result of a car crash in the Pont de l'Alma tunnel in Paris, Diana became the focus of pervasive public mourning, a process intensified on the day of her funeral, 6 September 1997.

Brown *et al.* (2003) state that over one million people lined the three-mile funeral procession route while approximately 2.5 billion people watched the worldwide satellite broadcast. Although such public outpouring of grief was critically assessed by some commentators as the result of either a form of mass hysteria or media representation and manipulation (Turnock, 2000), for Brown *et al.* the reason was the intense degree to which many individuals had forged a 'parasocial relation' with Diana. As they explain:

> Princess Diana embodied the archetype of the princess myth. She was a relatively unknown, beautiful young woman, discovered by the heir apparent prince, who became the 'people's princess'. Despite her personal moral failures, psychological struggles, and clashes with the house of Windsor, Diana was seen as one who reached out to help those less fortunate. These actions made her a heroine to many admirers who sought to protect her reputation. (2003: 588)

The mourning process created what Johnson refers to as the 'Dianized nation', a definitive period in which Britain was a nation that was 'in a state of shock' (2006: 525). The reason for this, argues Johnson, stems from Diana's apparent 'availability' when she was alive, her modification of traditional royal protocols of distance from the public to one of connection (frequently physical at official engagements and charity events). Thus, the keen sense of emotional connection with Diana as a famous figure manifested in clear examples of social 'solidarity' at the time of her death, as one commentator stated of the individuals who had come publicly to mourn her: 'the waiting crowd seemed as near as it was possible to get to a cross-section of the country: young and old, men and women, rich and poor, black and white' (Johnson, 2006: 526). In consequence, as Watson concurs, the death of Diana gave rise to widespread and authentic expressions of public grief, a Durkheimian example of the articulation of collective emotions and a collective ritual that constituted 'a uniform emotion that was common to all' and 'which created a sense of communion which encouraged a belief in shared values' (1997: 4). Similarly, shortly after the news that the pop singer Michael Jackson had died on 25 June 2009, the 'grassroots' user-created internet encyclopaedia *Wikipedia* had to be momentarily shut down due to the surge of individuals attempting to edit the Jackson entry (Whannel, 2010) and his death overwhelmed social networks such as Twitter and Facebook. While not all of the posts expressed feelings of grief or condolence (there were also jokes, rumours and spam), millions did (Hoe-Lian Goh and Sian Lee, 2011). As Hollander (2010) states, Jackson's death dominated news media and, as with Diana, more than one million people attended Jackson's memorial service, held in Los Angeles.

But, Hollander's appraisal of the public reaction to Jackson's death highlights an alternative perception of celebrity 'worship' that identifies its status and influence as an intrinsically *pathological* component of contemporary societies, and a sign that the social organism is distinctly unhealthy. Hollander, like many celebrity theorists, cites Daniel Boorstin's now classic book, *The Image: A Guide to Pseudo-Events in America*, originally published in 1961. Boorstin's view in *The Image* is quintessentially a pessimistic one. His central argument is that since 1900 Western culture has witnessed the transformation of the 'hero' into the 'celebrity', a process initiated by the 'graphic revolution' consisting of magazines, television, cinema, radio and newspapers. The major cultural impact of the graphic revolution was its ability to create famous people 'overnight', to fabricate 'well-knowness' (1992: 47). From a litany of classical heroes, such as Jesus, Joan of Arc, Shakespeare, Washington, Napoleon and Lincoln – individuals marked by achievements of 'greatness' – the prevalence of individuals promoted by the media system constitutes Boorstin's now classic definition of the 'celebrity', that of the individual 'who is well-known for their well-known-ness' (1992: 57). According to Boorstin's view, achievement is increasingly irrelevant with regard to the acquisition of fame, and the celebrities created by the graphic revolution are chiefly characterized by their contemporariness. By this, Boorstin means that they are not destined to linger in the popular consciousness; as he notes: 'Celebrities die quickly but they are still more quickly replaced' (1992: 66). Therefore, the popular cultural landscape of celebrity is one marked by rapid individual turnover and flux in which the famous are nothing more than superficial media-created diversions sustained by a series of 'pseudo-events' – purposefully produced publicity-seeking episodes initiated by studios or public relations professionals and representatives. Pseudo-events are deliberately planned and staged 'for the immediate purpose of being reported or reproduced', and arranged 'for the convenience of the reporting media' (Boorstin, 1992: 40).

Although highly pessimistic, Boorstin's analysis is prescient when one thinks of the parade of 'celebrity' figures produced by reality TV, particularly the Orwell-inspired and globally syndicated show, *Big Brother*; with its relentless wave of (usually) limited-lifespan celebrity figures, produced on a yearly basis, who, invariably, fade from the public consciousness once the 'white glare of publicity ... melts away' (Boorstin, 1992: 63). Hollander echoes Boorstin's scathing view of the trajectory of fame throughout the twentieth century as one in which celebrity and achievement have increasingly become mutually exclusive forces. As an example, he cites Paris Hilton as a key Boorstin-like figure who is famous for being famous, a celebrity figure who has attained this status without any discernible talent or capability bar that of her Hilton hotel heiress status, looks and sometimes scandalous lifestyle. However, as King (2010) notes, this has not prevented Hilton from successfully marketing her 'celebrity presence' from her personal fortune from the Hilton hotel empire, reality TV, acting, cosmetics and fashion lines, and her ability to charge $150,000 to $200,000 for a 20-minute appearances at upmarket parties.

Further twenty-first-century examples of Boorstin's assessment of the trajectory of celebrity could also be identified in the celebrity status of Kim, Kourtney and Khloé Kardashian, the daughters of Robert Kardashian, one of the attorneys in the O.J. Simpson murder trial in 1995. The Kardashian sisters have attained considerable celebrity status and media attention due to their reality TV series *Keeping Up with the Kardashians* broadcast on *E!*, which chronicles their various domestic activities but is also centred upon their fashionable lifestyles, conspicuous consumption and fame stemming from being themselves. Thus, it could be argued that the contemporary celebrity landscape accords keenly with Boorstin's critical view, reflecting a society that consumes celebrity that is removed from concrete or even notable achievement; and that 'greatness' is a thing of the past and tabloid antics a sufficient qualification for public adulation.

Yet, as Hollander concedes, although there is an economic, or 'power' dimension with regard to an entertainment industry that has progressively become an integral component of global economies (from Hollywood to Bollywood and beyond), which are strongly motivated to promote the celebrity system (creating entirely new industries such as public relations), this is not simply a case of capitalist ideological domination and manufactured desire. Rather, there is an authentic genuine demand for celebrity in contemporary society. And it accords with Durkheim's sociology perfectly: Hollander articulates this sense of need in terms of a celebrity 'worship' that acts as a substitute for some form of collective belief that has diminished. Thus, the 'cults' devoted to celebrities act in a manner akin to devotion to football, baseball or soccer teams serving as 'ersatz communities and sources of solidarity' (2010: 151).

DOES CELEBRITY ACT AS 'SOCIAL GLUE'?

The 'cult of celebrity' need not be pathological, as Hollander suggests, but rather could serve as a key vehicle for day-to-day social solidarity. 'Celebrity worship' need not be viewed as an aberrant form of behaviour, as it often is. Rather, an interest in celebrity coincides with a prevalent form of social interaction – gossip. As Brooks states, although frequently dismissed, gossip, or rather 'pointless conversation' is a 'powerfully healthy social elixir' (2004: 1) and the use of other people's lives, their problems and positives, can help individuals to define what they value as a culture. This is especially valuable, if not essential, in societies that have developed beyond small-scale settlements with close social proximity to industrialized 'multiple villages' – domestic spaces, work spaces, leisure sites – that individuals constantly move in and out of, with limited social contacts. As such, gossip about individuals who are located within an individual's home area is of no relevance to work colleagues. This is where the value of celebrity lies; because celebrity, argues Brooks, acts as a 'universal cultural currency' that can cover every social location within an individual's life. Consequently, talking about celebrities, their fashions, professional achievements, scandals, romances, failures, etc., acts as a 'social bridge' and one of the few that can successfully cut through class, ethnic, religious, sexual and a myriad of other cultural barriers. But, if a proportion of daily discourse invokes the critical views of Boorstin *et al.*, Brooks suggests otherwise because:

> The truth is, celebrity chat is not about them; it's about us. Far from being victimized by information about celebrities, we're using it for our own positive social ends. Far from worshipping the stars in a simplistic way, we're dissecting their lifestyle choices and their love lives to help us define who we are, to learn and reinforce our shared values, to build support networks and to reach out to people with whom we have little in common. (2004: 2)

In other words, to attain and reinforce a potent sense of solidarity in complex societies which have transcended the mechanical, small-scale ritualistic/religious sources of social cohesion. While the division of labour may be the primary and structural solidifying force in 'organic' societies, celebrity can be argued to act as a further form of 'social glue' because it is, love it or hate it, a universal cultural presence and a dominant force within the media system. Which is why Brown *et al.* (2003) argue that parasocial relationships are not aberrant but socially common due to the degree to which individuals are exposed to celebrity figures via the media with such regularity that they can be considered as 'friends' and acutely mourned when they die.

In his analysis of Barack Obama and his election campaign (which was heavily reliant on the internet and social networking sites) as a political celebrity, Sean Redmond (2010) draws on sociological work that explores the nature of later modernity, that of Zygmunt Bauman's 'liquid modernity' thesis (2000; 2003; 2006; 2007). Broadly, Bauman presents a picture of Western life in which the central components of individual and social lives (work, interpersonal relationships, politics, national identities, citizenship, community, production systems) have become ever more fluid, unstable, and subject to continual change: a society of 'togetherness dismantled' (Bauman, 2003: 119). For Redmond, celebrity culture acutely reflects this social condition as it is a world of fleeting spectacle and rapid bombardment by images. But, if we refer back to Durkheim, celebrity can (and commentators argue that it does) play a culturally stabilizing role.

For Lukes (1973), a key dichotomy in the sociology of Durkheim is that between the individual and society, celebrity represents a key contemporary example of the interrelationship between the two. Celebrity is a contentious issue and the critical view of Boorstin and Hollander is not without merit; the rise of reality TV and the prevalence of 'instant celebrities' created via viral videos validates key aspects of their arguments, although Boorstin arguably overstates the degree to which the media and public relations agencies can control the public reception of pseudo-events (Dyer, 1982). The issue of the parasocial relation is predicated upon individuals seeing celebrities as role models and as sources of moral behaviour (either as themselves or in roles that they portray on screen). Through their role as the arbiters of fashion, touchstones for body image, product endorsers and, increasingly, alignment with political campaigns, causes and candidates (from George Clooney's work in Darfur, Colin Firth's Oxfam association and Angelina Jolie's role as an ambassador for the UN Refugee Agency) celebrity figures hold a position of structural and cultural centrality. As such, it is a means with which to both identify and re-articulate the key components of Durkheim's sociology and link the individual to the social. As Inglis concludes on the subject and its social relevance: 'celebrity may massively mislead us, but I do not see that we can do without it. It gives us certain bearings' (2010: 285).

QUESTIONS TO CONSIDER

1. What role do religion and the division of labour play, according to Durkheim in the production of solidarity?
2. Why did the deaths of Princess Diana and Michael Jackson cause such widespread public displays of grief? Did these events collectively bind people together?
3. Do you think that celebrity gossip acts, as Brooks suggests, as a form of 'social glue' due to the 'universal' nature of the subject?

FURTHER READING

Key works for further reading by Durkheim should include *The Division of Labour in Society* and *The Elementary Forms of the Religious Life*. In terms of celebrity, Daniel Boorstin's *The Image* remains a classic critical text on the nature of fame, and Chris Rojek's Celebrity (2001), P. David Marshall's *Celebrity and Power* (1997) and Fred Inglis' *A Short History of Celebrity* (2010) provide historical and sociological accounts of celebrity culture. In terms of critical comparisons, readers should compare Brooks' short article, 'What celebrity worship says about us' (USATODAY.com), which suggests a socially cohesive function of celebrity, with Sean Redmond's 2010 article in *Celebrity Studies* entitled 'Avatar Obama in the Age of Liquid Celebrity'.

Simmel and pop fashion

4

Although frequently overshadowed by Marx, Durkheim and Weber, the German sociologist Georg Simmel (1858–1918) is nevertheless one of the major 'founding fathers' of the development of modern sociology as a distinctive discipline (Frisby, 1992). Born in Berlin, Germany, Simmel was (like Marx, Durkheim and Weber) interested in social change, but with a particular emphasis on how social transformation affected interpersonal relationships and was experienced psychologically. Consequently, Simmel's sociology would have a distinctive character that set it apart from his more famous classical fellow sociologists.

The author of numerous texts, including *On Social Differentiation* (1890), *The Problems of the Philosophy of History* (1892), *Fundamental Questions of Sociology* (1917), *The Philosophy of Money* (1907) and *The Metropolis and Mental Life* (1903), Simmel emerged as a foremost sociologist of modernity that took the form of a 'fleeting, fragmentary social reality' and the effect this had on the 'inner lives of social actors' (Frisby, 1985: 46). Simmel spent the majority of his career in Berlin and would be a decisive influence on a number of later thinkers, most notably Walter Benjamin and Siegfried Kracauer, and the urban setting of Simmel's life had a direct and evocative effect upon his work. As Carter (2003) states, Simmel immersed himself in, and loved, the metropolitan experience of Berlin. Consequently, his major sociological work concerned the nature of early twentieth-century modernity in urban settings that were characterized by a blur of sights and sounds; crowded streets filled with individuals who would never make meaningful human connections; and multiple sources of information assailing individuals in often bewildering ways. Simmel did not seek to provide a historical account of modernity, but was alternatively concerned with 'the modes of experiencing the social reality of modernity', believing that the analysis of society 'should coalesce around individual inner experiences' (Frisby, 1985: 61).

It is Simmel's *The Metropolis and Mental Life* that will form the basis of discussion within this chapter, but we shall also focus especially on his work on the role, function and use by individuals of distinctive fashion in heavily populated urban spaces in which social actors face a 'constant bombardment of the senses with new and ever changing impressions' (Frisby, 1985: 76). Although the study of fashion and its place and significance in popular culture (and economic and industrial systems) has now become common, Georg Simmel produced a seminal work as part of his analysis of the modern metropolis and individuality entitled *Fashion*, which emphasized not only the ways in which fashion was a means by which social groups were equalized (via the imitation of fashions), but also how it played a crucial role in establishing a space of identity in the rushing metropolis: that fashion could be the primary means by which individuals differentiated themselves from each other. In terms of popular culture, the chapter will relate Simmel's approach to the centrality of fashion and significant (if not outrageous) 'looks' in pop music, suggesting that contemporary pop performers, from Madonna to Rihanna, utilize fashion in ways that are akin to Simmel's metropolitan citizen: to be distinctive, to stand out in a crowd. In the metropolis it is to make a visual impact in a teeming city space, while on the pop scene it is to stand out in a crowded musical market place. As the chapter will demonstrate, in pop music the sound of a pop performer is equal if not often inferior to how that performer *looks*. As such, Simmel's sociology can be linked to the style evolution of Kylie Minogue, and the eccentric fashion statements of Lady Gaga.

SIMMEL, THE INDIVIDUAL AND FASHION

Broadly, Simmel's sociology is concerned with the status of the individual in relation to other individuals and wider society. But the relationship between an individual and society is dynamic and consistently two-way because society is essentially a structure which is made up of individual human beings who simultaneously stand within and outside of society. In essence, as Simmel states in *On Individuality and Social Forms*, there is a distinctive relationship between a society and its component individuals. Individuals are never completely subsumed into a social structure without establishing a distinctive relationship with it. Citing the example of religion, a key externally influencing 'social fact' in the sociology of Durkheim, Simmel states that although the religious man or woman feels gripped by a holy force or sensibility and have given themselves completely over to that belief, still 'some sort of self-existence/differentiated ego must be preserved – the religious experience must start from the existence of the individual: to be one with God is conditioned in its very significance by being other than God' (1971: 15).

The social picture that is established in this way sees humans as being the product of the functions and contents of their given society, and that which is the product of their own individual autonomous self. It is these two components coming together that, Simmel states: 'form the unit we call the social being' (1971: 18). The relationship between society and the individuals that compose it is a fundamental and significant feature of Simmel's work, and the nature of this connection is explored in his writings on the metropolis and the effects large-scale urban spaces have on the mental lives of social actors living in them. For Simmel:

> The deepest problems of modern life flow from the attempt of the individual to maintain the independence and individuality of [their] existence against the sovereign powers of society, against the weight of the historical heritage and the external culture and technique of life. (1971: 324)

According to Frisby's (1985) analysis, Simmel was concerned with the city as a sociological rather than physical space and stressed that a key challenge for individuals in large-scale metropolitan urban spaces is to resist being 'swallowed up' by them; to strive against forces that might level out individuality. Compared with the small town or rural setting, life in a major metropolis (such as Berlin) is, unsurprisingly, lived at a faster tempo, with a constant flow of individuals and sights, and is marked by difference, not uniformity, each possessing differing interests. Alternatively, the large city 'provides the possibility for the total indifference towards one's neighbours, not merely in the sense of those with whom one lives in close proximity but also those whom one confronts in everyday social contexts' (Frisby, 1985: 78). Thus, the metropolis is essentially characterized by a pervasive sense of impersonality, but one that impels some to create a particular individual style to combat this condition. As Simmel states, there 'is perhaps no psychic phenomenon which is so unconditionally reserved to the city as the blasé outlook' (1971: 329), an apparently nonchalant and relaxed urban attitude that is adopted in the face of an urban space defined by flux and constant movement.

Consequently, the metropolitan dweller presents a reserved outlook in the face of a social world that consists of fleeting contacts with fellow citizens, and in contrast to small-scale living spaces, individuals do not know their neighbours. Indeed, this is the primary reason why metropolitan residents can appear 'cold' and 'uncongenial' to 'small-town folk'. As such, even though individuals live and work closely together with a large mass of other individuals, this bodily closeness and lack of space actually results, for many people, in a condition of acute loneliness and desertion precisely because of the metropolitan 'crush of persons' (1971: 334). Added to this, the economic and productive life of the metropolis is based on a specific division of labour which leads to a further degree of specialization of individual members in terms of roles and services; individuals specialize in exclusive functions and further degrees of differentiation, which can be difficult to carve out as others may already have filled particular niches. While this enables societies to function and produce essential goods and services, it also, argues Simmel, results in a restricted kind of intellectual individuation of mental qualities amongst the metropolitan populace, and there are numerous reasons for this. As Simmel explains:

First of all there is the difficulty of giving one's own personality a certain status within the framework of metropolitan life. Where quantitative increase of value and energy has reached its limits, one seizes on qualitative distinctions, so that, through taking advantage of the existing sensitivity to differences, the attention of the social world can in some way be won for oneself. This leads ultimately to the strangest eccentricities, to specifically metropolitan extravagancies of self-distanciation, of caprice, of fastidiousness, the meaning of which is no longer to be found in the content of such activity itself but rather in its being a form of 'being different' – of making oneself noticeable. For many types of persons these are still the only means of saving for oneself, through the attention gained from others, some sort of self-esteem and the sense of filling a position. (1971: 336)

Therefore, the potentially alienating nature of the metropolis puts pressure on individuals to attempt to 'stand out from the crowd', as it were, to make an impact on others and be noticed, no matter how eccentric and extravagant this attempt may be. But how does an individual achieve this? How do you make a visual impact on a fleeting number of individuals that pass by in the blur of the metropolitan way of life? One method, argues Simmel, is via the deliberate use of fashion, which differs markedly from mere clothing.

The rich, complex and often contradictory nature of fashion is cogently and evocatively expressed by Juliet Ash and Elizabeth Wilson:

Fashion has dualities in its formation, a reputation for snobbery and sin. It separates individuals one from the other in appearance, and yet draws them together with common identities. It expresses inner selves, yet aids disguise. It is obsessive about outward appearances, yet speaks the unconscious and our deepest desires. (1992: xi)

Fashion and fashion brands have come to represent some of the most evocative and globally recognizable consumer brands in our economic and cultural system. From established fashion labels such as Dior, Gucci, Elsa Schiaparelli, Armani, Givenchy, Ralph Lauren, Prada, Chanel, Calvin Klein, Dolce & Gabbana, Donna Karan, Karl Lagerfeld, Gap, Versace and Bulgari, to L.K. Bennett, Moschino, Louis Vuitton, Red Or Dead, Tom Ford and Paul Smith, fashion brands are part of the cultural landscape. In *Adorned in Dreams*, Elizabeth Wilson (2003) states that prior to the development of mercantile capitalism and the expansion of cities in the medieval period in Europe, dress was not 'fashion', and there was no distinctive fashion 'system' in early modes of human organization. Although differing hairstyles and cosmetics were evident in ancient Greece and Rome, clothing (such as the toga) was generally uniform. As Christianity flourished within and beyond the Roman Empire throughout the Western world, simple 'ascetic' clothing was the norm. It was between the twelfth and fourteenth centuries (in Europe, at least) that clothing and dress began to take the form of a fashion system. From shaped dresses fastened with lace to elaborate doublets and ornately buttoned tunics and hats, clothing began to acquire symbolic social meanings. The differentiation between functional clothing worn for modesty and utility transformed in specific social and class groups in a distinctive way between the fifteenth and sixteenth centuries. It was here that clothes began to be discarded (by those with the financial means to do so) because they were considered to be out of date; to be 'unfashionable'. Social stratification could be visually observed as less affluent sections of societies adorned themselves in clothing that was outmoded in terms of style by the upper social echelons. Furthermore, the development of early capitalist production in the wake of the social shift from feudalism, mechanical production and the acceleration in the manufacture of cloth, expanded trade and the invention of productive technologies such as the spinning wheel resulted in the centrality of ostentatious styles among the new and emergent industrial class and an ever increasing turnover of fashions. This process developed throughout the seventeenth century (the sartorial lavishness of the court of Charles II, for example) and into the eighteenth, in which public displays in the increasing number of gardens, promenade spaces and theatres by members of 'society' were enhanced by status-communicating displays of fashion.

The consolidation and expansion of metropolitan cities exacerbated this development as the Industrial Revolution firmly established itself and transformed production processes in terms of factory manufacturing and a fashion industry that developed from the manufacture of cotton, wool and the importation of silk, to the manufacture of synthetic materials (nylon, polyester and acrylics) (Entwistle, 2000). Furthermore, the subsequent invention and proliferation of modes of transport, such as the railway, and communication technologies in the form of the telephone, then later cinema and the mass circulation of newspapers and magazines, contributed to intensify 'the rush and pace of modern life' and circulated images of fashion at greater levels of frequency and wider degrees of public consumption (Wilson, 2003). As a result, cities such as London, Paris, Milan and New York became hubs of fashion consumption, where first department stores and then the centre of the fashion world developed (Gilbert, 2000). Thus, there has been a long-standing and symbiotic relationship between fashion and the metropolis, and it is a connection, argued Simmel in the early years of the twentieth century, that was also evident at the level of the individuals who inhabited the metropolis and who consciously and deliberately utilized fashion to differentiate themselves from the urban crowd.

This seems a somewhat contradictory choice, though, as the essence of fashion is frequently associated with the practice of imitation and uniformity. In Simmel's analysis, acts of imitation are central psychological components of human behaviour that are rife in childhood, but which also provide a series of benefits in adulthood because they grant individuals a sense of collective feeling and satisfaction: 'whenever we imitate, we transfer not only the demand for creative activity, but also the responsibility for the action from ourselves to another' (1957: 542–3). A primary source of collective imitation is found in fashion, whereby copying the styles of others enables individuals to become 'a creature of the group' (Simmel, 1971: 295). Hence, the poorer sections of societies habitually imitate the sartorial styles (or cheaper approximations of them) of the fashionable upper social strata (usually spelling the end of that fashion). Then again, fashion also satisfies the individual need for a sense of differentiation from other individuals due to the dynamic nature of fashion and its constant emphasis on the 'new'. As Simmel explains:

> Fashion is the imitation of a given example and satisfies the demand for social adaptation; it leads the individual upon the road which all travel, it furnishes a general condition, which resolves the conduct of every individual into a mere example. At the same time it satisfies in no less degree the need of differentiation, the tendency towards dissimilarity, the desire for change and contrast, on the one hand by a constant change of contents, which gives to the fashion of today an individual stamp as opposed to that of yesterday and of to-morrow. (1957: 543)

The salient issue is that fashion can be utilized by individuals actively to demarcate themselves from others, and establish that moment of eccentric uniqueness in the teeming metropolis because the very nature of fashion is based upon 'the charm of novelty coupled to that of transitoriness' (1971: 302) and can, if employed knowingly, 'heighten an individualistic and peculiar character' (1971: 305). In the metropolis the pressure is on to make an impression as quickly as possible as fellow citizens pass by: fashion, and eccentric fashion in particular, is a potent means by which to do this, to imprint an image of individuality in a crowded sea of people. Clothing, according to Simmel, is a key aspect of the social construction of the self, of expressing one's individual identity (Svendsen, 2006).

It is, then, no surprise that Simmel's work on the philosophy of fashion has become enduring in the work of fashion commentators. For instance, in *The Fashioned Body* (2000), Entwistle relates Simmel's analysis of the socially communicative character of fashion to cultural movements such as Bohemianism and Dandyism – highly distinctive urban aesthetic lifestyles based on affected attitudes and outlandish clothing – typified by Charles Baudelaire's nineteenth-century metropolitan stroller, the *flâneur*. And there is a specific area of contemporary popular culture to which we can apply Simmel's sociology and the paramount role played by fashion in the process of individuation in a cyclical and volatile commercial landscape, and that is pop music: a 'scene' in which fashion-conscious image is as important as sound, if not frequently more so.

In Jennifer Craik's (1994) analysis, the use(s) of fashion by social actors habitually performs the function of a 'mask'; it enables individuals to disguise the 'true' nature of the body or person, to be someone else, or at least to suggest a specific appearance to wider society or even to themselves. Of course, this is the essence of what Simmel argued, and it is the key reason why Simmel's work on the nature and use of fashion has become a perennial citation in academic fashion literature. However, Simmel's approach to the strategic use of fashion as a means of constructing identity is arguably prescient with regard to one of the major and most dramatic tectonic knowledge shifts of the latter part of the twentieth century: the apparent movement from a condition of modernity to postmodernity.

Postmodernity, or postmodernism, is a body of thought concerned with the breaking apart of modernity, the linking of the project of modernity with the values and ideals of the Enlightenment, and the argument that Enlightenment's search for a position of absolute truth is impossible to attain. Although it is a diverse movement that includes thinkers such as Michel Foucault, Jean Baudrillard, Félix Guattari, Donna Haraway and Jacques Derrida, it was Jean-François Lyotard (1924–98) who emerged as *the* postmodern theorist *par excellence*. His now classic book, *The Postmodern Condition* (1984) introduced the term postmodernism to the academic world. In *The Postmodern Condition*, Lyotard rejects both Marx and the core of the modern Enlightenment. Its quest for truth was said to be allied with the establishment of social hierarchy and oppression. Lyotard appeals to a critical 'postmodern' knowledge that dismantles foundations and disrupts hierarchy. It is for this reason that at the end of *The Postmodern Condition*, Lyotard urges us to 'wage a war on totality' (1984: 82), arguing this because he considers 'master narratives' to be reductionist, simplistic and suppressing difference.

Although dismissed as inherently conservative, most notably by the critical theorist Jürgen Habermas, postmodernism became a significant cultural force throughout the 1980s, particularly due to the ways in which it manifested itself in wider culture and popular culture in the form of architecture, art, literature, cuisine, fashion, music and film. Furthermore, the lack of fixity and stability at the heart of the postmodern society that had allegedly arisen in this period also manifested itself at the level of individual identity. As Douglas Kellner argues, in 'traditional' societies, identity was commonly perceived to be fixed, solid, and stable, a function of predefined social roles. In the 'age of modernity', identity becomes more 'mobile, multiple, personal, self-reflexive, and subject to change and innovation'. Yet, the forms of identity in modernity are also relatively substantial and fixed; 'identity still comes from a circumscribed set of roles and norms' (1992: 141). From a postmodern perspective, as the tempo and complexity of modern societies has accelerated, identity itself has 'become more and more unstable, more and more fragile' and is a 'process whereby identity is a game that one plays, so that one can easily shift from one identity to another' (1992: 153). Thus:

> The Postmodern subject is conceptualized as having no fixed, essential or permanent identity. Identity becomes a 'moveable feast': formed and transformed continuously in relation to the ways we are represented or addressed in the cultural systems which surround us. It is historically, not biologically, defined. The subject assumes different identities at different times, identities which are not unified around a coherent 'self' ... The fully unified, completed, secure and coherent identity is a fantasy. (Hall, 1992: 277)

Postmodern identity is consequently a mode of self that is created 'theatrically', and so, in a postmodernist world, it is possible to change identities via the purchase of symbolic consumer items (most notably, fashion) and to effectively switch identities with the changing 'winds of fashion'. For the Marxist critic, Alex Callinicos (1989), however, this may be possible if one possesses the lifestyle of what was then known as the 'new-middle class', higher-income, white-collar workers, but what of the lower-paid, the unemployed? Can they engage in the playful process of masquerade and continual identity change, or are they in fact determined by class and external social forces? Callinicos favours the latter condition and therefore, whilst the notion of an essential, stable sense of identity is regarded as a mere fantasy by postmodern theorists, Callinicos suggests that it is the playfully, endlessly changeable postmodern 'subject' which is the fantasy.

In many respects, postmodernism is now considered to be somewhat *passé*, an example of a philosophical/cultural crossover that hit its peak from the 1980s to the mid-1990s. Many of the key examples of postmodern popular culture were produced in this period in areas such as literature (William Gibson's *Neuromancer* (1984), Don Delillo's *White Noise* (1985), Umberto Eco's *Foucault's Pendulum* (1988), Jonathan Coe's *What a Carve Up!* (1994), Brett Easton Ellis' *American Psycho* (1991), and Jeff Noon's *Vurt* (1993)); television (*Miami Vice* (1984–90) and *Twin Peaks* 1990–91)); music (hip hop); and cinema (*Blade Runner* (1982), *Blue Velvet* (1986), and the 1996 Wes Craven horror parody, *Scream*); although its fragmentary, non-linear qualities are still ably exhibited in Seth McFarlane's irreverent animated sit-com, *Family Guy* (Wisnewski, 2007) and its emphasis on knowing genre fusion is central to contemporary horror films such as *The Cabin In The Woods* (Drew Goddard, 2011). In a wider global context, the Japanese Manga and Anime comic/animated film cultural form represents a long-standing and evocative expression of core postmodernist themes. Although there are numerous examples (from the iconic 1988 film *Akira* to 2012's *Evangelion 3.0*), a classic example remains *The Ghost in the Shell* (Mamoru Oshii, 1995) with its narrative concerned with the cybernetic fusion of the human and the machine and the interrelationship between technology, gender and spiritual identity (Napier, 2000).

Yet, while postmodernist themes are plentiful in a range of cultural examples, it is fashion that has long been associated with the essence of postmodernism, characterized as it is by ceaseless transformation and instability (Connor, 1989; Wilson, 1992; McRobbie, 1994; Church Gibson, 2000; Forster, 2009). However, the conception, articulated by Simmel, of fashion as a means through which to mask the self, to construct a self that can stand out and be noticed in a crowded social world, *is* readily identifiable in popular culture in the symbiotic relationship between contemporary fashion and pop music. Within this cultural space, commercial necessity decrees that pop images must never be static, that the search for a fashionable and appealing 'look' is indeed a constant 'moveable feast' of performative identities that evokes the postmodern view, but also centrally the sociological theory of Georg Simmel.

POP FASHION

In the words of fashion and music impresario, Malcolm McLaren, the man who masterminded the controversial rise of the infamous UK Punk band, The Sex Pistols, in 1977:

> Fashion is the visual expression of a culture. Paradoxically, it can be both sublimely sophisticated and carnally bestial at once. Fashion is used as a means of sexual display, status symbol and tribal code ... Fashion has the ability to take over people's lives to an astonishing degree. Fashion can never be pinned down; it is constantly morphing into something else. (Cited in Gorman, 2001: 10)

In the view of Noel McLaughlin, the music and fashion industries are closely entwined to the extent that 'popular music is taken to play a powerful role in "window shopping" and selling clothes' (2000: 264). Although the distinctive (and ultimately iconic) suits of 1950s and 1960s performers such as Elvis Presley and The Beatles were the product of professional tailors (Lansky Bros Menswear, Memphis and Dougie Millings respectively), Mablen Jones (1987) argues that the reception of music in the 1950s and 1960s was primarily an 'aural' experience, that music, not imagery, was the salient attraction. However, during the 1960s this began to change as record companies increasingly took active control over how bands looked. In the wake of the global success of The Beatles, masterminded by manager Brian Epstein's recognition of the increasing salience of 'look', the ethos of image holding parity with the music became established (Rogan, 1988: 306). As the 1970s progressed, artists would emerge who were defined by distinctive and ever-changing image transformations, most notably David Bowie, who utilized fashion as a 'mask' to create a variety of musical characters (most famously, Ziggy Stardust) through costume in addition to sound. Furthermore, the worlds of fashion design and music increasingly came together in 1970s popular culture when the designer Bob Mackie created a series of extravagant costumes for Cher's television series and for Elton John's 1986 tour. Thus, the link between costume and popular music would become solidified throughout the 1970s and beyond. With regard to Punk, the association between Vivienne Westwood and The Sex Pistols ensured that 'playing music was subsidiary to how they looked' (Jones, 1987: 137), a process that continued in Britain with the 'pirate look' of early 'New Romantic' pop performers such as Adam Ant and Duran Duran. As the 1980s progressed, musical genres would be inextricably linked with specific fashions, perhaps most notably the commercial exponents of heavy metal music such as KISS, Ratt, W.A.S.P., Ozzy Osbourne, Poison, and Mötley Crüe, all visually defined by the distinctive and strategic wearing of leather, spandex, spikes, and make-up.

As E. Ann Kaplan (1988) argues in her analysis of postmodern popular culture, *Rocking Around the Clock,* in the past, with stars like Paul Anka, Elvis Presley, even the early Beatles or The Rolling Stones, the image that a star decided to promote remained relatively stable once a formula that produced commercial success had been found. This arguably began to change with the launch of Music Television (MTV) on 1 August 1981, and its repeated transmission of pop/rock star images. In consequence, Kaplan argues that an inevitable pressure to routinely change image in order to offset consumer boredom increasingly became the norm. Yet, certain genres of music embrace this ethos more than others, and with regard to 'pop' it is an ingrained aspect, because as Klein observes: 'Pop has always had fluid boundaries ... Pop constantly changes its faces and meanings' (2003: 42) and would be increasingly populated by pop performers who would continually 'transform and transfigure themselves' (Marshall, 1997: 194). The most notable post-MTV performer to articulate such image transfiguration is Madonna.

Madonna released her first album, *Madonna*, in 1983, and her subsequent recordings, videos and live performances have exemplified fluid image throughout a career that has moved through a succession of phases that reflected each album and live performance, each associated with specific 'looks' and the centrality of aesthetics in her musical career and development, be they the use of crucifixes, Marilyn Monroe-like hair and dresses, S&M imagery, Kabbalah and 'New Age' spirituality (Fiske, 1989; Bordo, 1993; Robertson, 1996; Lister, 2001; Hawkins, 2002; Gauntlett, 2004). Madonna would also form alliances with globally-famed fashion designers such as Jean-Paul Gaultier, most notably with the now iconic cone brassière he designed for her 1990 Blond Ambition world tour, and later, Dolce and Gabbana for her 'Love Kylie' tribute T-shirt (Craik, 2009).

Although commercially inspired, the ever-changing use of fashion by pop performers since the early 1980s can arguably be interpreted as a continuation of Simmel's emphasis on the pursuit of individuality. In place of the bustling metropolis, the primacy of fashion within pop music is based on re-invention and differentiation from other performers: the creation of distinctive and attention-capturing moments. These are often based on the music, but they are also frequently associated with distinctive fashion, be it items of clothing or eye-catching hairstyles. As Simmel states, compared with earlier phases of human societies:

> Fashion plays a more conspicuous role in modern times, because the differences in our standards of life have become so much more strongly accentuated, for the more numerous and the more sharply drawn these differences are, the greater the opportunities for emphasizing them at every turn. In innumerable instances this cannot be accomplished by passive inactivity, but only by the development of forms established by fashion. (1957: 546)

Contemporary pop music culture potently reflects this point: artists establish themselves and sustain themselves with an avowed and strategically planned emphasis on fashion-created image to sustain audience interest and differentiate their pop identities. So, many pop careers can be charted in terms of a series of distinctive fashion-conscious images. To explore the primacy of Simmel in twenty-first-century popular culture, I will focus on two distinctive musical case studies: Kylie Minogue and Lady Gaga, two very different female performers, but both defined by the primacy of costume-created image.

Although Kylie Minogue's career has become inextricably linked with costume and fashion – she has worn clothing by designers such as Karl Lagerfeld, Julien Macdonald, Dolce & Gabbana, John Galliano and Stella McCartney – she has also consistently engaged in a process of incessant invention that has resulted in a musical career marked by a series of 'personas' that can be broken into distinctive phases: 'Cute Kylie', 'Sex Kylie', 'Dance Kylie', 'Indie Kylie', 'Camp Kylie', 'Cyber-Kylie' and the 'Showgirl'. Kylie Minogue's career began in childhood acting with appearances in Australian television dramas, but it was at the age of 17 that she achieved mainstream cultural prominence when she was cast in the role of would-be mechanic Charlene Mitchell in the Australian soap opera *Neighbours*. Minogue was to play Charlene from April 1986 to June 1988, gaining popularity both in Australia and in Britain, and achieving iconic status through the character. It was during this 'Charlene' period that she also made her first foray into the world of popular music, recording 'The Locomotion', the Little Eva song from the 1960s, for Mushroom Records, which would ultimately reach number 1 in the Australian charts in July 1987. Subsequently, she signed a recording contract with the British writer-producer team Stock, Aitken and Waterman (SAW).

Minogue's first ten singles for SAW produced four number 1 hits, five that reached number 2, and one number 4. Moreover, she had hits overseas, in America, Europe and Australia. This recording success began with the track 'I Should Be So Lucky', released in December 1987 and achieving the number 1 spot simultaneously in the British and Australian charts. 'I Should Be So Lucky' deliberately exploited the 'cute' aspect of Minogue's *Neighbours* character to the extent that it 'was a song that the public could believe was sung by Charlene and there was little attempt to separate the two personas' (Baker and Minogue, 2002: 32). This was reinforced by a video that depicted Kylie dreamily thinking about a potential boyfriend and dancing in various rooms of an apartment, but particularly in her bedroom and wearing bright, inoffensive clothing. Minogue's evolution from 'Cute Kylie' to 'Sex Kylie' in the early 1990s reflected a growing sense of critical legitimacy regarding her image, whereby she transcended appearing exclusively in pop music magazines and began to grace the cover of magazine 'style bibles' such as *The Face* and *i-D*. Moreover, her image was a conscious and radical departure from the 'Cute Kylie' representation of SAW's earlier productions. Significantly, the music also differed from her initial formula, consisting of a slightly harder, dance-infused edge, as with her *Rhythm of Love* recording, a sound even flirting with R&B influences on the album *Let's Get To It*. Correspondingly, the video performances presented an identifiably erotic, sexualized content that was conspicuously lacking in 'I Should Be So Lucky'. This period did represent a marked transformation of the Minogue persona. The videos for 'Better the Devil You Know', 'What Do I Have To Do' and 'Shocked' now placed the emphasis firmly on exposed bodies, both Minogue's and those of male and female dancers, and visually depicted Minogue in a series of revealing outfits.

The emphasis on a sexualized gaze and revealing clothing continued in Minogue's first album for the smaller independent dance-oriented record label deConstruction, entitled simply *Kylie Minogue* and consolidating her search for a more mature sound and image, typified by the string-laden, dance-based single 'Confide in Me' and its accompanying video. 'Confide in Me' presents six images of Minogue framed within the concept of television help lines, or rather 'sex lines', with a garishly made-up Minogue singing to the screen as '1-555-confide' numbers repeatedly appear on screen, and anticipating her adoption of what can best be called 'Indie Kylie'.

'Indie Kylie' revolved around Minogue's 1997 recording, *Impossible Princess*, a title subsequently changed (although not in Australia) to the eponymous *Kylie Minogue* in the wake of the accidental death of Diana, Princess of Wales. The album presented a very different image in its active retreat from the glamorous aspects of 'Sex Kylie', replacing it with a pared-down vision of Minogue, emphasizing a simple sense of style, lack of overt make-up, and a short, elfin-style hairstyle. Moreover, the musical style of the album was a major departure from SAW and her first dance-orientated work with deConstruction. The 'indie' aspect derived mainly from the writing contribution of James Dean Bradfield from the politically charged rock group The Manic Street Preachers on the tracks 'Some Kind of Bliss' and 'I Don't Need Anyone', both characterized by a distinctive guitar-driven musicality. The *Impossible Princess* phase represented a period of diminished commercial success, marking the moment in which Minogue *consciously* began to engage in a playful awareness of image construction and self-referentiality, acknowledging her distinctive 'personas' up to that point. This was unmistakably manifest in the promotional video for 'Did It Again' which featured four Kylies, each defined by the labels that the media had created for her and in which Kylie was split into the various splinters of her pop star persona. Dance Kylie, Cute Kylie, Sex Kylie and Indie Kylie all struggled for supremacy. The overall victor, though, was none of these incarnations, but rather the construction of an entirely new one. Because, although Minogue was now reflexively alluding to her identity-shedding progression, 'Indie Kylie' did not gel with the wider record-buying public, and consequently, 'Indie Kylie' was discarded for 'Camp Kylie'.

In 2000, Kylie Minogue entered her third decade as a pop performer and regained the commercial success of her earlier career. Leaving the deConstruction label, she signed with Parlophone. Her comeback was inaugurated with the first single, 'Spinning Around', which went to number 1 in the UK charts. The single was soon followed by *Light Years*, an album dominated by an explicitly camp property, that principle which, according to Susan Sontag, chiefly involves 'a relish for the exaggeration of sexual characteristics ... a vision of the world in terms of style' (1994: 279). Furthermore, for Sontag, the camp sensibility seeks the theatricalization of experience. Unlike the prevailing motif of 'Indie Kylie', with its soul-searching angst, all of Sontag's camp attributes pervaded the *Light Years* album and especially the video for 'Spinning Around', because, as Sontag maintains, 'camp taste is above all, a mode of enjoyment' (1994: 291). 'Spinning Around' represented a decisive return to a pop music sound following the 'indie' experimentation of *Impossible Princess*. In the video, the emphasis is firmly on dance, fun and freedom as the setting is a disco and the video communicates no message other than to dance and enjoy life. But a crucial factor in Minogue's comeback was that it was propelled as much by a highly distinctive item of clothing as it was by her sound. In the 'Spinning Around' video, Minogue's body dominates the frame, dressed at various points in the now iconic gold lamé hot pants. The video presents a camp fantasy world, with neon-lit and slow-motion dance shots, and a sense of unreality created by costume changes, and marked by the easy-to-copy dance moves which could be re-created in real discos. But, maintaining the emphasis on a pop music sound, Minogue would construct yet another persona, don yet another performative mask and (partially at least) evolve from camp to a Minogue with a sleek, metallic sheen as 'Camp Kylie' segued into 'Cyber-Kylie'.

Although there were some three years between *Impossible Princess* and *Light Years*, it would take only one year for her next album, *Fever,* to appear. Moreover, the first single from the album, 'Can't Get You Out of My Head', further established Minogue's cultural and commercial relevance in the new millennium, giving her the highest-selling number 1 single of her career since 'I Should Be So Lucky'. 'Can't Get You Out of My Head', with its hypnotic 'la la la' refrain and the deceptively uncomplicated, catchily repetitive beats and synth sound marked yet another clearly defined transformation in image from the camp-infused *Light Years* to an emphasis on a cool, machine-like sexuality, a trait clearly identifiable in the song's video. For William Baker, Minogue's creative director (who had initially worked for the iconic fashion designer, Vivienne Westwood), Kylie Minogue's career is one of flux, a career typified by 'constant evolution, of construction and deconstruction' (Minogue *et al.*, 1999: 1).

Returning to her recording career, post *Fever*, Kylie Minogue has continued to toy with and adapt her image. For instance, the release of the 2003 album *Body Language* saw the creation of 'Bardot Kylie', with Kylie on the album cover adopting the French actress Bridget Bardot's archetypal 'sex goddess' image of 'long bleached blonde hair, heavy eye make-up, pink lipstick' (Vincendeau, 2000: 82); her 2007 *X* album was accompanied by a fusion of 1980s-style 'day-glo' outfits offset by a 1970s 'glam' sheen; while her look to accompany her 2010 release, *Aphrodite*, was based on glamorous couture. Hence, although her sound has seldom strayed beyond a broadly pop form, her costumes and specific looks have not remained static.

Minogue's musical career can be mapped into distinctive periods, each with a differing pop take (with Cyber-Kylie being radically different from Cute Kylie), but it is most notable for the highly distinctive images that mark each period. Like Madonna's, Minogue's career is one of identity shifts; of a series of 'masks' represented by clothing and style. In this respect, Minogue's pop music career has adopted the process of what Simmel dubs 'being different' – of making oneself noticeable, not in the context of a bustling metropolis, but in a turbulent pop market place characterized by unpredictable audience demand and defined by flux.

But Minogue is not alone in this fashion-focused approach to pop music. The twenty-first century has seen the arrival of another female artist who was to achieve enormous global success in the space of one year, but would also purposely combine pop music with fashion, and more specifically the nature of fashion, to the extent that it is as if Simmel was actually describing her: Lady Gaga. Unlike Madonna or Kylie Minogue, Lady Gaga (aka Stefani Germanotta) extravagantly and decisively links music with fashion into a distinctive and synergistic (sometimes controversial) artistic cultural project that recalls the fashion-created antics of Madonna, but also constructing herself with a determined and knowing use of fashion. As Miller states: 'Lady Gaga has become one of the most significant figures in not only global pop but also for the ways in which she vociferously connects fashion and music (and art) in all performances and representations' (2011: 151). While Gaga is perceived by Berger (2011) as a key contemporary example of Lyotard's postmodern subject due to the incessant ways in which she employs fashion as a series of props in order to continually re-invent herself, her professional strategy keenly evokes the sociology of Simmel. As Peters states of Gaga's image: 'Her dazzling outfits, oversized sunglasses, odd-shaped shoes, incredible hairstyles – all create an image that is unlike any of her rock-star competitors' (2011: 70).

Peters' use of the term 'competitors' is a key one, as the suggestion I have made regarding the application of Simmel to pop fashions is that the contemporary music market place is the 'metropolis' – an accelerated commercial space in which the ability to stand out visually is an essential corporate strategy to enhance consumer/fan interest and facilitate media exposure and career longevity. When viewed in retrospect, Madonna's and Kylie Minogue's careers are marked by distinctive image-based 'epochs', and are frequently tied to specific fashion 'looks' and items of clothing. Lady Gaga is a contemporary continuation of this process, but her relationship with fashion is more avowed, knowing and accelerated than the earlier examples. This is so because Lady Gaga is a self-conscious theatrical construct, creation or 'sculpture' (Miller, 2011) that is represented and maintained equally diligently both in performances and in off-stage environments.

In Simmel's view the intrinsic nature of fashion is based on 'the charm of novelty coupled to that of transitoriness' (1971: 302), a definition that aptly encapsulates Gaga's stylistic and visual approach. Influenced by Michael Jackson, Madonna and Queen's Freddie Mercury (her stage name is derived from the 1980s Queen song, 'Radio Ga Ga'), her video performances are predicated upon striking and frequently outrageous sartorial stylings and rapidly changing looks. Thus, while 'Just Dance' first introduces her now trademark large sunglasses, she also sports distinctly David Bowie-like make-up; 'Poker Face' sees Gaga emerge from a pool wearing a highly stylized mirror mask but subsequently (via rapid edits) transform from one eye-catching costume to another in a constant state of fashion flux. Meanwhile, 'Love Game' sees Gaga paying visual homage to 1980s pop culture in a video that melds the hyper-stylized sexuality of Madonna with the leather-and-chain-clad dance moves of Michael Jackson's 'Beat It' video. These videos all accompanied songs drawn from Gaga's multi-million-selling debut album, *The Fame* (2008), but on the release of her second album, *The Fame Monster* (2009), the primacy of fashion-based imagery progressed in ever more eccentric and conspicuous ways, with an increased focus on narrative and grand spectacle. For example, the video for 'Alejandro' is presented in the context of a science-fiction, Orwell-like dystopia in which a robotic Gaga, sporting outlandish goggles, presides over a squad of male dancers adorned in totalitarian militaristic uniforms. But as the video progresses, a number of differing Gaga 'personas' are presented, many foregrounding Catholic/religious visual motifs that range from crucifix-festooned rubber priest garb and perched atop a pair of huge platform shoes, to a customized nun costume. The tonal and visual quality of the video evokes Madonna's 1989 'Express Yourself' video, and an overt (but typically outré) stylistic nod to Madonna is unmistakable in the dance sequence that sees Gaga wearing a bra that sports two M-16 automatic rifles protruding from it.

However, it is the promotional video for 'Telephone' (featuring Beyoncé Knowles) that stands as her most visually outrageous. Framed as a mini-road movie (with a running time of nearly 10 minutes), 'Telephone' sees Gaga sent to prison and committing multiple murder by poison at a roadside diner. It also sees her sporting a series of outfits such as dresses with exaggerated shoulder pads, a stars-and-stripes bikini, a telephone-shaped hat, leopard-print bodysuit, and most memorably (and eccentrically) a pair of sunglasses that consists of lit cigarettes. The primacy of dress employed in such hyper-stylized ways can be argued to represent a key contemporary popular cultural example of the effect that Simmel predicted for uses of what he dubbed 'extreme fashion': its potential to heighten an individualistic and peculiar character, and to draw the attention of the public. Indeed, Gaga's fashion choices are frequently noted for their infractions of taste and conventionality. As Simmel states of the frequently contradictory nature of fashion:

> Judging from the ugly and repugnant things that are sometimes in vogue, it would seem as though fashion were desirous of exhibiting its power by getting us to adopt the most atrocious things for its sake alone. (1971: 297)

Lady Gaga's fashion-created looks frequently reflect Simmel's view, and although they are frequently created by the elite of the fashion design world, ranging from established designers such as Alexander McQueen, Dolce & Gabbana, Jean-Paul Gaultier and Thierry Mugler, to rising talents that include Terence Koh and Rachel Barrett, they are always designed to catch attention. The unconventional fashions created by such luminaries have included latex catsuits, spiked headdresses, lobster-shaped masks, robot armour and metal corsets, plastic bubble dresses, LCD screen shades, a light-up skeleton suit, a dress covered in Muppets and a PVC Elizabethan gown that included an immense ruff and 'an endless PVC-and-lace train' (Goodman, 2010: 131).

Lady Gaga's fashion-centred performances frequently transcend her pop performances and extend to her various off-stage appearances, accentuating her identity as an artistic project that is predicated on ostentatious and frequently bizarre fashion statements. This was nowhere better illustrated than in her attendance at the 2010 MTV Music Video Awards dressed in a dress, boots, purse and hat fashioned from dead animal flesh. Designed and made by the Argentinean fashion designer Franc Fernandez, the garment would subsequently be dubbed by the media that gave it global coverage 'the meat dress', and thus sealed Gaga's reputation as an individual who potently accords with Simmel's definition of the 'fashion addict', the individual whose awareness of self 'requires a certain distinction, attention and particularity' (Frisby, 1985: 99). Indeed, Gaga's penchant for overstated fashions recalls Simmel's figure of the 'dude', whose fashion sense is predicated on exaggeration and the taking of fashion to an extreme (see the 'Paparazzi' video for Gaga clad in a chrome and jewel-encrusted body cast and neck brace for a singular example). Thus: 'when pointed shoes are in style, he wears shoes that resemble the prow of a ship; when high collars are all the rage, he wears collars that come up to his ears' (Simmel, 1957: 549). Gaga arguably behaves in exactly the same manner, but to a far more prominent and outrageous degree, wearing fashion, not clothing, and consistently standing out from the cultural crowd via eye-catching, media-digested style.

SIMMEL GOES POP

In the barbed view of Camille Paglia (2010), Lady Gaga is merely a manufactured pop personality, who has not only borrowed much of her persona from Madonna (Paglia cites the 'Alejandro' video as not so much homage as theft), Cher, Jane Fonda as Barbarella, and Gwen Stefani, but who also lacks spontaneity due to her over-styled and eccentrically fashioned public appearances. But this view is not universal. As Church Gibson argues, Paglia misunderstands Gaga because 'Gaga is a fashion-created "construct" that is very different from the singer Stefani Germanotta. Gaga, via often outrageous fashion statements is geared to be culturally confrontational' (2012: 154). Thus, from Simmel's sociological perspective, there is a perfectly logical motivation for her to engage in such fashion-inspired attention seeking. The popular cultural media landscape of the twenty-first century is one that is not lacking in pop stars and pop trends. Not only is there the continual rise and fall of pop bands and vocalists, but reality TV talent shows such as *American Idol* and *The X Factor* (to be discussed in Chapter 5) have produced annual waves of pop singers emerging from the general public. Competition in the mass communication industries is fierce and audience/market attention spans are often short, thus visually standing out from the pop music crowd is a key part of ensuring, or at least encouraging, career longevity.

As such, at one level, we can see the landscape of popular culture itself, galvanized by the digital proliferation of television choices, Internet/YouTube culture and the ability to download and store thousands of songs using MP3 and I-pod technology as the media equivalent of the bustling metropolis. In this context, the primacy of fashion and image that has steadily become an intrinsic part of pop music culture is a key means by which pop singers demarcate themselves and forge individual identities, public selves that change with the 'winds of fashion'. Of course, as noted in Chapter 1, the motivation to visually imprint pop personas is intrinsically tied to the political economy of the music industry. While we may see Madonna, Kylie or Lady Gaga as key examples of postmodern 'fluid' identities, their motivation to transform themselves via distinctive looks is geared towards maintaining commercial appeal and viability. But the ways in which this is achieved, through the continual adoption of striking fashions, demonstrates the validity of Simmel's sociology. The nature of fashion that he articulated in the first years of the twentieth century was evident in the latter years of the century and is, as suggested by the on- and off-stage antics of Lady Gaga, manifest in the twenty-first. And there are numerous other examples that can be explored and cited: from the leather-clad 'gang' image of *Bad*-era Michael Jackson; the gothic, bondage-inspired style of heavy metal star, Marilyn Manson; the 'emo' styles of My Chemical Romance vocalist, Gerard Way; to the ever-changing hairstyles and hair colours of Rihanna, or the 'futuristic' clothing and distinctive pink and platinum blonde hair and differing public personas of female hip hop performer, Nicki Minaj (most notably her on-stage character called 'Roman'). Pop and fashion are synonymous. The music is important, of course, but the look of performers is central in the identity demarcation process, and this is achieved through the strategic use of clothing.

Consequently, such pop stars arguably unite (or their designers do, at least) both of Simmel's conceptions of the nature of fashion as a source of both imitation/uniformity and differentiation. In the most common sense, pop star fashions are perpetual features of 'steal their style' magazine features. However, pop stars themselves have increasingly capitalized on their status as sources of fan imitation by extending their careers into fashion design and releasing clothing ranges based on their pop identities. Thus, pop music stars such as Victoria Beckham, Jennifer Lopez, Beyoncé, Gwen Stefani, Lily Allen and Madonna have teamed up with designers to release distinctive lines of clothing and accessories (Tungate, 2008); and other performers including Kylie Minogue, Rain, Avril Lavigne, Jay-Z and Justin Timberlake have followed suit. The rationale is that fans of such star performers will be motivated to consume their fashions which are perceived to epitomize fashion vogue. And while they are not always successful (Jennifer Lopez's 2009 Sweetface brand line, for example), pop stars-turned-fashion-designers have become a common factor in contemporary culture, further cementing the centrality of practices and uses of fashion in pop culture.

In his analysis of Simmel, Frisby states that unlike other classic sociologists, Simmel's collected works do not present any overarching theoretical narrative, but rather a series of vignettes exploring and explaining key aspects of modernity. Arguably, the impressionistic qualities that Simmel observed, recorded and theorized about the metropolises of modernity can be readily identified in the sprawling shopping malls and the mega-cities of the contemporary world. And while fashion brands have emerged as key aspects of the cultural world and the symbolic power of fashion logos have attained iconic status, the use of fashion as a tool to communicate a self within a fast-moving world is a key component of popular music. So, when the latest promotional video of Rihanna, Kylie Minogue, Lady Gaga, or whoever the future pop equivalent of such figures is (and they are inevitable) appears on MTV, what they will be wearing is just as crucial as the song they are singing, if not more so. This is the sociology of Georg Simmel in action.

QUESTIONS TO CONSIDER

1. What is the connection between the nature of the modern metropolis and fashion?
2. Why does Simmel argue that imitation is central to the social use of fashion?
3. Do you agree that fashion is as important as music with regard to many contemporary pop stars? Why do you think that this is the case?

FURTHER READING

The essential reading regarding Georg Simmel is *On Individuality and Social Forms* to fully explore the nature of the metropolis, and the article 'Fashion' (published in *The American Journal of Sociology*, Vol. LXII, No. 6). For critical overviews of Simmel's work see David Frisby's books, *Simmel and Since: Essays on Georg Simmel's Social Theory*, *Fragments of Modernity*, and *Georg Simmel*. For a contemporary overview of the essential relationship between pop celebrities and fashion, see Pamela Church Gibson's book, *Fashion and Celebrity Culture*.

Adorno and reality television

5

In Raymond Williams' now classic 1974 book, *Television: Technology and Cultural Form*, he viewed television as a cultural and domestic technology. At one level it is a part of the 'furniture' as regards its physical presence as a technological piece of hardware. But, as television became entrenched within cultures, it transformed social actors' basic perceptions of reality and how they saw the world (Williams, 2003). Whether through news broadcasts, fictional drama or sport, prior to the mainstream development of the internet, television provided us with our information about world events. But its cultural prevalence has not occurred without critique. From the early technological developments of John Logie Baird and his work with the BBC producing 'televisors' through to the increasing prevalence of television set ownership in the 1930s and early 1940s, sets were expensive and consequently television viewing was restricted to a minority in society. In the United Kingdom television became the predominant home-based entertainment medium in the late 1950s and early 1960s. Initially, though, it was perceived (by the modernist poet, T.S. Eliot, no less) to be an inferior medium to radio and little more than a pernicious device through which to 'waste time' (Silverstone, 1994), establishing a perception of television as an expression of low cultural value. But sociological critiques have gone further than this, citing television as a major component of the mass culture industry and, through its dominant programmes, representing an ideological force that serves the needs and interests of capitalism.

Therefore this chapter returns to the themes raised in Chapter 1 as its focus concerns a theorist closely associated with the work of Karl Marx, or aspects of Marx's work – Theodor W. Adorno (1903–69), the author of a series of classic texts, such as *Dialectic of Enlightenment* (1947), *Philosophy of New Music* (1949), *The Authoritarian Personality* (1950), *Minima Moralia* (1951), *Negative Dialectics* (1966) and *Aesthetic Theory* (1970). Born in Frankfurt, Germany, but moving to America in the 1930s to escape the Nazi party, Adorno produced critical writings on culture (music, for instance) and would ultimately become associated with the 'the Frankfurt School', based around The University of Frankfurt's Institute for Social Research which included thinkers such as Max Horkheimer, Leo Löwenthal, Erich Fromm, Herbert Marcuse, and later Jürgen Habermas. The Frankfurt School would eventually become synonymous with what would become dubbed 'critical theory' and argue for a better social system that would be freed from the inequalities of capitalism and its consumerist system built upon false needs and instilled 'fetishized' desires. As Storey (2003) notes, unlike previous theorists of mass culture (Matthew Arnold, F.R. Leavis and Ortega y Gasset), who saw mass culture as a threatening cultural force of change, key members of the Frankfurt School argued that mass culture and its products represent the dominant agents of stasis and social, cultural and political conservatism.

The critical approach of Adorno (and Horkheimer) explicitly focused on the ways in which capitalist values had spread to areas beyond those articulated in Marx's work. Therefore, as How (2003) points out, Adorno applied Marx's analysis of the commodity to chart how it had, in the twentieth century, come to hold a dominant position in culture, or more specifically, mass culture: a culture that is commoditized, marketed, and standardized akin to products created on the assembly line of a factory. As the first six to seven decades of the twentieth century were dominated by the Fordist production system (derived from the car manufacturing plants of the industrialist Henry Ford in 1903) – of mass-produced, standardized products based on large economies of scale, so too would the nature and 'products' of mass culture take the same form, with new cultural artefacts simply representing copies of previously successful formats, with little innovation. To illustrate with reference to cinema, How states that:

> We know pretty much what will happen in a film within the first five minutes, in fact if we know *who* is starring in it we can equally predict much of its content. At the present time, if Clint Eastwood is in it, it will be a 'tough guy' movie, if Kim Basinger or Brad Pitt are in it [it] will be 'sexy', if Hugh Grant is in it, it will be a comedy of errors. (2003: 69)

If we add a few more contemporary examples, say Jason Statham or Dwayne 'The Rock' Johnson, Cameron Diaz, Eva Mendes, Olivia Wilde, Megan Fox, Anne Hathaway, Tina Fey, Bradley Cooper or Steve Carell then we can see the point: by and large, the kinds of star fronting a film will typically determine its content from the outset, irrespective of plot. The thrust of this argument is that the products of mass culture are invariably formulaic, undemanding and endlessly recycled for the generation of maximum profit. To illustrate this decidedly pessimistic view of the nature and content of mass culture, not to mention its stultifying effects on its consumers, Adorno examined a range of examples, most prominently music and television (but also, interestingly, astrology columns), and the example of popular culture chosen in this chapter will be television, but of a very particular form: the 'reality TV' talent shows *Pop Idol/American Idol* and *The X Factor*, highly popular (and lucrative) shows which are predicated on discovering new singing talent, and as such, endorsed by weekly public telephone voting, form a cogent synergistic bond with the music industry, but are predicated upon producing slick, highly managed singers firmly fixed within the pop idiom, and seldom granted the agency of individual creativity. The choice of *Pop/American Idol* and *The X Factor* therefore arguably combines Adorno's critique of both popular music and television and demonstrates how Adorno's cultural analysis is highly pertinent to the twenty-first century and arguably incisive in terms of evaluating the nature of contemporary mass or popular culture. Ultimately, the chapter will pose this question: if Adorno were alive today, would he say, having watched *Big Brother*, *American Idol* or *The X Factor*, 'Told you so'?

ADORNO AND THE NATURE OF MASS CULTURE

Writing with Horkheimer in *The Dialectic of Enlightenment*, Adorno argues that the key defining characteristic of mass culture in the twentieth century is sameness. The role of culture in Western capitalistic societies is to impose a pervasive brand of uniformity through its primary modes of mass communication products such as cinema, radio and magazines. The result is that:

> Under monopoly, all mass culture is identical. The technology of the culture industry results in standardization and mass production. The need which might resist central control has already been suppressed by the control of the individual consciousness. (Horkheimer and Adorno, 1973: 121)

Here then, we have an updated addition to Marx's super-structural forces: the major forms of the mass communication system impose themselves on the consciousness of individuals and define what can be consumed. Indeed, the forms of mass communication consumed in leisure time are exclusively defined and set by the mass culture industries, shutting off opportunities for alternative or amateur media production and viewing individuals as nothing more than customers. But the effect of this is not only articulated in terms of a financial nexus (individuals pay for mass communication products) but it also serves a key ideological function because, as Horkheimer and Adorno state, 'culture has always played its part in taming revolutionary instincts' (1973: 152). Thus, mass culture products are both a source of capitalist revenue and also, due to their function as entertainment, an alternative (with religion) 'opium of the people' – a means through which to transmit and instil a conservative message. But how do they do this, and what is it about the nature of mass cultural products that makes them so standardized and ideological?

As Adorno argues in *The Culture Industry*, mass culture should be the culture that develops from the masses themselves but this is not the contemporary meaning and operation of the term. Rather than some form of organic, spontaneous cultural art form arising from below, mass culture is systematically imposed from above. As such, the masses are not the primary force in the culture industry, they are firmly in a secondary position; they are nothing more than 'an object of calculation; an appendage of the machinery' (Adorno, 2006: 99). Thus, not only are the masses a proletariat within industry, but, in their private leisure spheres, they are intimately connected with the capitalist machine in terms of the entertainment they consume via mass communication. Moreover, whereas the division between high/serious and low/light culture was strictly segregated, the mass culture industry has collapsed such distinctions in the name of profit and incorporated it wholesale into the same total mass cultural system. Consequently, works of art and entire artistic movements have been utilized and incorporated into advertising campaigns (Adorno cites the use of surrealism in the 1950s as an example) and in consequence, commercialized. The power and influence of the mass culture industry is such that such appropriation constitutes the forcing together of 'the spheres of high and low art, separated for thousands of years' (2006: 98) and the products are nothing but commodities, and nothing else. As such, the dominating 'ontology', the nature and being of the mass culture industry, can be reduced to this, argues Adorno:

> What parades as progress in the culture industry, as the incessantly new which it offers up, remains the disguise for an eternal sameness; everywhere the changes mask a skeleton which has changed just a little as the profit motif itself since the time it first gained its predominance over culture. (2006: 100)

The scenario that Adorno presents is one of the commodity; the pervasive capitalist system's central object, infiltrating not only the major industrial components of society, but also its major expressions of popular culture. The result is not merely a wider source of profit generation – which it most assuredly is – but also a distinctive and cultural effect on cultural forms and the individuals who consume them. This process is not necessarily new: the literary works of eighteenth-century popular authors such as Defoe and Richardson demonstrated the ways in which literary works were tailored for mass market consumption, a quality that markedly increased and flourished in the twentieth century to the extent that it developed into a coherent and specific *system,* transcending novels to grasp what Adorno calls 'all media of artistic expression' (1954: 215). A key illustrative example cited by Adorno whereby the effacement of the division between high and low culture can be readily identified is popular music – a form that, according to Adorno, explicitly and demonstrably illustrates the extent of the decline of cultural taste throughout mass culture.

In Adorno's analysis, the message of mass culture can be found in all forms of music that are marketed for consumption. Indeed, the act of music, far from being a cultural event, a source of emotional or bodily pleasure, is intrinsically ideological. Thus, when a particular individual listens to a piece of music, 'the listener is converted, along his line of least resistance, into the acquiescent purchaser' (2006: 32). It does not matter if the form of music consumed is classical or popular, the underlining intent and effect is the same: the listener is exposed to a commodity and is being manipulated purely for reasons of marketability. Consequently, there are 'ominous experiences' to be found in even the most seemingly innocuous examples of light or popular music. This is so, argues Adorno, because any pre-capitalist sentiments that may have subsided within popular music have since been eradicated and its 'ethereal' or 'sublime' qualities converted into serving as advertisements for commodities in order to actually hear and experience these pleasurable effects (radios or music-playing technology). Indeed, freedom is curtailed with regard to music listening because consumers are faced with a choice that is strictly marshalled by the professional music industry and the examples chosen for broadcast and promotion on radio stations. The net effect of such curtailed and controlled musical choice is a wide-spread erosion of individuality, in which everyone does what everyone else does because the same cultural products are marketed to all members of society in a manner governed by the standardized production of consumer goods. And in terms of the content and form of this mass-marketed music, Adorno is unequiv-ocal: it is 'trash'. Thus, complex, demanding and 'authentic' musical forms, such as jazz, are downgraded and marginalized in favour of the simple and predictable. And the dominant promotion of such music has a critical effect because its thoroughly superficial and undemanding nature encourages the inat-tentiveness of listeners. But this is not a problem because the ideological forces transmitted by capitalism through its mass cultural agents have served their purposes effectively:

> The consciousness of the mass listeners is adequate to fetishized music. It listens accordingly to formula, and indeed debasement itself would not be possible if resistance ensued, if the listeners still had the capacity to make demands beyond the limits of what was supplied. (2006: 45)

The effect of the consumption of this music is decisive, argues Adorno, and essential for the continual production of such formulaic sounds. Indeed, prolonged 'exposure' to the light musical diet emanating from popular radio stations and syndicated through music stores (in the form of recordings and sheet music of popular songs) causes a process of what Adorno calls a 'regres-sion of listening', or more dramatically, a 'forcible retardation' of musical appre-ciation and taste and a general sense of 'neurotic stupidity' across mass society. But this is no accident; it is fundamentally a practice of design instilled by the mass culture industry to ensure that alternatives to the products of the indus-try are closed off and compliance enforced. As Adorno states: 'together with sport and film, mass music and the new listening help to make escape from the whole infantile milieu impossible' (2006: 47). This is partly related to the form that popular music takes, its increasing simplicity and strictly enforced stan-dardization – down to the number of beats per minute and the exact duration of songs, timed so that they have an immediate effect. Furthermore, hit pop songs are utterly disposable and are characterized by their short shelf life, replaced simply by more of the same; but this is precisely what the music-consuming public wants, as Adorno caustically concludes: 'Regressive listeners behave like children. Again and again and with stubborn malice, they demand the one dish they have once been served' (2006: 51). Consequently, the ideological power of the mass culture industry is such that the mass, having been successfully inculcated into the worldview of capitalism and its cultural products, have bought into the ideology and actually demand formulaic music; expecting a procession of similarity and rejecting innovative musical forms and genres, or at least driving them into specialist, subcultural minority ghettoes. But music is just one example of mass cultural industry. In addition to citing the ideological functions of popular cinema and sport, Adorno also focused upon a further pervasive example of mass culture: television.

Adorno articulates the 'nefarious' nature of television through comparison with classic works of literature, or more specifically, styles of classic popular literature of the type produced by Alexandre Dumas (*The Three Musketeers*, *The Count of Monte Cristo*), arguing that:

> Although the victory of the good over the bad was generally provided for, the meandering and endless plots and subplots hardly allowed the readers of ... Dumas to be continually aware of the moral. Readers could expect anything to happen. This no longer holds true. Every spectator of a television mystery knows with absolute certainty how it is going to end. (1954: 216)

Television, then, like popular music, is a standardized, mass form of entertainment characterized by predictability and sameness. Thus, television is filled with stock archetypes located in plots that are predestined, the effects of which lower viewer expectations and intellectual effort and demand less concentration. Furthermore, as the television industry has developed, it has divided output into a number of types, or 'genres', such as light comedy (contemporaneously dubbed situation comedies or 'sit-coms'), mysteries, dramas and the like. Yet, rather than representing dynamic forms of entertainment, these genres have established patterns for television formulae which have a distinctive effect upon the viewer: they pre-establish the 'attitudinal pattern of the spectator' which determines the ways in which precise television content is received. This is such a pervasive component of television programme production that the 'typing of shows has gone so far that the spectator approaches each one with a set pattern of expectations before he faces the show itself' (2006: 169). Therefore, when settling down to view a comedy, although the situation may be different from other comedies, the pattern is utterly predictable (some mishap, confusion, embarrassment or humiliation ending with a state of equilibrium leading to the next equally predictable episode). Furthermore, these programmes are populated by a core set of stereotypes and clichés that establish a sense of unchallenging stability: for example, the generally delimited characteristics of the cast of US sitcoms such as *Friends* or *How I Met Your Mother* maintain a comforting sense of sameness and a sense of predictable orderliness in the lives of spectators.

But although on the surface level television shows such as comedies may appear to be formulaic and banal, they do have pernicious attitudinal effects on viewers. According to Adorno's analysis, television shows consist of a number of layers of meaning, each superimposed on the others, which, cumulatively, have a specific consequence. Here, Adorno fuses Marxist-influenced analysis with his psychoanalytical commentary because television content has a precise socio-psychological effect on spectators; it contains hidden meanings and messages which are geared towards 'handling' or 'ensnaring' the television audience, positioning them to see the world and the prevailing social system in a precise ideological way. To illustrate, Adorno cites the example of a 'light comedy' in which an underpaid school teacher is repeatedly placed in a position of subservience by her authoritarian head teacher and her near-starving status. Nevertheless, rather than invoking feelings of sympathy, pity or outrage at the central character's plight, her 'hustling' for food from colleagues (which invariably fails) is the cue for laughter and the arch moments of comedy in the script. The only resistant attitude on the part of the 'heroine' is her persistent recourse to a self-defined feeling of intellectual superiority, and moments of wit and the articulation of a series of humorous 'wisecracks'. The overall effect, argues Adorno, is this:

> The script is a shrewd method of promoting adjustment to humiliating conditions by presenting them as objectively comical and by giving a picture of a person who experiences even her own inadequate position as an object of fun apparently free of any resentment. (1954: 224)

In other words, even a television show as light as a situation comedy is loaded with layers of meaning, the deepest (but most powerful) of which are based on a message of indoctrination into the prevailing economic and cultural order, and the naturalization of hierarchies and structural class positions of powerlessness. This is the inherent nature of the mass culture industry: forms of mass communication that both constitute an object to be purchased for the producer's profit, and provide the means to transmit the ideology of capitalism and the need for a conservative ethos to pervade the psychology of the social 'mass'. Indeed, this process could even be found in 'esoteric' examples of mass culture, such as the newspaper astrology columns that social actors read on a daily basis.

As Adorno stated in his essay, 'The Stars Down on Earth' (based on his content analysis of the *Los Angeles Times* 'Astrological Forecasts' by Carroll Righter), although it apparently channels the predictions of the heavenly constellations, the astrological column, filled with uncontroversial pronouncements, uncannily resonates with the prevailing American capitalist social order and its conservative ideology. Thus, a consistent motif within the astrological advice was that of suggesting feelings of social contentment and an adherence to conformist behaviour. This was most evident with reference to 'higher-ups', bosses and authority figures, with the advice explicitly skewed towards giving in to the demands of 'higher-ups', placating them and keeping in their good graces. Thus, the column advises those falling under the sign of Aries: 'Urge to tell off official would alienate helpful partner, so keep calm despite irritation' (1994: 58). What strikes Adorno as significant is that these otherworldly entities' counsel seems to be in 'complete agreement with the established ways of life and with the habits and institutions circumscribed by our age' (1994: 59).

The overarching premise of Adorno's critique of mass culture is that, whether it be music, television or sport, or even newspaper astrological advice columns, there is no neutrality. Even the most seemingly benign forms of cultural industry product are not only commodities to be consumed for leisure and entertainment purposes (thereby ensuring that the public/private zones of social actors' lives are totally inculcated into the capitalist system), but they possess messages that are geared towards the conservation of the prevailing capitalist system.

But can the cultural industry really have that much power? Are the mass communications technologies and forms impossible to resist, and universally standardized? Is the mass cultural landscape really as bleak as Adorno argues it is? As Rojek observes, a key critique of the Frankfurt School is that it is 'unduly pessimistic about the prospects of social change' (2007: 43). How (2003) also cites this typical view, especially the pessimistic tone and nature of Adorno's analysis, citing it as one of the reasons that his approach is somewhat out of fashion in contemporary cultural analysis and commentary. The reception of mass cultural texts has been extensively analysed in relation to the status of consumers, with an oppositional view proffered that consumers or 'fans' of the products of the cultural industries (be they cinema, music or television) are far from merely passive 'dupes' who uncritically absorb the latent messages of mass cultural products. Instead, they 'actively' engage with them, adapt them, re-read them and re-deploy them to enhance their lives and form a sense of solidarity with other like-minded social actors (Grossberg, 1992; Jenkins, 1992; Hills, 2002; Brooker, 2002). Furthermore, as Peter Golding, in his analysis of the mass media system, states:

> The term *mass* media and *mass* communication should not obscure the varia-
> tions within the audience and the vastly different ways in which people use
> the media. Even television, the mass medium par excellence, has by no means
> a homogeneous reception. (1974: 9)

Certainly, research into the 'uses' of soap opera, a genre one would assume falls directly into Adorno's 'predictable' and 'conformist' analysis, has been argued to elicit differing viewer reactions and even individually empowering readings, especially with regard to gender and ethno-cultural identification with characters and scenarios, irrespective of the narrative 'intent' (Hobson, 1982; Buckingham, 1987; Ang, 1996). However, Adorno did acknowledge that many social actors would 'see through' the standardized nature of the cultural industry, recognize the uniformity of the music industry and the inauthentic and improbable validity of newspaper astrology columns, but many would still 'buy into' the products (astrology columns in order to purposely mock the predictions, for example), thus reinforcing his pessimistic outlook.

We might also argue that Adorno's examination of the standardized and conservative nature of music and television is perhaps valid for the Western cultures of the 1940s and 1950s that he analysed, but not for the multi-faceted 'convergent' mass communication products of contemporary societies. Thus, the internet and digital broadcasting technologies have vastly expanded the range of radio formats, which includes many of an independent nature. Similarly with regard to television, in an era of limited channels, standardized or 'ideological' programming may have been in evidence, but the proliferation of satellite and cable television networks offers thousands of channels and numerous global news platforms that make it problematical to transmit a monolithic pro-capitalist ideological message. It is perhaps also difficult in contemporary society to agree with Adorno's assessment that television programming consists of a narrow band of clichéd forms that are ultimately predictable and leave the viewer with nowhere to go that cannot be discerned from the outset. For instance, are television series such as *The Sopranos*, *Lost*, or *The Wire* predictable? Could it be argued that politically liberal, critical and acerbic series such as *The West Wing*, *Generation Kill*, *South Park*, *Family Guy*, *30 Rock*, *The Newsroom*, or *Homeland* are conservative and supportive of the status quo? You would assume not, and we might conclude that Adorno's analysis has little or nothing to say about modern popular television.

But, in defence of Adorno and his critical theory, How (2003) argues that Adorno was well aware that his analysis was exaggerated, that this was indeed deliberate and that he overstated the seemingly irresistible power of the mass culture industry in order to draw attention to its nature and to galvanize resistance to it. As Adorno states in the final paragraph of 'How To Look At Television', he had revealed the psychological mechanisms by which television operated so that the social actors would not 'become blind and passive victims' (1954: 235). Adorno's 'mission' was to draw critical and political attention to commodified culture and, in How's assessment, his commentary represents a keen example of 'clear long-sightedness' (2003: 175). And How is perhaps accurate. Although television series such as *Family Guy* or *30 Rock* are not ideologically conservative, they are nevertheless 'products' and part of a profit-seeking television network system (acting as attractors for advertising revenue, for instance). Furthermore, and more fundamentally, the emergence of highly popular new television genres resonates strongly with Adorno's assessment, suggesting a contemporary relevance for his assessment of the nature of the mass communication industry and its tendency towards the standardized, predictable and ultimately conservative ethos.

ADORNO, REALITY TV AND 'TALENT' TELEVISION

If we are seeking to identify a twenty-first-century television genre that does suggest the applicability and validity of Adorno's critique of mass culture, we need look no further than the development and global popularity of 'reality TV'. Although commonly perceived to be a new form of television at the turn of the twenty-first century, the history of reality TV stretches back to at least the 1960s with 'people shows' such as *Candid Camera,* which played pranks on members of the public and filmed their reactions via hidden cameras for comic effect; and through the 1970s, 1980s and into the 1990s with so-called 'docu-dramas' and 'docu-soaps' including: *Seven Up!, The Family, An American Family, COPS* and *The Real World.* In terms of popular entertainment, reality TV's prime exemplar is undoubtedly *Big Brother,* originally developed by Endemol Entertainment in the Netherlands and since syndicated in numerous countries including France, Germany, Italy, Poland, South Africa, Australia and America. *Big Brother* was launched in the United Kingdom on Channel 4 in the summer of 2000 as an interactive reality TV game show with a visual symbol playing George Orwell's dystopic novel *1984.* Set in the specially constructed '*Big Brother* house' which is fitted extensively with cameras monitoring the inmates 24 hours a day, the point was for 'housemates' to nominate each other for eviction, the choice ulti- mately left to the voting public until the last remaining contestant emerged the winner and recipient of the prize money.

The show was positioned as an unprecedented psychological exercise and established an innovative 'convergent' media experience (viewers can watch an edited highlights programme or continual footage via the internet). Mark Andrejevic, in his book, *Reality Television,* cites Adorno in a way that appears to support the potential offered by *Big Brother.* Adorno's writings on the possibil- ities for 'authentic experiences' within contemporary cultures that are dominated by bureaucratic administration show that contrived experiential 'experiments' offer escape routes from such ordered and administered lives. Therefore, the *Big Brother* television set is an extraordinary incident for those who take part. It is a dramatic event and a 'once-in-a-lifetime' experience in an environment which is radically different from their daily routines. But while this may be true for the small number of contestants, what about the viewers, the mass communicative context, and the 'message' transmitted by the television programme? Here, we turn back to Adorno the mass culture critic. As reality TV developed from the early 2000s, distinctive cultural responses to its rise and proliferation initially bore a distinctly Frankfurt School-flavoured pessimism and critical cynicism. Contrary to any social-experimental 'mission statements', many commentators argued that reality television offered no social/psychological insights at all but instead merely represented nothing more than 'a mixture of banality and emotional pornography' (Barnfield, in Cummings *et al.,* 2002: 47). Such nega- tive approaches were supported and publicly illustrated with a distinctly Adorno-like edge in the case of the reactions to *Loft Story,* the French version of *Big Brother.* Whilst a significant ratings success, *Loft Story* was also subjected to various demonstrations by the protest group Activists Against Trash TV, which called for the programme to be taken off the air, and whose actions included demonstrators outside the television studio brandishing placards reading: 'With trash TV the people turn into idiots' (Hill, 2005: 4).

As the format has continued on a yearly (sometimes bi-yearly) basis, subse- quent editions of *Big Brother* (in the UK at least) progressively and strenuously emphasiszd the spectacle of the programme and its predictability (reflexively acknowledged by contestants who wish not only to win but to secure celebrity status on leaving the show) in the creation of stereotypical 'characters' in the media landscape and media discourses surrounding *Big Brother* (news media, celebrity glossy magazines, Internet gossip sites). Thus reality TV rapidly became a staple genre which was heavily marketed and inspired numerous spin-offs to the point of becoming something of a television cliché. Indeed, the reality TV 'genre' has become incorporated into mainstream television schedules in very diverse forms, ranging from self-improvement or 'makeover' shows (*Extreme Makeover*, *Ten Years Younger*, *What Not To Wear*, *The Swan*, *Queer Eye For The Straight Guy*, *The Biggest Loser*) and 'domestic' improvement shows (*Nanny 9/11*, *Supernanny*, *How Clean Is Your House*) to 'dream profession' shows (*American Inventor*, *Project Runway*, *Master Chef*, *America's Next Top Model*, *Hell's Kitchen*, *The Apprentice*). Many of these shows concern (often ruthless) individualistic competition, wealth acquisition and conformity with dominant social norms (makeover shows never question the social impetus to look 'good', or 'ten years younger', and critique the social forces of gender, bodily enhancement or ageism arguably reinforced by such programmes). Indeed, in the case of *The Apprentice* the onus on individual competition is the very raison d'être of its narrative and appeal. The show centres on the opportunity for an entrepreneurial individual to win the opportunity to work for the 'self-made' American billionaire Donald Trump (the UK's version is fronted by Lord Alan Sugar) if they can prove their capitalist acumen through a weekly series of profit-creating consumerist exercises. As such, 'the series is not only a vehicle for displaying Trump's business ventures and brands, but a lab for teaching/producing/inventing an ideal corporate citizen' (Ouellette and Hay, 2008: 188). As a result, the 'hidden mechanisms' of television identified by Adorno are arguably intact in mainstream, entertainment-oriented programming but with the difference that, as illustrated by *The Apprentice*, the ideological layers have risen to the surface to celebrate capitalism and the individualistic, entrepreneurial ethic that underpins it.

But the ultimate evolution of reality TV since the 'revolution' that characterized television production and programming throughout the 2000s is undoubtedly 'talent television' in the form of lavish and popular 'event' musical TV shows. *American Idol* and *The X Factor* combine two of Adorno's major productions of the mass culture industry: music and television. So, to what extent do these programmes illustrate Adorno's critical ideas in contemporary popular culture? To explore this question, let us take the example of *American Idol* first.

American Idol: The Search for a Superstar was first broadcast on 11 June 2002 and very rapidly established itself as one of the most watched programmes of the new century. Developed from the British series, *Pop Idol* (2001–03) created by pop manager and producer Simon Fuller and featuring the acerbic principal judge, Simon Cowell, the concept (complete with Cowell) was successfully franchised for the US and then global market, including Australia, Canada, Brazil, France, Israel, Japan, Russia, South Africa, Iran, and India. The concept is simple: the show seeks to find (from thousands of individuals who attend auditions) over successive weeks a solo performer who will be awarded a recording contract and thus realize their dream of pop music stardom. To date, winners have included Kelly Clarkson, Ruben Studdard, Fantasia Barrion, Carrie Underwood, Taylor Hicks, Jordin Sparks, David Cook, Kris Allen, Lee DeWyze and Scotty McCreery. Selecting the ultimate winner are a number of established and respected music producers and performers including Randy Jackson, Simon Cowell, Paula Abdul, Steven Tyler (lead singer with American rock group Aerosmith) and the actress and pop singer Jennifer Lopez, joined by an array of guest judges and mentors as disparate as Donna Summer, Gene Simmons, LL Cool J, Jewel, Olivia Newton-John and the film director Quentin Tarantino. The judges' decision regarding which performers are eliminated, however, is augmented from the semi-final stage by audience voting via telephone and text message. In addition to giving the series a 'dramatic' edge (viewers can vote for likeability over pure talent) the interactive, audience voting dimension has potently demonstrated the 'mass' appeal of the series. For example, prior to announcing the winner of the fifth season of *American Idol* in 2006, host Ryan Seacrest claimed that the 64 million votes cast to select the winner (Taylor Hicks) exceeded those of any American president, and were certainly more than George W. Bush received in his 2000 presidential election (Ouellette and Hay, 2008).

Thus, *American Idol* has rapidly become an entrenched part of popular culture, representing an example of reality television that dominates ratings and has successfully extended itself into a wide-ranging array of supporting media. But does the fact that *American Idol* is popular constitute an expression of Adorno's critique of the mass culture industries? Some of the critical reaction would seem to suggest that it does. For instance, Karla Peterson's journalistic critique of the series, hyperbole aside, keenly reflects the sensibility of Adorno's assessment of mass cultural artefacts. In assessing the cultural impact of *American Idol*, Peterson concludes that:

> American Idol was not a dumb summer fling, but a conniving multimedia monster. Shameless product placement. Bloodless nostalgia. Incestous corporate hype. Like the show's Stepford diva – who dutifully parroted every shriek, quiver and growl from the Mariah Carey catalog – American Idol has absorbed the sins of our debauched culture and spit them out in a lump of reconstituted evil. And because we were so dazzled by its brazen lack of redeeming qualities, we stepped over the mess and happily followed it over the abyss. (Cited in Jenkins, 2008: 61)

Adorno's sentiment, then, is alive and well. But how does what is clearly an innovative, if not unprecedented, television series garner such a negative critique? Petersen's review clearly evokes Adorno's assertion that the development of the mass culture industry initiated a period of declining cultural tastes, regression, cliché, repetition and the dominance of 'light culture'. It is also apt that Adorno refers to the 'schema of mass culture' as the 'dream industry'. *American Idol* is predicated on the individualized achievement of a 'fantasy' life, a recording contract and the celebrity lifestyle and wealth that are ostensibly associated with this status. Thus, having defeated their rivals and gained the judges' and wider audience's votes, it is a 'dream come true' for the winning contestant, a dream that is rapidly transformed into a concrete product: a pop song targeted at the very top of the charts.

American Idol was not only heralded, as Henry Jenkins states, as the early 2000s 'savior' of the American broadcast networks, but also constituted from the beginning of its run a potent and profitable example of a trans-media franchise:

> The show's first-season winner, Kelly Clarkson, signed to RCA Records and had an immediate number 1 hit single on the Billboard Hot 100, 'A Moment Like This'. The song went on to become the top-selling US single for 2002. An American Idol book made the best-seller list and the American Idol contestants played to sell-out houses on their nationwide concert tour. (Jenkins, 2008: 61)

Hence, *American Idol* is a prime example of contemporary 'synergy', that now classic mass communications concept that is the hallmark of media conglomerates such as News Corp which, as Morley and Robins (1995) note, involves the drive to control media production, distribution and the manufacture of hardware. *American Idol*, therefore, is a nexus of cross-media profitability, and its huge ratings popularity has made it the desired target for numerous corporate sponsorship deals from firms such as Coca-Cola and AT&T. Similarly, its unprecedented ratings success has enabled it to generate further financial success to the tune of hundreds of millions in advertising revenue.

Just as the success of *Big Brother* spawned further examples of reality TV, *Pop Idol* and *American Idol* have established a firm foundation for alternative talent TV programmes, for example *The X Factor*, first broadcast in the United Kingdom in 2004 but also franchised across the world (from Armenia, Belgium and Chile, to Kazakhstan and New Zealand). Created by Simon Cowell, *The X Factor* was developed to succeed *Pop Idol*, and although it would follow the same basic principle (the public search for a pop singer and audience voting for the ultimate winner of a recording contract and release of a single), it would have slight variations in that it had clear age categories (under and over 25s) and featured boy/girl singing groups. As with *American Idol*, Simon Cowell would be joined by a number of music industry-linked judges such as pop/rock managers Sharon Osbourne and Louis Walsh and the pop singers Dannii Minogue, Cheryl Cole, Kelly Rowland, Gary Barlow, and Tulisa Contostavlos (formerly lead singer of UK R&B/Grime act, N-Dubz). The role of these celebrity judges is to also act as 'mentors' to the group of aspirants who are whittled down from the thousands of hopefuls who attend the open auditions and who make the 'boot camp' stage – a residential stage in which contestants are given a specific song to learn and impress the judges on each successive show. Winners have included Shayne Ward, Leon Jackson, Alexandra Burke, Joe McElderry and the most internationally successful winner, Leona Lewis, who achieved hit singles in both the UK and America, and sang the theme song for James Cameron's sci-fi film epic, *Avatar*.

A key component of both *American Idol* and *The X Factor* is that it is based on genuine singing talent, and thus a pervasive sense of merit and a distinctive work ethic is central to the series and characterizes the individuals who ultimately win the public vote and the supreme prize. Furthermore, the interactivity of these shows marks a decisive sense of 'activity' on the part of the audience. With regard to *Big Brother* and its multi-media, or 'convergent' nature, some commentators have perceived the development of reality television as an unprecedented advance, viewing it as a medium by which the audience is actually *empowered*. In this analysis, reality television represents a dynamic development whereby the 'mass' is actually granted the ability actively to direct the narrative rather than simply receive transmissions in a docile, passive manner (Tincknell and Raghuram, 2002). As Centellas' (2010) research into student perceptions of *American Idol* in relation to the theoretical approaches of Karl Marx and Alexis de Tocqueville found, although many students read *American Idol* critically, seeing it as a bourgeois 'franchised empire', a capitalist television monopoly of the pop market, others had a different view – that the guidance given to contestants empowers audience members to achieve music success. A contestant making it to the top of the charts through publicly endorsed talent appeals directly to the record-buying/downloading public, by circumnavigating the standard industry routes and the conventional powerful gatekeepers such as producers. Musicians too, via convergent platforms such as MySpace and YouTube, can be similarly motivated to get their music out directly to consumers and not become part of the standard music industry corporate machine. According to this view, *American Idol* constitutes something of a 'revolution' within the music world.

Yet, from Adorno's perspective, the nature of *American Idol* and *The X Factor* suggests no revolutionary potential beyond the technological/convergent qualities and the scale of the 'events'. In terms of television and music, both of these programmes accord with the assessment of the nature and effect of the mass culture industry produced by Adorno decades before. Through the figure of Simon Cowell, *American Idol* and *The X Factor* have arguably enhanced the role of the producer, elevating a person who would typically have remained behind the scenes to the forefront of the stage and to global celebrity status. Thus, the producer in this instance becomes the arbiter of musical form and acceptability. Centellas' research shows that the contemporary music industry is not the monolithic entity it might have been at the time of Adorno's initial analysis. The internet and wider accessibility and affordability of musical recording equipment have enabled routes into the music industry to become more varied. However, the success and visibility that surround *American Idol* and *The X Factor* are of the very highest, and are extremely lucrative. As each series builds towards its climax, the battle between the remaining contestants, publicity and a fan base have been carefully constructed, factors that are elusive to the grassroots pop/rock acts supposedly revolutionized by these shows. Furthermore, the level of commercial expectation of the winner is acute: *The American Idol* winner is targeted at the number 1 spot in the US Billboard charts, while *The X Factor* champion is geared towards securing the prestigious Christmas number 1. Consequently, the 'monopolistic' qualities of the music industry and the prevalence of a form of music that can be perceived as an 'inescapable product' are readily identifiable with the ubiquity of *American Idol* and *X Factor* broadcasts, discussion and coverage, airplay and transmission of the winning song, and extensive reinforcing coverage within wider forms of media.

One aspect of reality TV and talent TV that would seem to disavow an Adorno-like analysis is the critique that television is thoroughly predictable from the outset. The key feature of *American Idol* and *The X Factor* is that the identity of the contestants who will progress to the 'boot camp' training stages, and then to the semi-final and ultimate final is unknown even to the producers, as it is in the respective hands of the judges and unpredictable voting public. However, both shows are arguably utterly predictable in their format, form, and structure. The only unknown is the identity of the winner, not that there will or will not be one. And the road to this ultimate revelation is one that is filled, week in, week out, with a standard format from series to series: early rounds that see a legion of unconsciously untalented individuals caustically dismissed by the acid-tongued Simon Cowell (the key component in his rise to celebrity status) and the 'pleasure' that the hapless and tuneless performers provide for the viewer. But beyond these stages come the ersatz drama and emotional expressions of performers and judges alike, the protracted pauses while contestants await the revelation of the judgement or the public vote, and the numerous established pop performers (from the Black Eyed Peas, Rihanna and Shakira, to Christina Aguilera, Katy Perry and Robbie Williams) who appear as mentors or sources of inspiration, but who invariably perform their own latest song in a further instance of synergistic music marketing. Furthermore, the predictability extends to the music that the contestants perform through the duration of the extravaganzas and invariably the winning song, which demonstrate the dominance of marketability and musical inoffensiveness that dominates the singing and the final product. Thus, *American Idol* and *The X Factor* are not concerned with any original compositions produced by contestants, but instead are rooted in the idiom of mass-appeal pop music or the soaring pop ballad. Indeed, on *The X Factor* it is in the familiar and pre-established form of the cover version. The cover version, which can be a source of musical innovation and creative expression, has, as Plasketes (2005) notes, a long-standing place in popular music and is a recording practice that frequently crosses musical styles, boundaries and genres, often to radical effect (think of Jimi Hendrix's version of Bob Dylan's 'All Along The Watchtower', Bruce Springsteen's interpretations of the music of Pete Seeger, or Tori Amos' piano/vocal re-interpretations of songs by artists as diverse as Eminem, The Beatles, Neil Young, Nirvana and Slayer). But no such radicalism tends to be present in the output of reality talent TV. Instead, it is about mass appeal and immediate hit record status; mainstream radio exposure and music channel video broadcasts. Indeed, while the interactivity and revolutionary technological aspect of the likes of *American Idol* are distinctly twenty-first century, and may constitute a form of 'audience democracy', this was not the intention. The purpose was to achieve the key goal of the mass culture industry: profits and mass consumption. As the creator of *American Idol*, Simon Fuller, has stated, following his managerial/promotional success with the UK pop group The Spice Girls, then the pop/TV crossover boy/girl band, S Club 7, the commercial role that television has in selling music was compelling. Inspired by this fusion, Fuller states:

> I developed an online idea called 'Fame Search' where the audience could nominate singers to appear in a new group. This then evolved into a TV format where the online voting element became phone and text voting. The interactivity was important because this would allow the audience to tell me who they liked best and this, in turn, would indicate to me who would have the most fans and eventually sell the most music and become the biggest stars. (Variety.com, 2011)

Thus, Adorno's view that contemporary music is dominated by the commodity form is inherent in the product of *American Idol* and *The X Factor*. The goal is not to expand the genres of popular music and uncover productive musical talent, but for popular performers to find approval with a mass audience, the audience that contributes to the ratings success of the respective programmes. As such, twenty-first-century popular culture exhibits examples that perfectly reflect Adorno's pessimistic critique, even to the point of reflecting the disposability of its winners, many of whom are forgotten by both the industry and the public as the next search for musical talent gears up. For Adorno, both popular music and television are characterized by a palpable lowering of concentration and intellectual effort in the act of consumption; this is so because the 'repetitiveness, the selfsameness, and the ubiquity of modern mass culture tend to make for automatized reactions and to weaken the forces of individual resistance' (2006: 160).

Nonetheless, if *American Idol* and *The X Factor* represent a contemporary expression of Adorno's insidious mass culture industry, it has also been the focus of resistance, and a novel form of opposition that has employed the technologies of convergence that lie at the heart of reality TV, and which implies that not all music consumers are passive 'victims' of the contemporary mass culture industry. Although we can take it as a given that many choose not to watch such programmes and do not purchase the music of the winners, *The X Factor* of 2009 was the target of a unique act of protest conducted on the social networking site, Facebook. Ultimately amassing over 500,000 followers, the campaign aimed to thwart a fifth consecutive *X Factor* Christmas number 1 single. The campaign urged opponents of *The X Factor* to download the Rage Against The

Machine track, 'Killing In The Name' (originally released in 1992). Based on the anarchist, anti-corporate politics of the band (see Chapter 1), with its expletive-laden defiant finale chant, the song was levelled both at the monopolistic nature of *The X Factor*, and explicitly at its chief associate and 'face', Simon Cowell. Although initially dismissed by Cowell, the campaign gained momentum and was successful in its goal: the 2009 winner Joe McElderry and his cover of a ballad originally released by the teen star, Miley Cyrus, 'The Climb', failed to secure the habitual Christmas number 1 slot, an event that had not occurred since 2005.

Although far from a revolutionary collective, this grassroots movement demonstrated the antipathy to the corporate nature of *The X Factor* and its factory-like production-line approach to the creation of mass-appeal pop music. Thus, modest as it may have been, it demonstrated a unique popular cultural moment of Marcuse-like 'great refusal', and showed that the negativity of Adorno and the wider Frankfurt School was not entirely exaggerated, but that critical voices could be articulated. Thus, with the growth of a 'talent TV industry' that serves as a nexus for a wide array of commercial and corporate interests, How's assessment of Adorno as a prescient thinker is, arguably, visible and valid. The twenty-first-century mass cultural landscape would do little to dissipate Adorno's pessimism.

QUESTIONS TO CONSIDER

1. Why is Adorno so pessimistic about the nature of mass culture?
2. What are the major objections to Adorno's cultural critique and the effects television and radio have on mass audiences?
3. Can TV programmes such as *American Idol* and *The X Factor* have 'democratic potential' for audiences?

FURTHER READING

For a wider understanding of the critical social thought of Theodor Adorno, readers should see his book, *The Culture Industry*, and the article 'How to Look at Television' (*Quarterly of Film and Television*, 1954, Vol. 8, No. 3, pp. 213–35), and (with Max Horkheimer) the *Dialectic of Enlightenment*. For a critical overview of Adorno's thinking see Ross Wilson's book, *Theodor Adorno*. Of related interest is Nick Stevenson's 2008 short article, 'Living in "X Factor" Britain: Neo-liberalism and "Educated" Publics'.

Feminism and sport 6

The relationship between feminism and popular culture is both acute and long-standing. This is no surprise, as popular cultural representations of femininity, particularly from the 1960s onwards, have provided a set of 'documents' that chart differing representations of women. From novels, advertising, girls' comics, pop music and music videos, and cinema, to television, the internet and video games, popular culture is the site of gender politics and apparent change. Thus, female passivity is represented in magazines that, according to Naomi Wolf (1991) establish a dominant code – the 'beauty myth' that reinforces the need for women to conform to regimes of beauty and bodily health; to the 'Girl Power' advocates, The Spice Girls, and the 'kick ass' heroines of various 'telefantasy' series made in the 1990s and early 2000s such as *Buffy the Vampire Slayer*, *Dark Angel*, *Charmed*, *La Femme Nikita*, and *Alias* (Beeler and Beeler, 2007; White, 2007); or to the confident consumer-driven independence of Carrie Bradshaw from *Sex and the City*. But while there is much scope for a 'pop cultural' analysis of feminism, this chapter will relate this subject to a more sociological cultural example: sport. Furthermore, although the chapter will provide an overview of feminism, it will be chiefly concerned with articulating a specific position: the relationship between 'proto-feminism' and contemporary 'post-feminism'. In the first section of the chapter I will focus on the arguments of the early feminist thinker Charlotte Perkins Gilman and relate her work to an interesting modern aspect of sport: the development of the 'WAG'. Coined by the UK tabloid press, the term WAG stands for wife or girlfriend of a male sports star, but (with a nod to Chapter 3) the WAG has become a distinctive celebrity category in her own right, and one that equates femininity with fashion, glamour and attachment to male status. Moreover, the cultural context that has seen the emergence of the WAG has also witnessed distinctive transformations in the representation of masculinity in sport, and this will also be examined, with reference to figures from sport such as the British footballer David Beckham and the NFL New England Patriots quarterback, Tom Brady.

Sport, I will suggest in this chapter, has become a prime cultural space within which to appraise transformations in gender relations and gender politics and to observe key shifts in terms of femininity, masculinity and the new life and validity that can be found for older cultural debates within modern cultural contexts and popular cultural consumption.

FEMINISM(S)

To define feminism is both straightforward and difficult. In Delmar's opinion, a base-line definition of feminism and the feminist is that a feminist:

> Is someone who holds that women suffer discrimination because of their sex, that they have specific needs which remain negated and unsatisfied, and that the satisfaction of these needs would require a radical change (some would say a revolution even) in the social, economic and political order. (1986: 8)

In Chapter 1, I outlined the problematic aspects of Marx and the economic and class basis of political action and revolution. Overthrowing the bourgeoisie would not necessarily eliminate *all* forms of inequality, only potentially that related to class, and nothing would necessarily change for women. And it is not just the revolutionary force of communism that could fail to address female subordination and the issue of patriarchal oppression. As Whelehan (1995) points out, the driving force that ignited the first wave of feminist thinkers and activists is usually attributed to Mary Wollstonecraft and the publication of her manifesto text, *Vindication of the Rights of Women* in 1792, developed by writers such as George Sand, Sarah Grimké, Margaret Fuller, Elizabeth Cady Stanton and Charlotte Perkins Gilman, who would form the foundation of the second wave. The key issue of political debate was the extent to which enfranchisement, the granting of the vote, was limited to males, and thus a concerted political movement to extend the right to vote to women and recognize women's rights was initiated, although it would not be until 1928 in Britain and 1919 in the United States that women were granted voting equality with men. Yet, the granting of the right to vote was just one issue; the power of patriarchy had many dimensions, not least of which was the rigid separation of the public and private spheres of human life, with women being expected to remain within the private, domestic space.

One of the most prominent liberal or first-wave feminist figures was Charlotte Perkins Gilman (1860–1935). Rather than adhering to the term 'feminist', Gilman actually preferred to be known as a sociologist and her central concern was that of economic dependence, a relationship between male and females that, she argued, was the main barrier in the way of progress for the female sex (in Schneir, 1996: 230). In her central text, *Women and Economics*, published in 1898, Gilman argues that there is a marked economic condition affecting the human race, and unparalleled in the organic world:

> We are the only animal species in which the sex-relation is also an economic relation. With humans, an entire sex lives in a relation of economic dependence upon the other sex. (1998: 5)

This unequal and patriarchal state of affairs is based entirely on history, not on innate or biological differences between males and females; males have controlled the economic components of societies for thousands of years. For Gilman, it is a global condition that in all societies throughout history economics and economic production are governed predominantly by the activities of males, and that the females obtain their share only through men. Thus, unlike other species (there is a distinctly Darwinian thread running throughout the text), females do not, indeed, cannot seek their own living but must be 'fed by the male' (1998: 18). This sense of dependency unites women into a collective state. As Gilman articulates:

> From the day labourer to the millionaire, the wife's worn dress or flashing jewels, her low roof or her lordly one, her weary feet or her rich equipage – these speak of the economic ability of the husband. (1998: 9–10)

In one sense, motherhood excludes women from the economic process; but this is simply a reflection of 'patriarchal ideology', argued Gilman, and when investigated historically it becomes apparent that the working power of the mother has always been a prominent factor in human life. Women represent the worker *par excellence*, but the nature of female work does not contribute to their economic status. Instead, a woman's 'living', from food, clothing and luxuries, has no direct relation to her power to produce wealth, to her services in the house, or to her role as a mother. Alternatively:

> These things bear relation only to the man she marries, the man she depends on, – to how much she has and how much he is willing to give her. The woman whose splendid extravagance dazzles the world, whose economic goods are the greatest, are often neither houseworkers nor mothers, but simply the women who hold most power over the men who have the most money. The female [of the human race] is economically dependent on the male. He is her food supply. (1998: 21–2)

For Gilman, this state of dependency had to be abolished so that men and women would be equal in terms of their economic relation, because only 'when the mother of the race is free, we shall have a better world' (1998: 340). Consequently (and predating Betty Friedan by decades), Gilman argued that women should be free to work outside their home. Furthermore, she advocated the socialization of housework: a society that employed professional housecleaners, communal kitchens and dining rooms and day nurseries for children in order for both men and women to work in the public social world.

On the outbreaks of the First and Second World Wars Gilman's predictions seemingly came true as the conflicts necessitated the use of women in typically male productive roles: factories, farming and munitions manufacture. But with the cessation of conflict, the sexual status quo and female 'dominance' of the household were quickly re-established in many nations, and women expected to find, as Friedan articulated in the landmark text, *The Feminine Mystique*, 'fulfilment as a wife' (1963: 13). Resistance to the idea of a woman's place being restricted to the domestic world (while men dominated the public sphere not only in terms of productive, wage-earning capacity, but also structural positions of social and cultural power) was expressed in a number of feminist texts, but there were also a number of differing feminist strands. Following Friedan's stark articulation of the socially restricted, subordinate plight of the American suburban housewife and the message for women to seek careers beyond the home, writers and key texts included Germaine Greer's *The Female Eunuch* (1970), which continued the classic second-wave writer Simone de Beauvoir's psychoanalytical/Freudian approach to female social and cultural status, as outlined in her seminal book, *The Second Sex*. In this text, de Beauvoir placed the status of women within a historic, mythic, and social context, weaving in literature (the fiction of D.H. Lawrence, for example), discussions of sexuality, the social positions of women (the married woman, the mother, old age) with a vision of female liberation that overcomes their suppression by patriarchy. Developing de Beauvoir's emancipatory vision, further psychoanalytically inspired texts included Kate Millet's *Sexual Politics* (1971) and Juliet Mitchell's *Psychoanalysis and Feminism* (1974). However, there were also radical texts such as Shulamith Firestone's *The Dialectic of Sex* (1971) that used the language of Marx and Engels to call for a revolution of women from men and from a deeply entrenched male culture that enforced the biological/maternal dependency of women on men.

As a result, these differing early approaches became united in a single sexual source of solidarity, 'the belief that women suffer injustice because of their sex' (Whelehan, 1995: 11). This rallying sentiment had been articulated earlier by one of the key 'liberal' feminists, Charlotte Perkins Gilman, who stated that:

> The Women's Movement rests not alone on her larger personality, with its tingling sense of revolt against injustice, but on the wide, deep sympathy of women for one another. It is a concerted movement, based on the recognition of a common evil and seeking a common good. (1998: 139)

Women, therefore, are oppressed because of their sex (Beasley, 1999: 54). The notion of shared oppression is intimately connected with a strong emphasis on the sisterhood of women; thus any woman has more in common with any other woman – regardless of class, race, age, ethnic group or nationality – than any woman has with any man (ibid.). To establish a foundational conception of feminism, then, this is arguably accurate. As stated earlier, feminism is an intellectual and political movement geared towards establishing equality between the sexes (or complete separation in some instances) and establishing a social system that enables women to live fulfilling lives freed from patriarchal oppression and control in both the private and public spheres. Nevertheless, a 'universalist' conception of womanhood and female status is a problematic aspect with any overarching approach to feminism. Although I have sketched only a few classic feminist theorists, it is perhaps more accurate to refer to *feminisms* rather than feminism. As feminist thought developed from the mid-1960s, a key characteristic of that progression has been its multi-faceted form, much of it emerging in critical reaction to second-wave feminism. Black feminism and post-colonial feminist voices – those of Patricia Hill Collins, Andre Lourde and Chandra Talpade Mohanty, for example – were underscored with a message of distinction from second-wave feminism; that the articulation of suburban white women was not and could not be comparable with that of black women and female experiences in various parts of the globe. To claim a universal female position was problematic and repressive itself. Caroline Ramazonoglu, in *Feminism and the Contradictions of Oppression* (1989), stresses the ways in which second-wave feminism is inherently oriented towards Western female experience, relations of exploitation that exist between the West and the South (Western women wearing clothing and fashion manufactured by women in poorly-paid 'sweatshop' working conditions in the 'Third World) and even the employment of working-class women for domestic service by middle-class women.

Returning to the theme examined in Chapter 2, differing levels of status can cut across and can act to negate any sense of gender solidarity, or render any Western claims to a 'global sisterhood' problematic, if not distasteful. Indeed, Ramazonoglu cites the Black Australian writer, Eve Fesl, who argues that in ethnic terms, black Australian women have faced far greater levels of oppression from white women than they have from black men. Consequently, bel hooks argues that the key text of second-wave feminism, *The Feminine Mystique*, with its revelation of 'the problem that has no name' referred to the domestic predicament of college-educated, middle-to-upper-class, married white women. Thus, hooks claims of the lived condition of American black women:

> Feminism in the United States has never emerged from the women who are most victimized by sexist oppression; women who are daily beaten down, mentally, physically, and spiritually – women who are powerless to change their condition in life. They are the silent majority. A mark of their victimization is that they accept their lot in life without visible question, without organized protest, without collective anger or rage. Betty Friedan's The Feminine Mystique is still heralded as having paved the way for [the] contemporary feminist movement – it was written as if these women did not exist. (2000: 1)

The issue of female difference rather than the 'universal sisterhood' quality of second-wave feminism would be such that it would lead, from the early 1980s, to a new period of feminist theorizing: third-wave feminism. The issue of sexuality and the differing levels of inequality that face homosexual women led to the emergence of Lesbian feminism, most typically associated with the work of Sheila Jeffreys, author of *The Spinster and Her Enemies: Feminism and Sexuality 1880–1930,* published in 1985. Furthermore, cultural debates would polarize feminist commentators into distinctive, oppositional factions, perhaps most notably with regard to the feminist 'sex wars' that raged in the 1980s over pornography, principally between the radical anti-pornography position of Andrea Dworkin and Catherine MacKinnon, and feminists who advocated an anti-censorship approach. Ethnic, class, religious and sexual diversity would form the key quality of third-wave feminist approaches, differences that cannot be subsumed beneath the umbrella of womanhood. Indeed, whereas issues such as sexuality and pornography were perceived to be key aspects of sexual socialization and oppression within second-wave feminist positions, third-wave approaches emphasized the issue of personal choice, that participation in the pornography industry or prostitution was always the result of oppressive structural forces and that women's choices were a factor. Therefore, as Tong observes: 'third-wave feminists maintain that a woman can be both a feminist and a porn queen' (2009: 288), and sexuality and feminist politics are not mutually at odds. In many respects, third-wave feminism reflected both the legacy of the poststructuralist turn in European social thought from 1968 (which in turn paved the way for postmodernism) – the concerted attack upon 'universal' and all-embracing, but 'oppressive' modes of thought. The French theorist Michel Foucault (1926–84) included in his work an analysis of sexuality, the history of madness and a historical 'anti-science' methodological approach which he called 'genealogy'. However, in his best-known work, *Discipline and Punish* (1977) he emphasized the multiple sources of power, or 'discourses', that pervade societies, and the multi-sources of power, sources which cannot be defeated in a one-off revolutionary event. Rather than one overarching form of dominating ideology, Foucault identified multiple forms of knowledge in societies, routinely used as a means to instil social power and domination within a range of institutions such as prisons, hospitals and schools. The issue here is that power is located at the level of micro-politics and is locally dispersed. Therefore, issues such as racism and sexism must be countered at the level where they arise and exercise power: a class-based revolution (as advocated by Marxists) will fail to alleviate such oppression.

Thus, a distinctive seam of postmodernist feminism arose in the 1980s, best illustrated by the work of Donna Haraway and Judith Butler. In one sense, a Foucault-inspired basis for third-wave feminism and its focus on difference and the multiplicity of inequalities, even within the gender category of 'woman', has advantages over approaches that subsume ethnic, class, religious and status differences beneath that of a general sense of solidarity due to being female and hence 'united' by the oppression faced by patriarchy. But the lack of a core agenda or set of defining values is seen as problematic for third-wave feminism: what does it stand for if it embraces everything? Furthermore, running parallel with third-wave feminism, if not emerging from it, was a curious, but ongoing, development: 'post-feminism'. This was identified most significantly by Susan Faludi and articulated in her classic book, *Backlash*. Looking at popular culture, Faludi discerned a potent message, and one that seemed to suggest that second-wave feminism had been too successful in its political quest for sexual equality. As Faludi observed:

> Women's magazines and newspapers alike are encouraging women to blame feminism for their exhaustion and disillusionment rather than a political structure which profits quite literally from the inequalities it perpetuates. It is argued that feminism spoiled women's fun, their right to be sexually attractive and dress up, to flirt and enjoy domestic bliss. (1992: 221)

Such claims of gender 'victory' were greatly exaggerated, increased female entry into the public workspace still tended to be in non-professional and low-paid jobs, and the practices of sexual and job discrimination remained rife. Nevertheless, the concept of post-feminism gained pace, especially with regard to popular culture, and I will return to it (in connection with Gilman and first-wave feminism) in relation to gender, equality and 'empowering' sport – an area of human experience which predates feminism, but which has always been a focus for gender issues and gender inequalities.

SPORT AND WOMEN (AND MEN)

In the view of Douglas Kellner, from 'the original Olympics in Ancient Greece and the chariot races and gladiator fights in Ancient Rome, sports have long been a major site of entertainment and spectacle' (2003: 65); furthermore, they represent a significant means by which social values are represented and transmitted. Sport articulates crucial societal components, such as power, nationalism, globalization, consumerism, ideologies, economics, representations of the body and class inequality (Hargreaves, 1994; Whannel, 2007; Giulianotti and Robertson, 2009); it has also, since its beginning within organized human cultures, been a source of gender socialization and sexist practices. According to Scambler (2005), sport emerged from the martial and military training practices employed by many ancient Greek armies and adopted and adapted in wider society, a development enshrined in the games first staged at Olympia in 776 BC and held every fourth summer until AD 261 – a thousand-year run with no cancellations, and revived by Baron Pierre de Coubertin in 1896. Moreover, the ancient world of sport included female competitors. As Cashmore (2010) states, history's first female sports champion was Cynisca, who triumphed at the Pan-Hellenic (meaning 'all-Greek') games in 396 BC in the quadriga event, a sport that involved a chariot drawn by four horses. Women also competed in hunting, riding and swimming in Greek and Roman games. Thus, the participation of female athletes in sporting activity and professional sports is as old as sport itself, but they have not competed on fully equal terms with male athletes. Cynsica won her victory in absence because although she owned and had trained the horses, she was not permitted to steer the chariot or even able to attend the games. Cashmore argues that later historical periods such as that of medieval Europe show evidence of female participation in activities such as running and archery; but as sport socially and professionally developed women were increasingly excluded from its practices, or marginalized to 'acceptable' sports. Consequently, as Boyle and Haynes argue:

> Sport has always been a sexual battlefield. The issue of gender, and the representation of biological difference between the sexes, has long been central to our perceptions of sport in society. Women's participation in sport has been blocked on several levels throughout the history of modern sporting practice ... Whether as athletes, coaches, administrators or sports journalists, women have found it difficult to establish the right and recognition of their place in the sporting world. (2000: 127–8)

Consequently, as Cashmore stresses, sport has reinforced and reflected the acute historical gender inequalities experienced by many women in relation to men and has illustrated an area of culture that the first-wave suffrage-focused form of feminism did not counter. While women may have been given the vote, inequalities experienced in the world of work and domestic social arrangements were also endemic within nineteenth-century professional sport, which was governed by a particular cultural perception of the 'fragile female' (Spears, 1978). In Great Britain, the omission of women from many sports was based on attitudes as to what constituted masculinity and, crucially, femininity. As distinctive sports, such as cricket and rugby, developed in nineteenth-century Victorian Britain, sport was associated with 'rugged' masculinity. Women, by contrast, were seen as 'gentle, delicate, and submissive'; associated with childbearing and childrearing, and thus not to risk the kinds of bodily harm associated with physical sporting activities. While clearly not indicative of 'universal' womanhood in this historical period and bearing a distinctive class orientation (middle to upper) the assumption was a potent one: women were less physically vigorous and strong than men and thus their bodies and natures were totally unsuited to sport. As a result, any women who did engage in sport were 'deviant' and unfeminine. So entrenched was this view that Pierre de Coubertin extended it to the Olympics and advocated the exclusion of female participants due to the frailty of their bodies; the Games were, rather, to be the 'exultation of male athleticism ... with female applause as reward' (in Cashmore, 2010: 207). Ultimately, though, de Coubertin relented and female athletes took part in the 1900 Games. As Cashmore identifies, women would participate in sports in the early part of the twentieth century, from the golfer Cecilia Leitch to tennis players Suzanne Lenglen and Maria Mednyanszky. The Women's Cricket Association was formed in the UK in the 1920s and the All-American Girls Baseball League was established in 1943. The track and field Olympic triumphs of Fanny Blankers-Koen followed in 1948. In spite of such displays of sporting prowess, the association of femininity with fragility and a lack of strength proved to be firmly entrenched, and a key obstacle to female participation in sport. The result, argues Jennifer Hargreaves (1994), is that there was no firm women's sporting history to inspire today's female would-be athletes, and consequently few role models to inspire future generations of sportswomen. And research has suggested that role models are a crucial factor in the socialization process. As Albert Bandura argues, individuals acquire values, attitudes and patterns of thought and behaviour by observing those of others, learning how to react and conduct themselves in similar social situations (in Adriaanse and Crosswhite, 2008), and this is of particular significance with regard to gendered behaviours.

In relation to sporting role models, male athletes remain associated with 'heroic' qualities: strong bodies, aggressive, and able to overcome hardships and break records. 'Heroines', however, are caring, kind and selfless, qualities not entirely compatible with the idea of sporting heroines, which is the key reason why female achievements in sport are culturally downgraded in relation to those of males. The salient issues are that the 'fragile female' ethos is still seemingly in evidence in twenty-first-century culture, and researchers such as McCallister, Blinde and Phillips have found that many adolescent girls associated the concept of the athlete with males. The research found that girls could easily provide a list with characteristics of male athletes such as 'big', 'tall', 'strong', 'muscles', 'runs fast' and 'healthy' while they struggled to name any such traits in relation to female athletes other than 'pretty' and 'has long hair' (cited in Adriaanse and Crosswhite, 2008: 386).

Yet, according to Roth and Baslow's (2004) research, the major factor that underpins sporting inequality is greatly exaggerated. They argue that Western culture's predisposition to perceive males as large and more muscular while females are small and thin does not reflect the norm, as the average man is only 10 to 15 per cent larger than the average woman. Therefore, if differences are not typically rooted in biological or bodily differences, they are arguably the product of a dominant social ideology that perpetuates and effectively *creates* 'weaker' females. Thus, while the societal masculine ideal is based on physical strength, the feminine ideal is diametrically opposed to this: it is predicated on beauty, and on bodies that are small or thin. This ideological message is socially pervasive and is communicated via key social and cultural institutions such as the family, religion, the professions and work, and the media. And where females do engage in sport, rules are enforced to ensure that respectable and acceptable expressions of female deportment are maintained. One such example is the prohibition on body-checking – physically charging into the body of an opposing player and pushing them against the wall – enforced in Canadian women's hockey but not applicable in the male National Hockey League. In other instances, physical sporting prowess is translated into sexual bodily display and sex appeal. For example, sports such as figure skating require the female skater to wear a revealing outfit (while the male skater does not) and incorporate dance into solo routines. As Roth and Baslow state:

> What could women/girls' legs being observable under a barely there skirt; a sparkling, sexy outfit; and a plastered on, lipsticked smile possibly add to the

performance of a triple axel? It certainly helps viewers forget the incredible amount of strength that is necessary to perform a triple axel. Instead of appreciating skaters' thighs for the power they possess and the feats they can perform, male viewers are given a perfect chance to appreciate those thighs as sex objects. And female viewers are reminded not that women's bodies are capable of incredible strength, but that they are expected to demonstrate incredible femininity. (2004: 252)

The association of sexual attractiveness and female sports star visibility is a key aspect of the gender/sport inequality debate, but the same association is seldom in evidence with male sporting figures. To illustrate this imbalance, Barry Smart cites the career of the Russian tennis player Anna Kournikova, who from the mid-1990s achieved modest success on the Grand Slam tournament circuit, but whose looks, long blonde hair and athletic body ensured that she received extensive media coverage whenever she played. Furthermore, the multitude of highly paid endorsement and sponsorship deals she was subsequently offered arose 'not from a consistent record of successful performances on the tennis court, but as a consequence of an image of sexual attractiveness and an associated media profile' (2005: 177). Cashmore (2010) makes a similar point in relation to another Russian tennis star, Maria Sharapova, similarly associated with a sexualized and highly feminized media image and who, although winning three Grand Slams from 2004 to 2008, saw her form slip and her ranking drop drastically; yet her marketable image still ensured that she negotiated endorsement deals with TAG Heuer and Sony Ericsson worth $20 million.

The issue of female sexual attractiveness and image in sport returns us to the subject of post-feminism. For example, examining sporting and fitness magazines produced expressly for the 'women's market', McDonald found them to be dominated by images of what she dubs 'culturally idealized bodies': young, physically fit and perfectly toned female bodies. In essence, McDonald reads this as the sign of the full entrenchment of post-feminism, an acknowledgement that the feminist battle is over, or all but won, and that the 'dour and now out-of-date uniformity of second-wave feminism' (2005: 26) has been rejected in favour of women being able to take pleasure in their attractiveness.

However, McDonald argues that the ways in which 'powerful' and 'fit' women are represented in sports magazines actually becomes associated with a 'New Right' neoliberal agenda (more on this in Chapter 8). What McDonald means here is that far from being seen as a politically and gender-based source of solidarity, the females featured in magazines epitomize individualism and individual achievement. Thus firmly linked with consumer culture, post-feminism (in the sports magazine context) emphasizes empowerment through bodily modification, and ignores issues such as social class, ethnicity and sexual female oppression.

In Angela McRobbie's assessment of post-feminism, she argues that it ignores pervasive and persistent expressions of patriarchy through 'celebrations of female freedom' (2004: 539) expressed chiefly via what she called 'commodity feminism'. McRobbie chooses the American HBO television series *Sex and the City* (1998–2004) as a prime popular cultural post-feminist 'text', and its central character, Manolo Blahnik-obsessed newspaper columnist, Carrie Bradshaw (Sarah Jessica Parker) as its post-feminist emblem. And her shoe obsession is a key feminist factor, as Anna König comments:

> This attitude neatly exemplifies post-feminist thinking within contemporary academic discussions of fashion: dressing up equals fun, and fun equals empowerment. Thus [Sarah Jessica] Parker has become a stiletto-heeled role model for women in our time. (2006: 140)

In McRobbie's view, the 'girlie' fashion-conscious behaviour of Carrie, endlessly looking at herself in mirrors and windows, represents only 'tedious narcissism, as she skips down the street wearing an ill-chosen hat and stupendously expensive shoes not made for walking' (2008: 540), but also a constant search for male approval from her wealthy on–off suitor, 'Mr Big' (Chris Noth), whom she subsequently marries in the first *Sex and the City* movie (2008). And this effective dismissal of one of the key icons of pop cultural post-feminism brings us back to liberal feminism, Charlotte Perkins Gilman, and sport.

CHARLOTTE PERKINS GILMAN AND WAGS

A salient development in the realm of sport is the ways in which it has become entwined with the social and cultural sphere of celebrity. This is hardly surprising, given the frequently global fame that many sporting figures command. And, in contrast to the diminishing nature of fame that Boorstin argues was symptomatic of twentieth-century culture (as discussed in Chapter 3), sports stars epitomize what Rojek (2001) calls the 'achieved celebrity': they possess sporting talent and ability. In the context of English football, a distinctly Boorstin-like development occurred that ostensibly seemed to illustrate the extent of post-feminism's cultural impact, but also, arguably, implies an older feminist critique. The development surrounded the 2006 World Cup and the creation by the British tabloid press of the 'WAGs' – the wives and girlfriends of the English players, many of whom travelled to Germany and engaged in numerous acts of conspicuous consumption and demonstrations of the glamorous and fashionable lifestyle that such a status entailed. Although sportsmen have obviously had families in the past, the term WAG was something culturally specific, in that it defined women as a distinctive type of new celebrity figure, whose qualification was that they were married or romantically attached to a player who was selected for the 2006 England squad. Thus, British tabloid newspapers popularized women such as Coleen McLoughlin (the girlfriend of Wayne Rooney), Carly Cole (the wife of Joe Cole), Cheryl Cole (the girlfriend of Ashley Cole), Abigail 'Abbey' Clancy (the girlfriend of Peter Crouch) and Victoria 'Posh Spice' Beckham (the wife of David Beckham). The issue is that the WAGs have become synonymous with the consumption of fashion, to the extent that they are frequently reported on solely within that context; that they are the arbiters of what is or is not fashionable; and that their status is reduced, in media terms, to that of women who consume designer-brand clothing and accessories. While it may be 'empowering', from a post-feminist perspective, that a woman can take pleasure in consumption and in the effects that fashionable clothing, shoes or handbags can grant (akin to Carrie Bradshaw or the Kardashian sisters), the apparent means by which the lifestyle is acquired is male-dependent, in terms of either economic dependency or the cultural currency that is essential for the WAG status. For example, in Watson's cynical assessment of the 'cricket WAG', she argues that 'WAGs will publicly bask, all expenses paid, in the reflected glory of a player's legendary status' (2007: 22). While this is not necessarily the case, for example both Victoria Beckham and Cheryl Cole carved out successful and lucrative careers in pop music with, respectively, The Spice Girls and Girls Aloud before their relationships began with footballers, the WAG tag is a pervasive one, and has a tendency to efface these previous successes (more so with Victoria Beckham, as Cole is separated from Ashley Cole and has had significant solo music success). The status of the WAG is entirely dependent upon male sporting success. In one sense, Gilman's theory of economic dependency is clearly relevant, as the enormous income earned by many footballers brings with it a lifestyle beyond the means of ordinary people. In this sense, what Gilman refers to as 'the comfort, the luxury, the necessities of life itself, which the woman receives, are obtained by the husband, and given her by him' (1998: 10) fit the WAG perfectly. But there is a cultural component too. The WAG represents not merely an economic relationship, but a cultural one whereby the fame and popular cultural status of the male sportsman is an equally dependent state. The celebrity status of the WAG is one of fame-by-association and is sustained by the cultural visibility this association ostensibly brings, as Frankel stated in the UK newspaper, *The Independent*, in the wake of the 2006 World Cup:

> If the damage the WAGS did to this country's sporting reputation is well charted, one can only imagine the havoc their public image is wreaking in the imaginations of any starstruck young girl worth her annual subscription to *Heat*. The message is loud and clear. Who needs a job? Bag yourself a Premiership footballer and fame, wealth, good fortune, not to mention many, many pairs of designer sunglasses, will be all yours. (2006: 1)

Again, to return to the words of Gilman in *Women and Economics*, 'the economic status of women individually depends upon that of men individually, those men to whom they are related' (ibid.), the WAG appears to reflect this hierarchic relationship perfectly. While the concept of the WAG may be a tabloid construct applicable to the minority of women who actually do marry or have a relationship with football stars, it is the aspiration, as Frankel refers, that has become seemingly desirable in contemporary culture, but it is a status that is utterly dependent on male economic and cultural power and the possession of sporting fame and wealth. Thus, the assertion of agency through fashion and the post-feminist 'right to be sexually attractive' is intrinsically tied to male patronage. Indeed, the term WAG has now become prevalent throughout many sports. Even women who have successful careers beyond their sportsmen partners, for example Coleen Rooney's (née McLoughlin) cosmetics business and Nicole Sherzinger's globally successful pop music career (with the Pussycat Dolls, then as a solo singer), are invariably linked in media discourse with their partners, respectively England and Manchester United striker Wayne Rooney, and Formula One racing driver Lewis Hamilton. Therefore, the WAG, at the level of popular culture, exhibits an image of women that emphasizes, on the one hand, fame and the fashionable consumption of luxury lifestyles, but on the other, a contemporary status that exists exclusively through being an 'other' – the wife or partner of a man who has achieved success. In this sense, it is not merely second-wave, but liberal feminism that seemingly still has something to say about a culture that is supposedly post-feminist. Gilman postulated that the period of women's economic dependence was drawing to a close, and while there have been shifts in the economic relationship between the sexes, popular culture has established a celebrity status that could have come from the pages of *Women and Economics*.

SPORT AND CHANGING MASCULINITIES

While sport has emerged as a key cultural space reflecting changing approaches to the status of women, it also reflects distinctive transformations within masculinity in the arena of sport, with fashion at its heart. While the issue of women-hood has, as this chapter has illustrated, an extensive and multi-faceted history as a category, the concept of masculinity has, until comparatively recently, been neglected. As Connell argues, the concept of femininity has no meaning unless it is related to an opposite – masculinity – which itself cannot exist except in contrast with 'femininity', and a 'culture which does not treat women and men as bearers of polarized character types, at least in principle, does not have a concept of masculinity in the sense of modern European/American culture' (2005: 68). Such a conception of masculinity, Connell states, has existed in this culture for only a comparatively short time (200 years or so) but was based upon particular features that formed the 'core' of masculinity. In Segal's analysis, a traditional view of masculinity is that *true* manhood involves toughness, struggle and conquest, stemming from the early nineteenth-century Western celebration of a distinctive 'Spartan' and athletic 'muscular manliness' (Segal, 1990: 104). As stated earlier, this notion of male 'toughness' was a primary cultural rationale for excluding women from sports participation. However, although physicality is clearly a key component within many high-level male sports, requiring optimum levels of fitness and precise physicality – in other words, 'tough masculinity' – such sports have also witnessed palpable changes in representations of such masculinity. For Whannel

(2007), a key reason for changes in sporting masculinity was the increasing relationship between television and sport, the tabloid press, and the development of celebrity culture. The result, argues Whannel, has been the emergence of what he dubs 'intersecting masculinities', and a prime example is the footballer, David Beckham.

By the age of fourteen, Beckham had signed on with Manchester United, and two years later, in 1991, became a full professional (Cashmore, 2002). In August 1996, he scored a goal of such distinction against Wimbledon that he made headlines nationally. The 'wonder goal' gave Beckham a national audience (2002: 20) and he subsequently played for the England squad in international competitions. However, far more influential in the ascent of Beckham's cultural stock was his relationship and subsequent marriage to Spice Girls singer Victoria Adams. Dubbed 'Posh and Becks', their relationship became a media narrative that symbolized the increasingly blurred distinction between the two cultural worlds of football and entertainment – thus the first 'WAG' was created. However, Beckham's association with celebrity and fashion also signalled distinctive changes in representations of masculinity, beginning the association of football with the trappings of consumption that would become synonymous with the WAG phenomenon.

In Rahmin's view, Beckham has long been able to balance competing conceptions of masculinity, simultaneously representing hetero-family/masculine status and that of a gay icon related to his consumption of fashion and cosmetics that has ranged from sharp designer suits to sarongs and pink nail varnish, combinations that have led celebrity magazines such as *Heat* to describe him as being 'macho and absolutely beautiful' (2006: 225). Consequently, Beckham came to be read as a distinctive representative of a new form of twenty-first-century masculinity. As Parker and Lyle (2005) argue, recent decades have seen dramatic shifts in constructions of masculinities. For many theorists British society and culture have see the demise of 'old traditional/industrial' man – the bread-winning and decidedly unemotional male who was located at the focal point of the nuclear family – and the rise of the 'new man' in the 1980s, initially in the form of the 'yuppie', the entrepreneurial 'buccaneer' reflecting the individualist economic philosophy of Margaret Thatcher's social and economic reforms and characterized by selfish ambition. The second was a more domesticated 'new man', even a 'feminized' man – a man who nurtured and cared and was committed to emotional labour. Although this apparent form was challenged by the emergence of the 'new lad' in the 1990s – based around Britpop music (principally bands such as Oasis) and the embrace of excessively masculine lifestyle habits such as excessive consumption of alcohol and hedonism – traces of the 'new man' would remain, with a masculinity focused on visual appearance: the 'cosmetically conscious male', the 'metrosexual', the socially mobile cosmopolitan man. Metrosexuals are typically young males who live in and frequent the social and occupational spaces of major cities – the metropolis (which accounts for the prefix 'metro'). The hallmark of the metrosexual ethos is the knowing proclivity for clothes and cosmetics and the creation of precise looks with a particular narcissistic attitude.

Hence, at the level of popular culture, Beckham provides a perfect example of the modern 'metrosexual' man who is cosmetically aware and fashionably astute, and who promotes these identifiers strongly as part of his public image. Beckham demonstrates a socially mobile and decidedly 'middle-class' form of conspicuous consumption. In Whannel's view:

> Beckham's image, with its concern with fashion, appearance and hairstyle, has been part of a reconstruction through which the objectification of masculine bodies and appearance has interacted with more traditional concepts of sporting masculinity. (2007: 12)

Following a period with Real Madrid, Beckham joined Los Angeles Galaxy in a deal worth some $250 million, and subsequently launched a lucrative fashion brand with wife Victoria called dVb (David and Victoria Beckham) that specializes in clothing and a range of fragrances (Vincent, Hill and Lee, 2009). Consequently, the consumerism/fashion/femininity nexus that characterizes the WAG emerged to a large extent from the union of Beckham with Victoria Adams, a marriage that established an economic brand partnership and the primacy of gendered image related to conspicuous consumption and the fusion of sport and celebrity.

Nor is Beckham alone in representing apparent metrosexuality in football. For example, the Manchester United and Real Madrid star Cristiano Ronaldo became equally famous for his modelling of the Emporio Armani underwear range (following Beckham), while even the physically aggressive world of American football has seen distinctive shifts in masculine representations principally with regard to the New England Patriots' quarterback, Tom Brady. Brady joined the Patriots in 2000, has played in three Super Bowl winning teams; has been the recipient of a number of MVP (Most Valuable Player) awards; and has received numerous sports journalism accolades such as Sportsman of the Year and Male Athlete of the Year. In terms of professional prowess, Brady is considered one of the NFL's (National Football League) best quarterbacks, having achieved a number of game records (most touchdown passes in a season; fifth highest career passer rating in the NFL's history) in a sport that is physically demanding and fundamentally brutal with regard to style of play and the physical effects of the game on players (quarterbacks in particular). Football is, then, a game that is ostensibly predicated on the Victorian 'Spartan' principles that underpinned sport and the culturally perceived masculine characteristics required to participate in it. Conversely, as Pierce states, although Brady is regarded as a prime example of a 'tough' contemporary sportsman, he is also represented in distinctly Beckham-like ways. For instance, in addition to *GQ* magazine fashion shoots, Brady has endorsement deals and advertisement links with fashion brands such as UGG, Stetson Cologne and Gap, a connection cemented by his marriage to 'supermodel' Gisele Bundchen. However, Brady's particular expression of 'hybrid' masculinity is evident within his professional life, as Robert Kraft, the owner of the New England Patriots, states in his evaluation of Brady's character:

He's a what? What do you call it now? That term they use in gossip? Metrosexual? Something like that, but at the same time, he's an old-time football player. You can connect with him and feel that you have a special bond with him. He's soft and gentle, but he can be really, really, tough when he has to be. (Cited in Pierce, 2006: 25)

GENDER AND SPORT: AN ARENA FOR CHANGE?

From W.G. Grace, Joe DiMaggio, Muhammad Ali, and Pelé, to Billie Jean King, Michael Jordan, David Beckham, Tom Brady, Tiger Woods, Yao Ming, Roger Federer, Li Na, Sachin Tendulkar, and Usain Bolt, sport has produced iconic figures who are world famous and are central and significant parts of popular cultural consumption and entertainment, but who are also representatives of gender politics and changing representations of femaleness and maleness. Given the history of sport and its increasing centrality in the leisure lives of individuals (the alignment of sport with television and global broadcasts), it is an arena in which female and male representations are readily perceptible, and changes evident. The issue of female inequality is, as this chapter has discussed, a long-standing one, and cultural perceptions of physical differences between men and women are still evident. Furthermore, the differential divide between male and female within contemporary sport is a global issue. As Wu observes, in China women's sport receives considerably less media exposure than men's. This division was explicitly demonstrated during the 2004 Athens Olympics in which, although female athletes won more gold medals than male athletes, 'the Chinese media still gave preferential treatment to men's sport events during the Olympic Games' (2009: 73). And when female athletes such as diver Guo Jingjing were granted media coverage, the dominant journalistic emphasis was upon her physical characteristics rather than her athletic prowess, with bylines such as: 'Beautiful Goddess on the Springboard'.

The issue of post-feminism has potentially complicated critiques of such perceptions with its emphasis on pluralism, and some feminist commentators (Juliette Fretté, Joan Morgan and Laura Doyle) finding 'empowering' potential in overt displays of female sexuality (such as posing for *Playboy*) and selective submission to patriarchal power in the home as a way of enhancing feelings of femininity (Snyder-Hall, 2010). In this sense, the proximity of sport, celebrity, fashion and women that the media-tagged WAGs represent might be seen as post-feminist expressions of consumption-based 'power'. However, the application of Charlotte Perkins Gilman that I have suggested arguably problematizes this in relation to the dependency of the WAG (itself a derogatory media-enforced label) on male sportsmen, to the extent that female achievements (in the worlds of pop music, fashion and business) are eclipsed by their relationships with powerful and culturally influential male figures. This relationship is compounded by distinctive and newer modes of masculinity that are evident in sport and which have effaced the boundaries between the worlds of sport, fashion and celebrity. This is not to suggest that traditional models of masculinity that have long been associated with sport are no more; indeed, it is difficult to apply any 'metrosexual'/fashion-conscious representative label to Manchester United's Wayne Rooney, or to the French national and Racing Métro 92 rugby player, Sébastien Chabal.

Sport, then, in addition to representing a primary source of media spectacle in contemporary popular culture, is a potent site for the analysis of gender politics and gender representations. Further, sport has emerged as a space for female empowerment, as Mariah Burton Nelson, a former professional basketball player, states:

> While playing sports our bodies are ours to do as we please. If in that process our bodies look unfeminine – if they become bruised or bloody or simply unattractive – that seems irrelevant. Our bodies are ours. We own them. While running to catch a ball, we remember that. (1996: 35)

In an American context, although its full efficacy has been critically assessed, Title IX of the 1972 Education Amendments produced a generation of female athletes such as the Washington Freedom soccer player Mia Hamm who enjoyed high-profile sporting careers and represented potent female sporting role models (Cole, 2000). And there are newer expressions of feminist politics, such as Islamic feminism, which, through reinterpretation of Islamic texts from a female perspective, is helping Muslim women to re-enter public life and pursue equality within an Islamic framework. Part of this process is the recognition that there is nothing in Islam that prohibits female participation in sport, and consequently opportunities in sport can lead to the 'empowerment of girls and women through all arenas of sport, education and physicality' (Benn et al., 2011: 7). Furthermore, the 2012 London Olympics served as the stage for the achievements of a number of globally mediated female gold-medal-winning athletes celebrated for their athletic skills in a variety of sports (cycling, swimming, pole-vaulting, judo, boxing, and the heptathalon) such as Victoria Pendleton, Kayla Harrison, Cate Campbell, Melania Schlanger, Alicia Coutts, Brittany Elmslie, Ye Shiwen, Jennifer Suhr, Nicola Adams and Jessic Ennis. As such, the world of international sport has an increasing number of fermale role models who are celebrated due to their sporting prowess. Therefore, from Ancient Greece and classic first-wave feminism, through fashion-conscious WAGs and metrosexual football stars to cutting-edge contemporary feminist scholarship, the relationship between gender, sport and popular culture seems set to play on for the foreseeable future.

QUESTIONS TO CONSIDER

1. What is Charlotte Perkins Gilman's principal argument in *Women and Economics*?
2. Do you agree with the view that 'female achievements in sport are culturally downgraded in relation to those of males'? Is this changing with the impact of post-feminism?

3.   Have representations of masculinity been transformed in relation to sports stars such as David Beckham and Tom Brady? Can you think of further examples?

FURTHER READING

For a comprehensive overview of sport and its role within contemporary societies, see Ellis Cashmore's *Making Sense of Sport*. With regard to feminist thought, readers should explore Charlotte Perkins Gilman's *Women and Economics* in more detail. However, in addition to her work as a sociologist, Gilman also communicated her ideas in the form of fiction, most notably her short story 'The Yellow Wallpaper' but also in the novella *Herland*. In *Herland* Gilman conveys a utopian society that exists without men, and essentially presents, in a science fiction format, the fundamental argument of *Women and Economics*.

Semiotics and tattooing

7

Having examined popular culture in terms of music, film, celebrity, television, sport and fashion, this chapter turns to perhaps the oldest mode of communicative culture, predating even sport: tattooing. Archeological data suggests that tattooing, the insertion of ink into the deep layers of human epidermis, was practised in the Stone Age and was in evidence in ancient civilizations such as that of Egypt. Indeed, as Sanders argues, 'proof of the antiquity of the practice is derived from the mummified body of a priestess of Hathor (dated 2,000 BCE) that bears parallel line markings on the stomach, thought to have had medicinal or fertility functions' (2008: 9). In Bryan Turner's analysis of the sociology of the body, the 'pre-modern' body was a primary site for the display of a range of key cultural factors such as social status, family position, tribal membership, age, gender and religion. The issue here was that early tribal societies physically marked out status differentials through scarification and the act of tattooing. Such marks signified key moments in an individual's life, particularly with regard to rites of passage between differing statuses (age being a prime example). However, tattooing has developed through the ages and has survived (and flourished) in a range of contemporary societies. In Turner's view the religious or rite-of-passage functions of tattooing have diminished and shifted into the realm of fashion, but still retain a role in demarcating social membership of what he dubs an 'urban tribe' (1991: 6).

The idea of tattooing as a contemporary mode of social inclusiveness is an important one in tattooing research; however, Turner's view of the anthropological roots of tattooing identifies a crucial factor: that tattoos are highly *symbolic*, they *communicate* specific meanings of social, cultural and individual significance. Although tattoos and tattooing have developed from social and spiritual practices to become, contemporaneously, 'consumer products' (Sanders, 2008), sociological readings and popular cultural expressions of the art of tattooing and, crucially, the decision to have a tattoo, have retained communicative and highly symbolic functions. In essence, tattoos frequently tell stories and signify key moments and developments in a life. Although no longer typically socially or culturally enforced as a widespread practice, tattoo culture concerns individuals mapping out their own rites of passage on their bodies, for others to read, but often for themselves – inked art that symbolically represents biographical moments: band insignia and lyrics, poetry, superstitions, private jokes, religious expression, corporate logos and inspirational codes. In effect, tattoos did and do speak to the world *semiotically*. And it is semiotics which forms the theoretical subject of this chapter.

Within the study of media and popular culture, semiotics is, Jonathan Bignell (2004) argues, a long-established methodology for 'reading' the meanings of cultural texts as disparate as newspapers, magazines, cinema, television, computer games and advertising images. In some cases to discern their overt meanings, in others to potentially uncover what they 'really mean' (is ideological practice present in an advertisement, for instance, or specific gendered/patriarchal representations in television, cinematic or magazine texts?). However, although social actors are faced on a daily basis with increasingly diverse forms of media, all of which transmit and communicate meanings, social life itself is replete with messages, from shop signs and the diverse fashions of people passing by (many bearing fashionable or pop/rock music logos) to the signs that ensure that society functions harmoniously and lawfully – traffic lights, for instance, which communicate their precise (and crucial) meanings without words, but through colours which are 'read' by drivers. But while meaning can be communicated through spoken and written language, it can also be transmitted through symbols that speak to society or simply to the individual.

This chapter will explore the major parameters of semiotics, but it will subsequently consider how deliberate semiotic communication frequently lies at both the heart of the art of tattooing and the motivation for many of those who elect to be tattooed. Consequently, the chapter will critically examine the major principles of semiotics through an analysis of the symbolic basis of tattooing, historically, culturally, and within popular culture in terms of the recent proliferation of television programmes devoted to tattooists and their clients (who tell the stories behind their tattoos), specialist tattoo magazines and the emergence of tattoo artist celebrities such as Kat von D. From antiquity to the modern world, tattoos have been a cultural constant, and although the practice has ebbed and flowed and social reactions have wavered between censure and celebration, tattooing has transcended cultures, ethnicity, gender and class, with an increasing number of individuals communicating meaning through ink inscribed into their skin.

SEMIOTICS

As articulated by Roland Barthes in his classic 1957 text, *Mythologies*, cultures transmit various messages or 'myths' that convey meaning. In some instances these can include instances of speech, but they are not confined to such communication. Rather, mythic messages are diffused and supported through a range of media such as photography, cinema, journalism, sport and publicity materials. Therefore, cultures 'speak' through mythic messages, and the focus of what Barthes dubs 'semiology' is based on the operation of reading or deciphering these myths. In his analysis of myths and the ways in which they work to communicate meanings, Barthes analyzed cultural examples as diverse as a photograph of the actress Greta Garbo, magazine covers, toys, soap powders, the science fiction of Jules Verne, striptease, steak and chips, and wrestling. With regard to the example of steak, Barthes examines how specific foods have come to signify specific qualities and cultural values. In the case of steak, it is a food that consists of bovine meat, and eating steak sates hunger and provides the body with energy. However, although it evidently achieves this, the eating of steak, argues Barthes, represents distinctive cultural meanings, too: strength and power. Thus, objects acquire wider significations, a factor that underpins the advertising industry in its drive to associate empowering emotions and desires with the consumption of material goods. Myths as such are what Barthes called a second-order semiological system in that they draw on signs which belong to first-order systems, such as language or the animal kingdom in the case of the origin of steak.

Barthes' most famous example of mythology in action is that of the cover of the French magazine, *Paris Match*, that depicts a black soldier in a French uniform saluting (presumably to the French flag). Here, myth is argued to operate in a distinctly ideological way as the magazine serves to reinforce the fact that the French colonial empire displays no discriminatory practices, and demonstrates the enthusiasm the 'colonized' have for their 'so-called oppressors' (Barthes, 1993: 116). In terms of explaining the science of semiology, Barthes argues that there is a *signifier*, the image of the black solider saluting, and a *signified*, the mixing of Frenchness and militariness. Signification comes with the fusion of these two components. However, these concepts were initially conceptualized by the originator of semiotics: Ferdinand de Saussure (1857–1913).

Ferdinand de Saussure is notable in that the text that formed the foundation of semiotics, *A Course in General Linguistics*, was assembled and published in 1916 by his students following de Saussure's death. However, de Saussure's approach was so influential that he would become known as the 'twentieth-century father of the science of signs', which he called 'semiology' (from the Greek *semeion*, meaning 'sign'). Semiology was intended to be a systematic means by which to explain what constitutes signs, and, more importantly, 'what law governs them' (de Saussure, cited in Leitch, 1983: 7). Signs are drawn from the system of language that exists within a society (what de Saussure called *'langue'*, meaning language, in opposition to *'parole'*, meaning speech), and all signs are derived from the system of language. Most famously, de Saussure's theory of the sign is reducible to the way in which all signs adjoin a form and a concept, what he famously called a signifier and a signified. As de Saussure explains:

> A linguistic sign is not a link between a thing and a name, but between a concept and a sound pattern. The sound pattern is not actually a sound; for a sound is something physical. A sound pattern is the hearer's psychological impression of a sound, as given to him by the evidence of his senses. This sound pattern may be called a 'material' element only in that it is the representation of our sensory impressions. The sound pattern may thus be distinguished from the other element associated with it in a linguistic sign. This other element is generally of a more abstract kind: the concept. (2008: 66)

What de Saussure means here is that the signifier creates in the mind of a listener a distinctive mentally registered image, be it a cat, a tree or whatever. Nonetheless, although this all sounds straightforward and we can routinely recognize this process, de Saussure claimed that the relation between a signifier and the signified, the word and the mental concept that it creates, is entirely arbitrary. Thus, there is absolutely no natural link between the word and the concept. So there is no intrinsic reason why the word 'tree' should create the image of a tree; it is simply a name that was given to the woody plant at some point and which became fixed and culturally recognized, but there is no essential link between the word, either when spoken or written, that intrinsically bears any relation to trees. To further illustrate this process, Crow cites the example of the English word 'dog' that refers to a four-legged canine animal. However, in French dog is *chien*, in Spanish it is *perro*, in Italian it is *cane*, while in German it is *Hund*. Consequently, the word culturally employed to signify dogs has no relation to the animal it represents; the only exceptions are onomatopoeic words which do directly reproduce the objects they represent through the sounds they make (2010: 17–18).

In the view of de Saussure, the signifier is capriciously formed and a cultural construction that is subject to change. As an example, Leitch observes that the word 'relay' originally meant 'a set of fresh hounds or horses posted to take up a chase', while in computer-powered twentieth-century culture it means 'an electro-magnetic device for remote control of other devices in a circuit' (1983: 8). But if this is so, how do signifiers acquire their meaning? For de Saussure, the meaning of signs derived from their relations of difference. Words and concepts get their meaning by differing from other words and concepts. Consequently, the relations of difference between signifier and signified fix meaning and a linguistic system is a series of differences of sound combined with a series of differences of ideas. Basically, any sign is what all the others are not: thus, night is in a binary opposition to day; dog is dog because it is not cat.

However, the key issue is the way in which sounds can signify and inspire mental images and explain how meanings are culturally communicated. And it is this foundation provided by de Saussure that paved the way for an approach to cultural understanding that would become known as semiotics. Barthes' work was invaluable as it stressed, as Crow (2010) points out, the way that semiological readings had to take in a wider system of signs than merely the verbal. Furthermore, Barthes stressed the crucial role played by the reader of signs, a factor further developed by Umberto Eco in his classic text, *A Theory of Semiotics*. Eco argues that although de Saussure did not define the signified clearly, seeing it as a fusion of a mental image, concept and psychological reality, he did emphasize the nature of the signified as the mental activity of an individual receiving a signifier – and this is crucial. As Eco states of de Saussure's essential insight: 'sign is implicitly regarded as a communicative device taking place between two human beings intentionally aiming to communicate or express something' (1976: 14–15). Eco, who employs the term 'semiotics' as opposed to semiology, as postulated by the American linguistic philosopher, Charles Sanders Peirce (1839–1914), is concerned with approaching cultural processes as being processes of *communication,* but communication that results in an interpretative reaction from the receiver of the message. But the important point is that words can be substituted for signs of various kinds that can be read as expressing the same meaning. Therefore, in defining its role and function, Eco states that semiotics is concerned with everything that can be *taken* as a sign, and a sign is anything that can be seen as meaningfully substituting for something else. Consequently:

> Something is a sign only because it is interpreted as a sign of something by some interpreter ... Semiotics, then, is not concerned with the study of a particular kind of objects, but with ordinary objects, insofar (and only insofar) as they participate in semiosis. (1976: 16)

Although separated by decades, de Saussure, Barthes and Eco are united in their emphasis on the ways in which objects within cultures can 'speak' and be substituted by alternative objects or symbols that are then read by other social actors. But the idea of communicating via symbols that substitute for distinctive ideas or words is one that we can readily discern within contemporary culture, from art, cinema and advertising, to graphic design, theatre and graffiti. Nonetheless, there is also the development and expression of symbolism within tattoo culture, past and present, that offers itself as a potent means of critically exploring the nature of semiotic communication within contemporary culture. This is such because, as tattoo culture has changed radically in the last few decades, the central motivation and function of many tattoos is to communicate distinctive meanings that may be understandable only to the wearer of the tattoo, but which can be read (in numerous ways) by wider society. As Margo DeMello states, 'except when worn in private areas, tattoos are meant to be read by others' (2000: 137).

TATTOOING CULTURE: 'SCARS THAT SPEAK'

In his anthropological and cultural history of tattooing, published in 1925, Wilfrid Dyson Hambly traces the roots and cultural function of tattooing back to religious, magical and status-communicating practices. For example, Maori warrior Moko tattoos were not designed for ornamentation but to signify specific meanings such as prowess in battle and to convey advancing levels of social status in tribal groups. Meanwhile, in early European history, the Picts, the ancient tribal groups populating the British Isles (whose name derived from the iron tools used to create tattoo designs) adorned themselves with animal tattoo designs to inspire fear in their invading Roman enemies, but this actually inspired many of the occupying Roman legionnaires to adopt the practice, until forbidden by the Emperor Constantine on the grounds that tattoos 'violated God's handiwork' (Sanders, 2008: 13).

While tattooing continued in Europe in the Anglo-Saxon period before again being banned by the Church, it returned during the Crusades. These designs took the form of religiously inspired symbols, principally crucifixes, frequently designed to ensure that soldiers would receive a Christian burial should they be killed in action. Religion-themed tattoos would ensure that the practice of tattooing continued within Western culture, but it was with the expeditions of Captain James Cook that tattooing became a widespread Western cultural phenomenon. Until Cook and his crew reached Tahiti on their second voyage (1772–1775), tattooing was actually called 'pricking' in the West, but seeing the practice performed extensively in the South Pacific, 'Cook introduced the Tahitian word "ta-tu" meaning "to strike" or "to mark" and soon "tattoo" became the common term' (Sanders, 2008: 14). Moreover, many of Cook's officers and sailors were tattooed and thus brought their designs back to England where they soon initiated a European 'tattoo rage' that manifested itself primarily in heavily tattooed sailors and soldiers touring with carnivals. Although legitimacy was temporarily bestowed on the practice by the wearing of tattoos by numerous members of the aristocracy, including Czar Nicholas II of Russia and Kaiser Wilhelm of Germany (Parry, 2006), tattooing rapidly 'came to be seen as the vulgar affectation of the unsavoury types who frequented the Bowery and similarly disreputable urban areas' (Sanders, 2008: 17).

The correlation of tattooing with social disreputability was reinforced by the work of the early Italian Positivist criminologist, Cesare Lombroso (1835–1909). In his classic book, *L'uomo Delinquente* (*Criminal Man*), published in 1876, Lombroso approached the explanation of crime from an anthropological/Darwinian perspective and, through the analysis of a number of 'criminal' craniums (studying 2,734 subjects), concluded that individuals who commit crime have distinctive physical abnormalities including ape-like lower faces, large jawbones, receding foreheads and small cranial capacities. Consequently, criminals were essentially physically different from law-abiding individuals; atavistic or 'primitive'; regressions back to previous pre-civilized states; and 'born with evil inclinations' (2006: 48). Thus, criminals are biologically determined towards anti-social behaviour and acts of criminality. However, in addition to their distinguishing bodily traits Lombroso also observed that:

> One of the most singular characteristics of primitive men and those who still live in a state of nature is the frequency with which they undergo tattooing. This operation, which has both its surgical and aesthetic aspects, derives its name from an Oceanic language. In Italy, the practice is known as *marca* [mark], *nzito segno* [sign], and *devozione* [devotion]. It occurs only among the lower classes – peasants, sailors, workers, shepherds, soldiers, and even more frequently among criminals. (2006: 58)

In Lombroso's view, although some tattoos specifically denoted identity in terms of membership of criminal groups (most notably the Italian Camorra criminal organization) all of the tattoos worn by his criminal sample acted as *signs*, and he discovered a limited set of design categories of tattoos centred on love, religion, war and profession, but representing 'external signs of belief and passions predominant among working-class men' (ibid.). Lombroso's work has been the subject of extensive criticism, from the weak statistical basis of his empirical approach and the recognition of environmental and social influences on criminal behaviour and motivations, to later genetic theory that has categorically invalidated the idea of criminal 'throwbacks'. Furthermore, his inclusion of tattooing as a sign of inherent criminality is also viewed as a major weakness of this thesis because tattooing is 'the result of cultural fashions which have tended to have been concentrated in the lower classes' (Taylor *et al.*, 1973: 42). But the association of tattooing with 'deviance' and disreputability would become a perennial feature of tattooing culture and social attitudes to it.

As Michael Atkinson argues in his book, *Tattooed: The Sociogenesis of a Body Art*, there have been a series of distinctive eras in the development of tattooing, with the early period, the Circus/Carnival Era (the 1880s–1920s) popularizing tattooing both as a source of public entertainment and also as a 'form of social deviance' (2003: 36). As sailors bearing numerous tattoos returned from their travels, they sought work in carnivals that promoted them as 'wild men', generating widespread public interest in viewing heavily tattooed bodies, both male and female. However, as the carnival attraction of the tattooed waned, tattooing as a practice developed, and tattoo artists and tattoo parlours were increasingly established in numerous American cities, with a clientele drawn predominantly from the military and the working class. Furthermore, the nascent body modification industry had a distinctly illicit nature. The parlours were located 'down dirty alleys, in pool halls, and generally spread across areas of cities characterized by poverty and crime' and they effectively represented a 'social club' for individuals that existed 'on the margins of society' (2003: 36). The standard form of design offered consisted of 'Flash' art, tattoo designs displayed on the walls of parlours that were chosen by clients and would typically consist of military insignia, names, hearts and banners, cartoon characters, skulls and daggers, eagles, snakes and flags. Yet these designs were seldom random and devoid of meaning. In *Tattoo: Secrets of a Strange Art* (2006), in addition to validating Lombroso's claim that tattoos were linked to atavism, Albert Parry finds that numerous Flash designs carried distinctive symbolic meanings. For example, serpents are symbols of wisdom and eternity; tiger motifs signify strength; and roses symbolize love and constancy. But the wider social 'reading' of such motifs etched in skin was dominated by its association with the disreputable strata of society. And this connection would endure throughout the next phase of tattooing culture, the Rebel Era (1950–70).

The Rebel Era, developing in the immediate post-World War II period, saw both the proliferation of tattooing as a Western cultural practice and its degeneration in terms of widespread social reactions. In part, this was because many individuals elected to wear tattoos as deliberate badges of defiance against social conventions, to 'advertise their collective discontent with society', and as such, tattooing became popular 'among members of the social underbelly – deviant groups' (Atkinson, 2003: 38), cementing the tenacious association between tattooing and practices that signify 'danger and transgression' (Rojek, 2007: 79). As such, youth cultures and particularly motorcycle gangs in the 1950s and 1960s used tattoos in keenly semiotic ways, in a process of symbolic transmission and social reception. Consequently, North American motorcycle gangs adopted tattooing as a deliberate signifying practice and their 'highly visible tattoos were an encoded language of rebellion' (Atkinson, 2003: 40); and their symbolic 'messages' were 'decoded', argues Atkinson, by wider social groups as visible indicators of the wearer's 'predisposition to crime' (2003: 41). Although Lombroso's Positivism had been long relegated in terms of its validity, the essence of his ideas, that tattoos, and the choice to have them, were an outward sign of criminality, has been reinforced by individuals who acquired them because of their power to symbolize rebellion and social non-conformity. While having tattoos is manifestly not a sign of innate criminality, they were culturally read as belonging to individuals associated with the 'criminal and outlaw spheres' (ibid.).

Yet, while regarded as a 'dark age' in terms of the respectability of tattooing in the West, the Rebel Era also flagged up symbolic and communicative codes within prisons as a further instance of the use of tattooing in criminal cultures. Although already evident in the early twentieth century among North American prisoners, a distinctive communicative tattoo culture developed in America during the 1950s and 1960s. However, the link between incarceration and tattooing is a long-standing one. Although the South Pacific and early Europe have been named as sites of early tattoo cultures, Japan is a further example of a society in which the practice of tattooing can be located in antiquity. The initial period of Japanese tattooing spanned from the fifth century BCE to the fifth century AD but it was revived in the thirteenth century as a method of permanently marking criminals with tattooed symbols that denoted the type and location of the crime they had committed. Subsequent developments in Japanese tattooing art would consistently be the subject of state censure. Thus, the technique of *irezumi*, the tattooing of highly ornate designs of heroic and mythic figures covering large sections of the body, would burgeon in Japan until it was banned in the mid-nineteenth century by the Emperor Meiji who regarded it as immoral, but also as a potential signifier of barbarism to Western visitors. As a consequence, *irezumi* became an underground practice, most associated in modern times with the Japanese organized crime group, the Yakuza (Sanders, 2008).

It was initially in American prisons in the 1960s that tattooing is perceived to have taken on a clear semiotic significance and function. Tattooing was a system 'of "communicative encryptions" to denote gang affiliation within prisons or one's feelings of capture and confinement' (Atkinson, 2003: 40). However, a significant body of work has been devoted to the status and function of tattooing in the Russian prison system during the Soviet era and beyond the fall of the Communist regime, revealing a rich culture of communication through tattoo designs. In Baldaev *et al.*'s extensive pictorial analysis of Russian prisoners bearing tattoos, they map out a complex system of 'prison folklore', an argot that symbolically communicates a range of information, from dates and places of birth to the crimes committed. While the historic Japanese penal system inscribed such information, in the Russian prison system prisoners tell their own stories. As the researchers state of the tattooed bodies of convicted thieves, their bodies are 'a linguistic object', and the tattoos within this culture represent a 'unique language of symbols and the rules for "reading" them are transmitted via oral tradition' (2009: 27). The crucial factor in this regard is that the tattoos act as a secret or 'esoteric' idiom that encodes precise information that cannot be interpreted by 'uninitiated outsiders'. Consequently, tattoo designs that may seem common and meaningless (a devil, a burning candle, a snake or a cat) are symbols imbued with precise social, and often political significance. For example, snakes represent fate; a cat symbolizes agility and the thief's luck; a skull motif frequently alludes to an individual's status as a thief; and anti-communist symbols (Lenin depicted with horns, for example) are not intrinsically representative of specific political grievances, but frequently express a rejection of state power and symbols of resistance against the forces of authority.

More precisely, a thief's tattooed body represents a 'full-dress uniform' in that it is adorned with regalia and badges of rank and status distinction according to the number of tattooed military designs, rings, crosses on chains, bracelets and star-shaped badges and crowns. Read in a semiotic manner:

> These tattoos embody a thief's complete 'service record', his entire biography. They detail all of his achievements and failures, his promotions and demotions, his 'secondments' to jail and his 'transfers' to different types of 'work'. A thief's tattoos are his 'passport', 'case file', 'awards record', 'diplomas' and 'epitaphs'. In other words, his full set of official bureaucratic documents.

Therefore, in the world of thieves a man with no tattoos has no social status whatsoever. (Baldaev *et al.*, 2009: 27)

Hence, these intricate collections of tattoo designs (which appear a mere random jumble of images to those who are not instructed in the symbolic world of the culture) represent a 'voice' that speaks of personal history, thoughts, feelings, memories, and, sometimes, regret. Accordingly, tattoos represent a 'chronicle of a life' and the men who bear them are 'tattoo texts' whose bodies form what Baldaev *et al.* term 'a kind of thieves' mass media' (2009: 29). Furthermore, these bodily tattoo 'texts' accord perfectly with Barthes' conception of semiotic signs, in that a single body can constitute an array of differing communicative signs from the verbal (written language), to the 'representational, allegorical and symbolic' (2009: 31).

Baldaev *et al.*'s research is a highly innovative, complex and sub-cultural example of the practice of tattooing used to communicate secret/coded meanings. As such, it represents a potent example of tattooing as an avowedly semiotic phenomenon whereby each symbol is deliberate and, if the code is known, readable by others. However, although manifestly not a common communicative system, the motif of symbolic self-expression via tattooed symbols is one that has become widespread, if not dominant within the contemporary tattooing culture initiated by the 'tattoo renaissance', or the New Age Era that began in the early 1970s. This was the beginning of a period in which, as Susan Benson states, tattoos came to be recognized as 'statements of the self' and were no longer the result of 'drunken impulse or forcible subjection', but 'chosen after much deliberation' and representing declarations of 'me-ness' (2000: 244–5). This period marked a decisive shift away from the association of tattooing with social stigma or disreputable and/or 'criminal' classes, and into the embrace of tattooing as a means of self-expression. A driving force in the rise of the 'tattoo renaissance' was improvements in tattoo machine technology and a greater array of ink pigments, greater levels of sanitation, practitioners from art school backgrounds, and professionalism in studios (consultations and appointments rather than drop-ins), all of which facilitated greater opportunities for 'clients' to acquire customized tattoo work in lieu of stencilled Flash art; designs that were explicitly tailored for the person to be tattooed that were distinctive, if not unique. Consequently, from the 1970s onwards, tattoos progressively became '"chic products", "personal ornaments", "cosmic jewellery" and pigments of imagination – not gaudy kitsch souvenirs' (Wroblewski, 2004: 21). Tattooing, therefore, became more personalized: motivations linked to self-expression and marked transformations in class and gendered attitudes to tattooing developed as women and the middle classes became increasingly interested in tattoo culture and in having tattoos applied. Alongside the emergence of new, socially diverse audiences was the increasing availability of 'globalized' tattoo styles, including Japanese, New Zealand, South Pacific and African, as well as a resurgence of interest in 'American traditional' – the style synonymous with the early twentieth-century 'Bowery' tattoo parlours.

In her cultural history of American tattoo communities, Margo DeMello identifies a range of motivations by those who have elected to have tattoo designs with consciously communicative functions and significances. As such, the impetus for being tattooed includes group affiliation, commemoration of a significant life event, dissatisfaction with wider society, but also, from the 1980s onwards, the re-interpretation of tattoos as an ill-considered sign of a lack of discipline and bodily foresight (due to their permanence). This was in part, argues DeMello, related to issues as politically disparate as the development of feminism and women's spirituality, ecology groups, and New Age and self-help movements. Consequently, 'Tattooing began, for the first time, to be connected with emerging issues like self-actualization, social and personal transformation, ecological awareness, and spiritual growth' (2000: 143).

At one level, the tattooing process itself was interpreted as a 'spiritual' act, expressed in terms of Christian symbols, or distinctive tribal designs drawn from non-Western religions and ethnic traditions. In this regard, the tattooing of religious/tribal motifs acts as a source of inspiration, or a symbolic mechanism by which individuals mark or confront personal life issues. At its extreme, adherents of the tribal styles have, in conjunction with other techniques of body modification (piercings, scarification, branding) utilized tattooing as part of a symbolic rejection of the dominant mores of Western culture. Dubbing themselves 'Modern Primitives', they critique a society that is held to be 'alienating, repressive, and technocratic and that lacks ritual, myth or symbol' (DeMello, 2000: 175). But in a less extreme form, the embrace and use of tattoos as a way of using symbols also became increasingly associated with personal 'storytelling' within wider, mainstream adherents of tattooing. A key issue in the 'tattoo renaissance' has been the extent to which individuals have mapped out on their bodies specific designs that represented values, events or memories that were exclusive to their lives, and created via customized, 'only-for-them' work. Returning to Eco's conception of the nature of semiotics and semiotic study, a sign is anything that can be seen as meaningfully substituting for something else, and a significant contemporary reading of tattooing culture has focused on the way that tattooed social actors 'speak' through symbols and use them as 'an expression' of the self and for 'self-realization' (Benson, 2000: 250).

TATTOOS AS STORYTELLING SIGNS

Reinforcing the positions of DeMello and Benson, Sanders (2008) argues that although there are individuals who select tattoo images to wear simply based on liking them or their colours, many decide on designs that symbolize personal issues, or even important leisure interests, hobbies and fan-dom. For example, at the level of popular culture, the increased visibility and commercial popularity of, and interest in, tattooing is qualitatively indicated by the proliferation of specialist tattoo magazines devoted to the culture, its artists and tattoo designs. Recent years have seen the publication of international magazines such as: *Tattoo, Inked, Tattoo Society, Savage, Flash, Skin Art, Rise, Skin and Ink, Total*

Tattoo, *Skin Deep* and *Tattoo Energy*, with glossy presentation featuring visual strategies that stress the changes in tattoo culture and its mainstream acceptance; these are underpinned by the preponderance of tattooed young women who habitually feature on the covers. While at one level this strategy arguably represents an 'alternative' take on Naomi Wolf's (1991) now-seminal charge that popular magazines are dominated by a pervasive and oppressive female 'beauty myth' (the models have slim, toned, but extensively tattooed bodies), it could also illustrate the degree to which a gender divide regarding tattoo wearing is no longer significant and the traditional social censure of the practice as 'unfeminine' has diminished (Sanders, 2008). These magazines typically consist of editorials concerning developments and trends in global tattooing culture, artist features, reportage on tattoo events, and frequently cover model profiles. However, a substantial degree of content is, unsurprisingly, extensive photographic examples of tattoo work, and it is in these sections that the 'communicative' nature of many designs is evident. In some instances this consists of showcases of styles (American Classic, Japanese or Tribal, for instance), but more commonly pictorial features demonstrate the extent to which tattoo wearers communicate statements of cultural/identity interests that 'advertise' their consumption of popular culture. Consequently, while various examples of religious iconography are commonplace (Jesus, crucifixes, the Virgin Mary, angels, Hindu images and Buddhist figures and symbols), contemporary images range from portraits of cinematic horror icons such as Bela Lugosi's Dracula, Freddy Krueger, Jason Voorhees and Hannibal Lecter, to a wider assortment of historical and cultural figures from Marilyn Monroe, James Dean, John Wayne, Audrey Hepburn, Judy Garland, Johnny Cash, Buddy Holly and Clint Eastwood, to Hunter S. Thompson and Charles Darwin. Additional images are drawn firmly from popular comics, television and film in the form of various Transformers, ET, Edward Scissorhands, Tony Soprano, Dexter Morgan, Captain Jack Sparrow, The Ramones, Slipknot, Superman, Tank Girl, Heath Ledger's Joker and characters from *Toy Story* and *Star Wars*. In essence, such personalized communicative practices that draw on the raw materials of popular culture to adorn aficionados of that culture epitomize the era of tattooing Atkinson calls the Supermarket Era that covered the later 1990s and the 2000s. This era is characterized as a consumer market in which clients shop around for the best artists (who charge market-dictated fees) in a field that is (as opposed to the classic Flash tradition) driven by the principles of freedom of expression and self-exploration and in which tattoo culture is a heterogeneous practice underscored by the provision of highly personalized designs. As one artist interviewed by Atkinson stated of his artistic ability and approach to clients: 'If you can think it up, I can do it' (2003: 47). It is with regard to such prowess (and clients now extensively research tattoo artists' capabilities and portfolios) in tandem with the profusion of specialized tattoo magazines and periodicals, that the industry has witnessed the rise of celebrity tattoo artists such as Ami James, Chris Garver, Hannah Aitchison, Corey Miller, Louis Malloy and

Katherine von Drachenberg (aka Kat von D). This development has been facilitated by the popularity of a series of tattoo-centred documentary/reality TV shows that appeared from 2005 onwards such as: *Miami Ink*, *LA Ink*, *London Ink* and *NY Ink*. Although punctuated with biographical and human interest factors (most notably interpersonal conflicts) that veer towards the generic foundations of reality TV, the foundational component of shows like *Miami Ink* is the focus on clients, and more importantly, the 'stories' which accompany each prospective tattoo design.

Although obviously selected by producers for inclusion on the basis of possessing a 'story' to tell, the clients who appear on *Miami Ink* (this extends to all the other TV shows identified) come to the artists with tattoo ideas that represent a key life issue, and which, symbolically, communicate a facet of their identity either to themselves, or to the wider world, via external tattoo markings. Thus, examples include mermaids in tribute to a father's sailor past; guardian angels to ward off 'tough times'; a lotus flower to symbolize 'staying focused on career goals'; Eastern religious imagery (hands and a snake) that represent temptation and act as visual reminders to 'stay grounded' and resist 'inner demons'; a tiger lily flower that represents a deceased mother; a skull and roses motif that celebrates extensive weight loss; and butterflies that are worn as symbols of self and creativity. The dominant motif is that of tattoos acting as coded 'mile-markers of life', classic rite-of-passage symbols (many clients mark turning 18 with a tattoo), childhood memories and periods of change; or tattoos are a communicative means of coping with bereavement. Whether as part of the 'tattoo renaissance', or captured on TV shows such as *Miami Ink*, many individuals who elect to have tattoos see them as symbolic artefacts, as visual indicators of their personal identities, representing in numerous cases 'highly symbolic objects' (Sanders, 2008: 149). DeMello concurs, citing interviews with individuals who 'look like they should not wear them', and who, when asked about their specific designs, have 'created lengthy narratives to explain them' (2000: 151).

SEMIOTICS, TATTOOS AND THE PROBLEM OF MEANING

In Orend and Gagné's ethnographic interviews with people who have corporate logo tattoos, from Harley-Davidson brand insignia to Nike, Adidas, Ford, Budweiser, Volkswagen, Lego and Apple, a semiotic function was also evident from their respondents. They expressed the opinion that tattoos should communicate specific meanings related to the wearer. As one respondent stated of the signification of tattoo designs: 'It's like you send out signals of what you're into' (2009: 501). The rationale for sporting corporate brands ranged from brand loyalty, identifying with the products and establishing 'communities' with other aficionados of the brands, and creatively identifying with a brand (as one Lego fan stated), to 'oppositional' stances as evidenced by the respondent who wore the IBM logo, not as a celebration of the classic computer company, but as a representation of '"resistance" to corporate America' (2009: 506). The tattooing of corporate brands and logos, therefore, acts in a distinctive and multi-dimensional manner, but all united by the individual desire to communicate something via brand symbols. As Orend and Gagné state:

> All of our respondents used corporate logos to convey meaning about themselves, their communities, or their lifestyles. Although most had reservations about why others get tattoos, all believed they were exercising personal autonomy and agency and that their tattoos represented something intrinsically real about themselves, their communities, and their lifestyles. (2009: 509)

Certainly, group affiliation is a key motivating reason for many tattoo acquisitions and is evident within the key ethnographic studies of tattooing culture cited in this chapter (DeMello, 2000; Atkinson, 2003; Sanders, 2008). Moreover, the popularity of tattooing across class and gender lines from the 1980s onwards has been interpreted as a means by which individuals attempted to secure a sense of stable identity in a potentially bewildering, fluid postmodern world through the permanence of tattooed symbols and signs (Sweetman, 1999).

Yet any sense of intention and stability with regard to semiotic communication is problematic in terms of how signs are formed and used, but is especially contentious in relation to tattoos by dint of their permanence. With regard to the tribal and prison cultures referred to earlier in the chapter, within these micro-social settings the use of symbolic markers that signify rites of passage or warrior status is understood in a small-scale interpretive community. Similarly, the tattooed symbolic substitutes for written language evident in certain prison cultures represent a distinctive argot that is shared by a specific group. In this regard, tattoos operate as semiotic devices that render entire bodies as readable texts. In terms of wider cultures, it is also clear that many tattooed people consciously seek to communicate, or at least, symbolically inscribe meanings through specific signals that act as communicative signs, but this can be problematic.

For instance, Orend and Gagné found that, regardless of the various motivations for adorning their bodies with symbols of corporate capitalist culture, there is nothing to offset the overall reading of individuals' bodies as representing a 'human billboard', or walking advertisements for companies. Thus, while the respondent who marked himself with the IBM logo did so as an act of rebellion against capitalism, outside interpretations of that symbol may (and commonly will) read it as an *endorsement* – as an extreme act of brand loyalty. But the permanence (or the difficulty in removing) tattoos brings with it further illustrative points concerning the nature of semiotics and the functions of signs.

In *Mythologies*, Barthes argues that there is 'no fixity in mythical concepts: they can come into being, alter, disintegrate, disappear completely' (1993: 120), and one of the key aspects of semiotic communication is the fact that signs are seldom neutral, and subject to readings that may be radically different from intentions. In referring to de Saussure within the context of cultural studies, Longhurst *et al.* (2008) stress that that de Saussure maintained that signs were made up of precise components consciously 'put together' by an individual, and motivated by intent. But be that as it may, this does not guarantee that the sign will be interpreted in that way. Indeed, many commentators would argue that it is unlikely, if not impossible, for this to be the case. At one level, this is because meanings of words, concepts and signs historically change, to the extent that they may come to mean radically different things (Williams, 1976). Indeed, signs can mean different things to different readers due to the nature of signs themselves. This is the concept of polysemy, typically drawn from the work of the Russian Marxist theorist, Valentin Voloshinov (1895–1936) and his classic text, *Marxism and the Philosophy of Language*. (Voloshinov argued that de Saussure did not acknowledge the influence of ideology within the workings of the language system.) However, the concept has been widely applied in readings of popular culture.

Writing in relation to audience responses to television, John Fiske (1990) identified how audiences can decode meanings in a variety of ways. Thus, they are not 'monolithic', but are potentially polysemic, as they can contain a number of possible meanings and accordingly allow for a range of interpretations that may be very different from that intended by the producer. For instance, Fiske argues, television delivers semiotic experience, and an experience characterized by openness and polysemy. This sense of textual openness would also be central to core commentators who were critically opposed to structuralist theorists such as de Saussure, and who alternatively argued that meanings could never be fixed. Postmodernism was underpinned by such an approach: that there is no essential truth and that meanings are marked by plurality, and arguably the most significant figure in this tradition in this regard was Jacques Derrida (1930–2004). It was Derrida who famously established the concept of deconstruction, a complex method of close reading that demonstrated that texts cannot sustain definitive meanings. As Derrida states in *Of Grammatology* (1997), deconstruction means the displacement and dismantling of meaning and the rejection of the supposition that any text can ever be universal, timeless and stable.

Although the concepts of polysemy and deconstruction are now classic examples of social and cultural theory, they are especially significant when applied to tattoos, the semiotic example of this chapter, as they are expressly worn to be timeless and stable; and yet they are subject to extensive social, cultural and individual polysemic and deconstructive readings that circumnavigate the wearer's intent with the choice of a design. For example, one of Atkinson's interviewees, 'Doug', sported swastika symbols as a political gesture of cultural and symbolic reclaiming. However, as Doug stated:

I know when most people see the swastikas I have tattooed on my arms, they immediately think I'm a Nazi. They don't get that it's one of the oldest symbols used by men, and I'm trying to steal it back as a meaningful cultural symbol. I hate all that white power bullshit, but I am not stupid enough to believe that I don't look like that to people on the street. (Cited in Atkinson, 2003: 229)

Irrespective of communicative intention, symbols can be read in oppositional and negative ways, and a symbol such as the swastika will be forever frozen in its Nazi connotation. Tattoos as a form of semiotic communication can therefore be problematic and the meanings open to uncontrolled (and uncontrollable) deconstructions. The polysemic nature of signs was acknowledged by Barthes, but as Strinati (1995) critically states, if texts are negotiable in terms of multiple readings, then what weight does the semiologist's reading of them have? Barthes' analysis of myths is also without context and empirical substantiation, argues Strinati. To illustrate, he cites the example of roses which are interpreted as being symbolically resonant with romance. However, without contextualization, the giving of roses could mean many other things, such as a joke or a mark of respect in bereavement. And so it is with tattoos – they may mean something very specific, but without the context (as the swastika example cogently illustrates) readings can be unpredictable.

Nevertheless, tattoos arguably do reflect the principles of semiotic communication in a cultural setting. They communicate messages, frequently through the substitution of symbols for words, and as such, they serve as a potent way of demonstrating the everyday presence of semiosis in action. This is certainly the essence of Sanders' definition of tattoos: 'mechanisms of social communication'. They provide symbolic information about the bearer's personal interests, social position, relationships, or self-definition (2008: 21). But tattoos also illustrate how signs and signifiers change over time, and this is especially problematic with designs that are literally inscribed into the skin. As we have seen, tattoo culture is characterized by changing social attitudes and mores. However, it is not that long ago that the possession of a tattoo, regardless of design, signified deviance within wider society, and although that has changed extensively, there are no guarantees that once the tattoo's current fashionable status wanes, such censorious attitudes might not return. It is interesting to note a chapter in Stephen Bayley and Roger Mavity's business/lifestyle book, *Life's a Pitch* (2007) that recommends the would-be future captain of industry *not* to acquire tattoos. Although it has been endorsed at the level of global popular culture by figures such as David Beckham, Bayley and Mavity regard tattooing as a form of fashion conformity and, in their rejection of the practice, turn to none other than the classic thinker Cesare Lombroso, suggesting that the signification of disreputability is still evident with regard to tattoos, irrespective of design. Therefore, the space between the connotation and denotation of signs is unpredictable and although the tattoo is currently fashionable, it may not always have this status. However, in cultures where a myriad of tattoos is on public display, try some semiology ...

QUESTIONS TO CONSIDER

1. What are the main differences between the approaches of de Saussure and Barthes in terms of explaining how signs semiotically function?
2. What are the major 'eras' of tattooing and how do they differ from one another? How would you describe current social and cultural attitudes to tattooing?
3. Does the fact that social and cultural reactions to tattooing have undergone major transformations make semiotic communication through tattoo designs problematic?

FURTHER READING

The two obvious texts to consult to deepen an understanding of the principles of semiotics are Ferdinand de Saussure's *Course in General Linguistics* and Roland Barthes' *Mythologies*. However, to place semiotics within a media and cultural studies context, Jonathan Bignell's *Media Semiotics* is a very informative text. Clinton Sanders' *Customizing The Body* and Michael Atkinson's *Tattooed: The Sociogenesis of a Body Art* are highly sociological discussions of tattooing as a social and cultural practice, while Orend and Gagné's 'Corporate Logo Tattoos and the Commodification of the Body', *Journal of Contemporary Ethnography*, 2009, Vol. 38, pp. 493–517 examines how individuals identify with specific tattoo designs. For a wider context of tattooing and body modification that examines the ways in which 'tribal' cultural designs have become incorporated into Western tattooing see Vivian Vale's *Modern Primitives* (1989, reprinted as Vale and Juno, 2010). Among literary texts, John Irving's novel, *Until I Find You*, contains numerous references to the cultures of tattooing and tattooing practices (including numerous references to real-life tattoo artist pioneers such as Sailor Jerry).

Neoliberalism and literature

8

In this final chapter I intend, to a certain extent, to turn the focus back full circle to where the book began in relation to the work of Marx. Yet the subject of this chapter is the theoretical antithesis of Marx's approach because it will focus on a body of thought that has not only united economics, politics and social thinking, but dominated Western, and increasingly global, economic life for decades: neoliberalism. Included under this heading are thinkers such as Adam Smith, Milton Friedman, Ludwig Von Mises, Friedrich von Hayek and Robert Nozick, and political and economic figures such as Margaret Thatcher, Ronald Reagan, Paul Volcker and Alan Greenspan. Furthermore, in addition to charting the rise of neoliberalism and exploring its major characteristics, the discussion will contextualize and critically engage with neoliberalism via an example of popular literature, the fiction of Ayn Rand. In David Harvey's view:

> Neoliberalism is in the first instance a theory of political economic practices that proposes that human well-being can best be advanced by liberating individual entrepreneurial freedoms and skills within an institutional framework characterized by strong private property rights, free markets, and free trade. (2007: 2)

Thus, as it developed, the major tenets of neoliberalism would settle into a series of major criteria for the social, political and economic well-being of individuals and societies: individual liberty, free markets, and a limited or minimal state. Only societies that embrace such values can provide true freedom and social justice for their citizens. Although the 'end of history' was to be the collapse of capitalism and the embrace of socialism according to Marx's social vision, from the neoliberal perspective (for example, that of Friedrich von Hayek), socialism ultimately constitutes a threat to the survival of modern civilization, personal freedom and responsibility, the production of wealth and social justice (Gamble, 1996). Still, if Marx were able to survey the dominant economic systems of the contemporary world, he would not see many instances of socialism. On the contrary, he would perceive the dominance of neoliberalism, a force that traces its roots back to economic doctrines produced in the eighteenth century and taking root globally from the late 1970s.

Born in St. Petersburg, in 1905, Alyssa Rosenbaum left Russia for America in 1926 in the wake of the Bolshevik revolution and the subsequent Soviet Communist regime, never to return. Once in the US, Rosenbaum worked in Hollywood at the legendary film director Cecil DeMille's studios in a variety of roles that included wardrobe supervisor, filing clerk and script reader before beginning her own writing career in the form of plays, novellas and finally three novels. It was during this period of her life that Rosenbaum 'decided on a pseudonym: "Ayn" after a Finnish author (Aino Kallas) by that name, "Rand" after her Remington-Rand typewriter' (Bell-Villada, 2004: 229). Rand produced four substantial works of fiction: *We The Living* (1936), *Anthem* (1937), *The Fountainhead* (1943) and *Atlas Shrugged* (1957). Although each features different plots, settings and characters, they are united by the distinctive philosophy Rand communicated in each work, especially in *The Fountainhead* and *Atlas Shrugged*, of what she termed 'Objectivism'. Objectivism had its roots in the classical Greek philosophy of Aristotle, and as she outlined in her non-fiction work, *The Virtue of Selfishness* (1964), the key to the survival of humanity lay in the use of two components: thinking and productive work. The Objectivist position posited rationality as humanity's basic virtue, and as the source of all other virtues. As Rand explained: 'the virtue of Rationality means the recognition and acceptance of reason as one's only source of knowledge, one's only judge of values and one's only guide to action' (1964: 28). In terms of ethics, Rand argued that the basic social principle of the Objectivist is that every living human being is an end in itself; they are not the means to the ends or the welfare of others. Therefore, humans must strive to live for their own sake, neither sacrificing themselves to others nor sacrificing others to themselves. As a consequence, the Objectivist ethics Rand constructed advocates and endorses rationally inspired selfishness and that humans must act for their own rational self-interest (Rand, 1964: x). In terms of social organization, Rand argued that the principle of trade is the only rational ethical principle for all human relationships (Rand, 1964: 34), and the only proper, moral purpose of a government is to protect an individual's rights, that is, to protect him or her from physical violence – to protect his or her right to their own life, liberty and property and to the pursuit of their own happiness (Rand, 1964), and to ultimately protect their ability to trade. For Rand, capitalism at its purest, that is, full, uncontrolled, unregulated laissez-faire capitalism is the ideal economic system. Indeed, as she states: 'Capitalism is not the system of the past; it is the system of the future – if mankind is to have a future' (Rand, 1964: 37). In Rand's vision of this perfect society, all aspects of society would be privately run, from the postal service to schools. Only the police, armed services and the law would be state-controlled. Rand rejected any form of mysticism, especially belief in God and religion. Ultimately, Rand argued that capitalism is the only system that can be defended and validated by reason (cited in Boaz, 1998: 165).

From 1958 until the end of her life in 1982, Rand would articulate the philosophical contours of Objectivism in a series of non-fiction texts, including: *The Virtue of Selfishness, Capitalism: The Unknown Ideal* (1967), *The Romantic Manifesto* (1969), *The New Left: The Anti-Industrial Revolution* (1971), *Introduction to Objectivist Epistemology* (1979), and *Philosophy: Who Needs It* (1982). However, these ideas were unswervingly present within her fiction, indeed, her fiction was created as a popular mode by which to transmit her message of the ideal ethics and the ideal economic social system: capitalism. And, although slow to start, once Rand's popularity grew and her books began to sell in millions, her valorization of selfish, exuberant entrepreneurship found a substantial young audience. As Margot Adler states:

> If Marxism, with its promise of a proletarian utopia, was tailor-made to the aspirations of the working-class crusader, Objectivism and its ethic of self-sufficiency and achievement was intoxicating to the sons and daughters of the 1950s middle class. (1986: 287)

What Rand's fiction communicated was the essence of liberalism, but with a prescient yearning for a future period of 'pure capitalism' and the capitalist/industrialist hailed as the true heroic figure in free-market 'libertarian' nations that contain a state which contents itself with only ensuring national security and the enforcement of laws to ensure the harmonious dynamic of free trade. Rand's fiction, as we shall see, acts as a means through which to explore liberalism and later neoliberalism expressed in an idealized form, and thus to identify critical aspects of the social and economic system of ideas. Rand's work is, furthermore, significant as a way of pop-culturally exploring economic ideology as her work has proven to be surprisingly durable. Highly controversial and dramatically divisive in terms of reception and evaluation (reader reviews on the Amazon website vary between one and five stars), what Bell-Villada calls her 'thick, preachy epics' continue to sell hundreds of thousands of copies annually.

At the level of popular culture, Rand's controversial ideology and persona have found (often critical) references in a range of forms, including the progressive rock music of Rush (who set Rand's novella, *Anthem*, to music on their 1976 album, *2112*), *Dirty Dancing, The Simpsons, South Park, Mad Men*, and the popular video game, *Bio-Shock* (Burns, 2009). They have also found new contemporary audiences in an era that is characterized by chronic economic recession which appears to point to the failure of the liberal/neoliberal project. Indeed, many members of the American Tea Party anti-government group, which was formed in 2009 and is pledged to block Democrat spending plans and health care initiatives, 'subscribe to the philosophy of [*Atlas Shrugged*] and believe in the writing of Ayn Rand and her view of individual liberty' (Boerma, 2011: 1). Arguably, then, the principles of liberalism and the neoliberal basis of contemporary economics can be found in novels that, although written in the 1940s and 1950s, potently resonate with the political and economic global world of the twenty-first century and articulate, in an extreme and unfettered form, the essence of neoliberal thought and what many supporters of neoliberalism would like it to become.

THE RISE OF NEOLIBERALISM

The development of neoliberalism, argues David Harvey (2007), lies in the liberal theory that emerged from the group of economists and historians who came to surround the political thinker Friedrich von Hayek. Such was the sympathy for Hayek's work that the group, which included Ludwig von Mises and Milton Friedman, became known as the Mont Pelerin Society (formed in 1947). Initially, the group characterized themselves as liberals, reflecting the thought of classic exponents of liberalism such as Jeremy Bentham and the principle of 'laissez-faire' (let it be) capitalism. The term 'neoliberal' emerged from an alternative brand of economics proposed by figures such as Alfred Marshall that, from the mid-nineteenth century, decisively broke away from earlier traditions associated with David Ricardo, Karl Marx and Adam Smith. With reference to the latter thinker, as Friedman and Friedman (1980) state, the genius of Smith's seminal work of economics, *The Wealth of Nations* (1776), was his analysis of how a market-based economic system could combine the freedom of individuals to follow their goals with the necessary large-scale co-operation and collaboration required in the larger economic social structure to guarantee the production of essential human goods such as food, clothing and housing.

Smith's key insight was the argument that both parties involved in an economic/goods exchange can benefit: indeed, to the extent that co-operation remains voluntary, no process of exchange will occur unless both parties do benefit. For this reason, there is no need for any form of external force or coercion to be applied to the economic exchange process for it to operate harmoniously. As such, no infringement of an individual's freedom needs to be enforced to produce co-operation among individuals meeting on the market. Yet, this process had wider social implications, as Friedman argues:

> Adam Smith's flash of genius was his recognition that the prices that emerged from voluntary transactions between buyers and sellers – for short, in a free market – could coordinate the activity of millions of people, each seeking his own interest in such a way as to make everyone better off. It was a startling idea then, and it remains one today, that economic order can emerge as the unintended consequence of the actions of many people, each seeking his own interest. (Friedman and Friedman, 1980: 14)

The only problem, argue Friedman and Friedman, comes when this efficient price system is prevented from functioning by state interference. Without any such social meddling, a society based on voluntary co-operation is a society that is able simultaneously to preserve and expand the realm of human freedom. It is a free-market-driven society that 'keeps government in its place, keeping it our servant and not letting it become our master' (1980: 37). The state is an essential component within a free-market liberal society. As Robert Nozick argues in *Anarchy, State, and Utopia*, 'the minimal state is the most extensive state that can be justified. Any state more extensive violates people's rights' (1974: 149). Thus, as Friedman articulates in *Capitalism and Freedom*, the social and political scope of government must be limited to one major function: 'to protect our freedom both from the enemies outside our gates and from our fellow-citizens: to preserve law and order, to enforce private contracts, to foster competitive markets' (1982: 2). This is a view that finds support with another eminent figure of the liberal tradition, Ludwig von Mises, who, in *Liberalism*, held that a factor within peaceful human co-operation was the threat of force. Accordingly, the restricted function of the state, in accordance with liberal doctrines, is reducible to 'the protection of property, liberty, and peace' (2007: 17); or, as Friedman pithily expresses it, government is indispensible as a medium for 'determining the "rules of the game" and as an umpire to interpret and enforce the rules decided on' (1982: 15). The problem, argues Friedman, is that in numerous post-war democracies, government and the state did not diminish to provide such protections for individual freedoms, but rather emphasized welfare over freedom to the extent that many constituted threats to individualism.

In Harvey's analysis of the 'revolutionary' emergence of neoliberalism as a political and economic system, the period 1978–80 stands as a crucial historical moment for a number of reasons. First, it was in 1978 that Deng Xiaoping, leader of the Communist Party of China, initiated the liberalization of the Chinese economy. Second, in the United States, Paul Volcker was appointed Chairman of the Federal Reserve in 1979 and changed monetary policy to combat rising inflation. Meanwhile, in Britain, Margaret Thatcher was elected Prime Minster in 1979 on the basis of a mandate that specifically promised to reduce trade union power and combat the economic stagnation that had dominated the 1970s. The final component fell into place with the 1980 election of Ronald Reagan as President of the United States, who supported Volcker's decisions at the Federal Reserve and thus 'instigated a blend of policies to curb the power of labour, deregulate industry, agriculture, and resource extraction and liberate the powers of finance both internally and on the world stage' (Harvey, 2007: 1). The theoretical principles set out by the likes of Friedman were thus being enacted on the global stage. Consequently, the state assumed the role of protector of the quality of money in addition to setting up the key 'military, defence, police, and legal structures and functions required to secure private property rights and to guarantee, by force if need be, the proper function of markets' (Harvey, 2007: 2).

A leading cause of the decisive turn to neoliberalism was the apparent collapse of the post-war economic systems that had dominated the West. As Harvey explains, many nations restructured their state systems to ensure that capitalism would not succumb to the economic slump and depression that had characterized it in the 1930s. In Europe, the United States and Japan, state re-structuring centred on the recognition that full employment, economic growth and the welfare of citizens should be the key objectives of the state, and, if neces-sary, the state should intervene in market processes to ensure the realization of these social and economic goals and establish welfare systems with regard to health and education. This ultimately became known as the 'Keynesian' approach, after John Maynard Keynes (1883–1946), author of classic economic texts such as *The General Theory of Employment, Interest and Money* (1936). Keynes' approach advocated the need for states to sometimes intervene, for instance to increase expenditure in order to stimulate economies because 'unless a market economy could create jobs, it could not survive' (Stiglitz, 2010: 239). It was an approach that would be implemented in many capitalist countries in a form Harvey calls 'embedded liberalism', and which would produce substantial rates of economic growth. The defining factor of this Keynes-inspired system was the ways in which market practices were enclosed by distinctive social and political constraints that saw trade unions achieve considerable influence within state processes. But it was not to last.

Towards the end of the 1960s the embedded liberal system experienced debil-itating problems and began to collapse as unemployment and inflation rose dramatically. Thus, as the 1970s progressed, acutely in response to the OPEC oil crisis of 1973 and the global property market crash that led to the folding of a number of banks and even the bankruptcy of New York city in 1975 (Harvey, 2010), the neoliberal project arose. This economic system aimed to remove 'welfare' constraints from free-market forces; to deconstruct the welfare state and union power; to encourage entrepreneurialism and private enterprise; and to valorize individualism, private property and personal responsibility. Consequently, from 1979 capitalist countries progressively enforced processes of deregulation, tax cuts, the 'financialization of everything' (Harvey, 2007: 33), freely functioning markets and free trade, underpinned by a state that enforces the rule of law and establishes a secure society for such processes to take place, dismantling all traces of the preceding Keynesian doctrines. But within the developing neoliberal system the freedoms of the individual within the market-place are upheld and secured by law and law enforcement while individuals are rendered responsible for their own actions and, crucially, their own personal well-being. Individuals were thus encouraged not to look to a welfare state for the provision of health, education or pensions, but to assume individual respon-sibility. As Francis Wheen (2004) illustrates, Margaret Thatcher was judicious in her application of Friedman's neoliberal principles, especially her policy of cutting public spending and her hostile approach to organized labour (princi-pally steel workers and miners), approaches mirrored in the US by the Reagan administration.

I will raise critical issues regarding the consequences of neoliberalism at the end of the chapter, but Harvey, evoking Marx, stresses that although the system may appear to be a blueprint for the re-organization of capitalism, it is in essence a system predicated upon re-establishing capitalist accumulation, and a potent way of re-articulating the power of the economic elite and the established concentrations of corporate power in key areas of social and cultural life, from energy, transport and pharmaceuticals, to retailing and media/mass communication conglomerates. Consequently, Harvey stresses that the system is inherently unjust because:

> To accept it is to accept that we have no alternative except to live under a regime of endless capital accumulation and economic growth no matter what the social, ecological, or political consequences. (2007: 181)

AYN RAND AND THE FICTION OF NEOLIBERALISM

Rand's overall philosophical approach is typically labelled libertarian in outlook, which is, in Boaz's assessment, 'a species of (classical) liberalism, an advocacy of individual liberty, free markets, and limited government rooted in a commitment to self-ownership, imprescriptable rights, and the moral autonomy of the individual' (1998: xiv). However, in her assessment of the status of the individual, her rabid rejection of all forms of political collectivism, and her understanding and assessment of the nature of capitalism, Rand articulated the aspects of liberalism that would form the bedrock of neoliberalism. Indeed, her definition of capitalism was such that she argued that it was not merely an economic system founded on the recognition of individual rights, but also a moral system (Douglas *et al.*, 1998). As Rand articulates in *Capitalism: The Unknown Ideal*, everything that humans need must be discovered by the mind, therefore systems of production are the application of human reason to the challenge of survival. Thus, while some humans may choose not to use their reason or not to work, their subsequent sole means of survival is by 'looting' the productive activities of individuals who do so, and whose labours have ensured that the conditions necessary to ensure the continued existence of humans are created and secured. Consequently:

> Since knowledge, thinking, and rational action are properties of the individual, since the choice to exercise his rational faculty or not depends on the individual, man's survival requires that those who think be free of the interference of those who don't. Since men are neither omniscient nor infallible, they must be free to agree or disagree, to cooperate or to pursue their own independent course, each according to his own rational judgment. Freedom is the fundamental requirement of man's mind. (Rand, 1967: 17)

Throughout history, capitalism is the only economic system that has established the freedom whereby human relationships are voluntary and geared towards mutual benefit. As Rand states, a capitalist society bestows on its citizens the right to agree and to disagree and this 'is the cardinal difference between capitalism and collectivism' (1967: 19). Unlike communist societies such as the Soviet Union (prior to its collapse in 1989), Rand argues that the material wealth of the United States was not established via any desire for the 'common good', but alternatively 'by the productive genius of free men who pursued their own personal interests and the making of their own private fortunes' (1967: 29). Consequently, any call for a redistribution of wealth is 'obscene' and it was state intervention in the nineteenth century and the early decades of the twentieth that stopped the laissez-faire trajectory from establishing pure capitalism. The various economic downturns, crises and depressions argued (by Marx, for example) to be the central contradiction and failing of the capitalist system – its 'boom and bust' cyclical nature – were, according to Rand, 'caused by government interference, not by the capitalist system' (1967: 31).

As one would imagine, Rand was an ardent critic of the Keynesian approach of government intervention to stimulate economies and its critique of the 'hands-off doctrine of laissez-faire' (Burns, 2009: 72). But a significant aspect of Rand's criticism of state intervention and her veneration of pure capitalism underpinned by individual self-interest is the frequency with which (in *Capitalism: The Unknown Ideal*, for example) she cites incidents and characters from her own fictional novels as supportive evidence for her more philosophical and economic views. It was through her fictional writing that Rand both attained considerable commercial (if not always critical) success, and consciously transmitted her ideas concerning individualism and the strengths of pure capitalism and the primacy of the entrepreneur. It was also her fiction that brought her into contact with key figures of the neoliberal movement, most notably Ludwig von Mises and Alan Greenspan. The latter, who was Chairman of the Federal Reserve from 1987 till 2006, held firm to the principles of laissez-faire capitalism throughout his tenure and remained committed to Rand's ideology, having becomes friends with her in the 1950s and been privy to early drafts of *Atlas Shrugged*. Therefore, Rand's views on individualism, capitalism and deregulation were being expressed at the heart of US neoliberal policy and ideology; but it was a message that she expressed most potently in her works of fiction, not in standard works of philosophy or economics.

The plot of Rand's first novel, *We The Living* (1936), concerned the plight of the character Kira Argounova in 1930s post-revolutionary Communist Russia. In Burns' view, 'Rand's anti-communism is woven into every scene in the novel and its overall structure' (2009: 31). Expelled from university because of her bourgeois class background, Kira begins an affair with Communist Party member Andrei Taganov in order to save her real lover, Leo Kovalensky, the son of an executed aristocrat, who eventually becomes a 'food speculator', a private black market trader, a practice which is highly illegal, and which results in his arrest and sentence to death by Taganov. Consistently, and unsubtly, *We The Living* depicts the 'evil' of collectivism, that any society dominated by an overbearing, intrusive and controlling state is fundamentally at war with the concept of the sovereign individual, and this is illustrated by the following exchange between the committed 'Comrade Sonia' and Comrade Taganov in relation to a speech concerning the future development of Communist economic policy:

'Don't you agree with the speaker?'

'I prefer not to discuss it.'

'Oh, you don't have to,' she smiled pleasantly. 'You don't have to. I know – we know – what you think. But what I'd like you to answer is this: why do you think you are entitled to your own thoughts? Against those of the majority of your Collective? Or is the majority's will sufficient for you, Comrade Taganov? Or is Comrade Taganov becoming an individualist?' (1996: 311)

Rand employs fiction to highlight her philosophical stance on the battle between the individual and the collective, a debate articulated consistently through the mouths of her characters. Spurred on by Kira's words and her belief that the individual outweighs the state, the once loyal Taganov rebels during a Party gathering, denouncing the Communist ethos, and in doing so, perfectly expresses Rand's philosophy:

Every honest man lives for himself. Every man worth calling a man lives for himself. The one who doesn't – doesn't live at all. You cannot change it. You cannot change it because that's the way man is born, alone, complete, an end in himself. No laws, no Party, no GPU will ever kill that thing in man which knows how to say 'I'. (1996: 408)

The primacy of the value of 'I' was the central theme of Rand's next work, the science-fiction novella, *Anthem* (1937). *Anthem* takes place in an imagined collectivist society. The hero of the novel is Equality 7-2521, a state-enforced street cleaner (the state assigns all employment) who begins to show dangerous signs of individualist behaviour. This is dangerous because there is no concept of 'I' within this society, only 'We'. As the social mantra of the society makes clear:

We are one in all and all in one.

There are no men only the great WE,

One, indivisible and forever. (1995: 19)

Such is the centrality of collectivism within this society that the use of the word 'I' by the populace is a crime punishable by death. Equality 7-2521 discovers a light bulb which constitutes proof of an earlier and better civilization that had mastered technology, but when he presents it to the rulers, the Council of Scholars, they reject the object and destroy it. Disillusioned, but enlightened, Equality 7-2521 rebels against the Scholars and subsequently escapes with a female, Liberty 5-3000, into the surrounding wilderness where they discover an abandoned house that contains books, sources of the 'old world' that will enable them to master the skills of production and consequently forge a new life. And most vitally, it is beyond the world of the Council of Scholars that Equality 7-2521 makes the breakthrough to individuality by at last proclaiming: 'I Am. I Think. I Will' (1995: 94) and discovering what brought the old civilization to ruins: 'What disaster took their reason away from men? What whip lashed them to their knees in shame and submission? The worship of the word "We"' (1995: 102).

While *Anthem* articulated Rand's individualist themes in 88 pages, Rand's next work, *The Fountainhead* (1943), expressed such themes on an epic scale (679 pages in the HarperCollins edition), becoming her first major success. *The Fountainhead* charts the career of Howard Roark, Rand's first fully formed 'ideal man' (Sciabarra, 1995). Roark is a brilliant architect, a man of integrity who is expelled from the Stanton Institute of Technology for refusing to compromise his vision of true architectural design and for refusing to conform to traditional architectural styles. Thus, Roark is an arch-individualist whose work is revolutionary to the extent that few recognize his genius. As a counterpoint to Roark, Rand presents his fellow student, Peter Keating, a less talented, but more successful architect, who at one stage copies Roark's ideas to win a coveted design competition that results in fortune and a partnership with a prestigious architectural firm. Meanwhile, Roark elects to labour in a granite quarry and steadfastly refuses to compromise his architectural vision. Even when he does design according to his own standards, his work is criticized and ridiculed, most notably by the 'socialist villain' of the novel, the architecture critic Ellsworth Toohey. Indeed, at one stage Toohey and his cronies debate the 'true' nature of society, the virtue of unselfishness and the need for state control. As one character states: 'It's stupid to talk about personal choice ... It's old-fashioned. There's no such thing as a person. There's only a collective entity. It's self evident' (1994: 543).

By contrast, Roark perfectly sums up Rand's ideology in one of his most memorable statements when, challenged to work on a project as part of a team, he caustically replies: 'I don't work with collectives. I don't consult, I don't co-operate, I don't collaborate' (1994: 500). The stark difference in beliefs between Roark and Toohey forms the crux of the novel, with the latter glorifying collectivism in opposition to Roark's rugged and dogged individualism. Toohey's embrace of collectivism, his staunch anti-individualism is the product not of altruism, but of his own personal weakness and failings. For Rand, Toohey is unable to attain values through productive effort and can only achieve greatness in the eyes of others by crushing and ridiculing the heroic in his reviews and in his circle of slavish acolytes.

The climax of the novel comes when Roark, via Paul Keating, designs the Cortlandt public housing project, but on the strict condition that the blueprints, submitted in Keating's name, are not changed in any way. But they are altered significantly and the project is built in a manner that differs from Roark's vision. In response to such a violation of his singular vision, Roark dynamites the completed project and is arrested and brought to trial, only to defend himself in court by enunciating the principles of individualism. His attitude is that no-one had the right to alter his plans, arguing that a 'man thinks and works alone' (1994: 668), and that he destroyed his creation because altruists debased his vision, because 'I recognize no obligations towards men except one; to respect their freedom and take no part in a slave society' (1994: 670). In the face of such stirring words dedicated to the sovereignty of the individual, the jury vindicates Roark, clearing him of all criminal charges. He agrees to rebuild the project according to his own specifications. The novel concludes with Howard Roark triumphant and his ethos recognized by society.

The interlinking theme that unites *We The Living*, *Anthem*, and *The Fountainhead* is that of anti-collectivism and the need for free individuals to live their lives beyond the control of state interference and enforced collectivism. The result of such systems is portrayed in each of these novels as oppression, stultification and domination of the creative spirit of humanity. In terms of liberal/neoliberal ideas, these early works focus on the ideal conditions for humans to exist and work, and stress (with little subtlety or balance) the inferiority and danger posed by communist or state-controlled social and economic structures. However, it was in her final work of fiction, the epic 1069-page *Atlas Shrugged* (1957), that Rand fully wove her sustained ideology of individualism into a tale exclusively devoted to the veneration of both capitalism and the capitalists who create and sustain it.

In terms of structure and theme, *Atlas Shrugged* is an unremittingly polemical novel, and tells the sprawling story of the principle and value of the labour process strictly from the perspective of the capitalist entrepreneur. The most notable characters are: Dagny Taggart, head of Taggart Transcontinental Railroad; Hank Rearden, owner of Rearden Steel and inventor of a new type of steel that is superior to existing metals; and the mysterious, but ultimately all-powerful John Galt, who does not appear until late in the story, but whose presence dominates from the outset, usually in the form of the question, 'Who is John Galt?', a recurrent motif and catchphrase throughout the novel. Dagny, Hank and Galt (not forgetting Francisco d'Anconia, Midas Mulligan, Ellis Wyatt and Ken Danagger) are the rugged and noble heroes of the novel, the staunch economic individualists pitted against their polar opposites: the 'moochers' and 'looters', industry-halting unions and corrupt state-socialists intent on equalizing opportunities and curbing entrepreneurial zeal, who are symbolized by the character of Wesley Mouch. Mouch is the initiator of 'Directive 10-289', which decrees that private enterprise must be turned over to the interests of the state, underpinned by the rule that 'all wages, prices, salaries, dividends, profits, interest rates and forms of income of any nature whatsoever, shall be frozen at their present figures, as of the date of this directive' (1992: 498), and driven by the desire to control and limit capitalist activity and 'run the world for the sake of the little people' (ibid.). In the novel, capitalism emerges as the ideal social, economic and moral system. Socialism is a failure and is argued to be evil. The ideal society is one in which the capitalist individual is given the freedom to pursue profit. The anti-collectivist sentiment of the novel is captured in this dialogue between the millionaire industrialist Rearden and his 'moocher' brother, Phil: 'You don't really care about helping the underprivileged, do you?' Philip asked ... 'No, Phil, I don't care about it at all' (1992: 47). Running through such rejections of altruism is a commitment to pure liberalism, and indications of the untrammelled, 'pure' capitalist ethos that it would develop into. This is articulated on numerous occasions throughout the novel, but is perfectly expressed in a speech given by Rearden to a committee devoted to limiting capitalist profit-making:

> I work for nothing but my own profit which I make by selling a product they need to men who are willing and able to buy it. I do not produce it for their benefit at the expense of mine, and they do not buy it for my benefit at the expense of theirs; I do not sacrifice my interests to them nor do they sacrifice theirs to me; we deal by mutual consent to mutual advantage – and I am proud of every penny that I have earned in that manner. I am rich and I am proud of every penny I own. I made my money by my own effort, in free exchange and through the voluntary consent of every man I dealt with. (1992: 444)

The essence of *Atlas Shrugged* is that the industrialist is the true artist and hero within society, and should be perceived and celebrated as such. As the composer, Richard Halley, explains to Dagny: 'That sacred fire which is said to burn within musicians and poets – what do they suppose moves an industrialist to defy the whole world for the sake of [their] new metal, as the inventors of the airplane, the builders of the railroads...?' (1992: 718). This ethos is perfectly captured in the argument made by the pirate character, Ragnar Danneskjold, who attacks ships carrying the products of capitalists and redistributes the wealth (in the form of bars of gold) to their deserving and 'exploited' creators. In terms of justifying his actions, which of course turns Marx's political goal upon its head, Ragnar explains that the most evil man in history was Robin Hood. Why? Because:

> He was the man who robbed the rich and gave to the poor. Well, I'm the man who robs the poor and gives to the rich – or, to be exact, the man who robs the thieving poor and gives back to the productive rich. (1992: 532)

As the narrative progresses the members of the capitalist class steadily withdraw from society into their utopia, the 'New Atlantis', or its official title, Galt's Gulch, and set up their own free enterprises, rather than submit themselves to state intervention. Indeed, the ideology of individualism is so dominant and entrenched for Galt and his persecuted entrepreneurs, that the maxim of this capitalist idyll is that it is the place 'where one doesn't ask for help' (1992: 692). And such is the exclusivity of this world that loyal employees are discarded and forgotten, most notably Eddie Willers who displays nothing but slavish devotion to Dagny and Taggart Transcontinental throughout the narrative, but whose only reward is to be left to die in the crumbling society, abandoned in the wilderness as a passenger on a train that has ground to a halt – due to the inefficient and myopic actions of rail unions, of course.

Although it runs to more than 1000 pages, characters celebrating capitalism and advocating ultra-individualism can be found on almost every page of *Atlas*

Shrugged. But the quintessence of the novel is distilled in a speech made by the true hero, John Galt, which lasts for almost 60 pages (pp. 924–79 in the Signet edition). Having taken over a radio broadcast to the US and the entire world, Galt proceeds to set out his vision of the perfect society, but starkly emphasizes that in depriving America of its key industrialists and entrepreneurs, he has potently and decisively destroyed the collectivist world: 'I have stopped your motor. I have deprived your world of man's mind, because, we are on strike, we the men of the mind' (1992: 924). Thus the strike, symbolically the main channel of the proletariat's resistance *against* the owners of the means of production, is an act of defiance in the face of a society that castigates the deserving industrial rich, a world that considers business leaders to be 'ignoble' when it should be adopting a 'reverent' stance. While eulogizing Rand's focus on the power of reason and mind as the key drivers of human productive society, Galt's speech also extols the virtues of the capitalist system they have created, and the individualist/limited government ethos that underpins it (or should do so). Consequently, the result of Galt's withdrawal of capitalists and the giving over of society to the collectivists is complete social and economic disaster. At the end of the novel, America is reduced to an anarchic and collective-created dystopia: a ruined society that can deliver no services and has no foundation for generating the means of production. Accordingly, *Atlas Shrugged* champions capitalism by depicting the fate of a world that is abandoned by capitalists. Thus, the collective forces of the novel, from the Locomotive Engineers' union to the corrupt 'collectivist' government, only serve to impede the progress of the various capitalist individuals who populate its pages. Indeed, the book ends with the forces of collectivism having destroyed themselves, and, in doing so, signalling the moment in which pure capitalism will now triumph:

> 'The road is cleared,' said Galt. 'We are going back to the world.' He raised his hand and over the desolate earth he traced in space the sign of the dollar. (1992: 1069)

Written expressly as a capitalist fantasy, *Atlas Shrugged* presents the ultimate neoliberal utopia: a world in which the free market is supreme and the state serves only to establish a secure basis for individuals to engage in free trade. Furthermore, even as the novel was being written, Rand steadily instilled it with the fundamental ideas that would inform later neoliberal thinking and policy, due principally to her friendship with one of its economist architects, Ludwig von Mises. Although it was a volatile relationship (as most of Rand's friendships were), Mises' liberal economic thought greatly influenced Rand, particularly his conviction that capitalism was an absolute social and economic system, his fervent attacks on and rejection of socialism as a means to provide the social good, but also his 'vision of an economy centered primarily on entrepreneurs rather than workers reinforced Rand's individualistic understanding of production and creativity' (Burns, 2009: 142). This was a conviction that would be held and expressed by the primary political 'icon' of neoliberalism, Margaret

Thatcher, who held that the true heroes of society were 'buccaneering entrepreneurs' whose mode of living was 'truly virtuous' (Wheen, 2004: 29). Furthermore, the 1980s neoliberal 'Reagan Revolution' adopted distinctive Randian motifs of economic self-centredness (Bell-Villada, 2004) and George W. Bush adopted a 'swash-buckling model of rugged American individualism ... with his cowboy boots and manly swagger' (Stiglitz, 2010: 281).

In his critique of neoliberalism, Pierre Bourdieu argues that it is an ultra-right utopia shaped by the forces of 'mega capital' (Mitrović, 2005); a utopia, or 'infernal machine', predicated on the principle of endless exploitation and the systematic destruction of collectives by a 'pure and perfect market made possible by the politics of financial deregulation' (Bourdieu, 1998: 2). For Bourdieu, the dynamic for the neoliberal project comes from stockholders, conservative politicians, and principally industrialists who are imbued with the 'free trade faith' and motivated only by an 'individual quest for the maximization of individual profit' (1998: 4). The results of the rise of neoliberalism nationally and globally have been twofold in their immediate effects: the destruction of the key collective institutions able to resist the effects of neoliberalism; and a distinctive 'moral Darwinism' at the level of the individual – a pervasive and powerful 'cult of the winner' that relegates collective ties of solidarity with fellow social actors. Although not referencing her work, Bourdieu's critique of the dominant tenets of neoliberalism perfectly captures both Rand's liberal ethos and the plot and ideology of *Atlas Shrugged* – a text that pushes to excess the most extreme edges and qualities of a laissez-faire world dominated by profit and self-reliance and the single-minded, if not frequently brutal, acquisition of profit and wealth.

Not surprisingly, the negative consequences of unbridled capitalism and unceasing market-driven economic expansion are not acknowledged by champions of neoliberalism, nor are they addressed in the fiction of Ayn Rand. As Harvey argues, states that have embraced (or been impelled to embrace) neoliberal economic policies may have seen productivity dramatically increase (as in the case of China), but they have also had to pay (and continue to pay) a high price. This ranges from the heaping of blame for economic failure upon 'proletariat' individuals, the diminution of trade union power, flexible working patterns based on short-term fixed contracts lacking security and benefits, and rising crime rates, to the ecological consequences of increased carbon emissions from industrial states (predominantly America and China) and the destruction of rain forests. Nevertheless, none of these issues are to be found in the pro-market/pro-capitalist fiction of Ayn Rand. For Rand, welfare and compassion for the 'unproductive' poor are not issues worth considering, and, as *Atlas Shrugged* relentlessly reiterates, unions are 'evil' and nothing but a brake on the free-marketeering heroics of entrepreneurs. As for ecological degradation, the environmental devastation caused by a rampant, perpetually expanding neoliberal capitalist system were actually a sign of success according to Ayn Rand, as she praised pollution as a definitive sign of progress in the human struggle against nature (Shermer, 1997).

RAND AND THE MODERN NEOLIBERAL WORLD

The fiction of Ayn Rand is a literature that reflects by neoliberal ideas, but one that depicts it at its most uninhibited and most ruthless. Within her vision of the perfect economic and social world order, capitalism begins and ends with the capitalist. The proletariat are either entirely excluded from consideration, utterly beholden to their 'superiors', or trouble-making union agitators intent upon destroying free trade and with it, the true human spirit. So, while Bret Easton Ellis' controversial 1991 novel, *American Psycho*, presents Patrick Bateman, a consumer-driven, product-obsessed, sexually motivated serial killer 'Yuppie' as the face of 80s Reaganomics, and Jonathan Coe's *What a Carve Up!* (1994) equates Thatcher's neoliberal Britain with the wealthy, corrupt and cruel Winshaw family, Rand acknowledges no weaknesses in the liberal project. From the hyper-individualism of *We The Living*, *Anthem*, and *The Fountainhead*, to the hymn to capitalism that sings out from virtually every page of *Atlas Shrugged*, popular culture can mirror economics and economic aspirations perfectly, and Rand's work was, as Bell-Villada ruefully notes, read voraciously by subsequent generations of entrepreneurs, from the steel industries of the 1960s to the dotcom boom of the twenty-first century.

In spite of this, the beginning of the twenty-first century has been marked by capitalism's apparent failings and limitations, and by extension this has raised critical issues concerning the system's neoliberal foundation. Although the cyclical instances of boom and bust have always been endemic to the system (as Marx observed), the e-commerce economic wave faltered, and, more chronically, from 2006 capitalism faced what David Harvey (2010) describes as the 'mother of all crises', and Joseph Stiglitz calls an economic 'freefall'. This began in America with the sub-prime mortgage crisis, which, in the wake of the housing 'bubble' bursting, saw global credit markets begin to melt down. The scale of the crisis was dramatically symbolized by the collapse of the financial services firm, Lehman Brothers, on 15 September 2008. Subsequently, within the US economy, consumer spending fell, unemployment rose, housing construction slowed markedly and numerous manufacturing plants closed, crises that were rapidly experienced in the British economy and in many parts of the European Union. More importantly, neoliberalism reneged on its basic principles as the state intervened to bail out a number of banks and industrial producers, including General Motors, the US car manufacturer that had come perilously close to bankruptcy, and in the United Kingdom the Bank of England bailed out the bank Northern Rock. In order to move on and ensure that lessons are learned from what Stiglitz calls capitalism's 'near-death experience', fundamental transformations to the philosophy of economics must be made:

> The model of rugged individualism combined with market fundamentalism has altered not just how individuals think of themselves and their preferences but how they relate to each other. In a world of rugged individualism, there is little need for community and no need for trust. (2010: 289)

Consequently, Stiglitz argues, there is a need for an adjustment to be made to the dominant model of economics that arose in the latter decades of the twentieth century and which has experienced almost cataclysmic breakdown in the first decade of the twenty-first. As it is, the foundations of liberalism, and later neoliberalism, conceptualize humans as nothing more than self-serving and self-interested individuals existing (and often profiting) in a system that has 'no room for human empathy, public spiritedness, or altruism' (2010: 249). In Harvey's more radical view, capitalism in its current neoliberal state has run its course, and an alternative economic system needs to be instituted. This could be the Marx and Engels-inspired communist revolution, or an anti-capitalist 'Party of Indignation' that is 'ready to fight and defeat the Party of Wall Street and its acolytes and apologists everywhere' (2010: 260). Less radically, the solution may be to turn the clock back to the era of the New Deal, and re-establish a more just and humane form of economic production that balances capitalist endeavour with necessary state invention: effectively, the resurrection of Keynes (Harvey, 2007).

Nevertheless, within this period of acute economic recession, the popularity of Ayn Rand, and *Atlas Shrugged*, soared. As the recession escalated from 2006, sales of *Atlas Shrugged* increased dramatically in spikes that *The Economist* linked to specific state actions, such as the Bush administration initiating its interventions with banks to assist mortgage holders; the Troubled Asset Relief Program, which saw the US government purchase stakes in a number of banks to prop them up; and the publication of Barrack Obama's economic stimulus plan (Coleman, 2009). Reasons for the popularity of Rand in a period that apparently illustrated the chronic weaknesses of capitalism are that the system is not sufficiently pure; that the era of 'true' capitalism as exemplified by Galt is yet to come; and the US Tea Party's enthusiasm for Rand and commitment to a stricter version of neoliberalism. *Atlas Shrugged*, a novel published in 1957, not only maps out the trajectories of a dominant economic landscape as it has developed since the late 1970s, but also points to what it could potentially become in the future, quite aptly, as the novel is a work of science fiction.

And so, I began the book with Marx and his rallying call for the proletariat to gather in his *Communist Manifesto*, but Rand produced her own version, in what she called her 'Individualist Manifesto', that subverted Marx's words and replaced his collectivist message with her own unique (but somewhat paradoxical) appeal: 'INDIVIDUALISTS OF THE WORLD, UNITE!' If the Marxist-inspired hip-hop music and the literature of Ayn Rand are compared as regards reflecting contemporary economic, social and political conditions, it is not difficult to see which is the more evident. Although the march of neoliberalism is not unopposed across the globe, the 'infernal machine' remains, and while its foundations can be gleaned from the economics of Milton Friedman, Robert Nozick or Ludwig von Mises (Rand did not consider von Hayek to be sufficiently devoted to the market or individualism), the memoirs of Ronald Reagan, Margaret Thatcher and Alan Greenspan, or the websites and literature of the Tea

Party, it can also be found within the fiction of Ayn Rand, a writer who has become, in the words of Jennifer Burns, the 'Goddess of the Market'.

QUESTIONS TO CONSIDER

1. What are the major principles of neoliberalism?
2. Why does Pierre Bourdieu find these principles (and their practice) so problematic?
3. What are the central ideas of Ayn Rand's theory of Objectivism, and how do they relate to contemporary neoliberalism?

FURTHER READING

For an authoritative overview of the major ideas and thinkers associated with neoliberalism, see David Harvey's *A Brief History of Neoliberalism*. With regard to Ayn Rand, her major novels, *Anthem, The Fountainhead,* and *Atlas Shrugged* are required reading and give extensive insights into Rand's philosophical and economic views. In terms of situating Rand within a philosophical and contemporary context, see Chris Sciabarra's *Ayn Rand: The Russian Radical* and Jennifer Burns' *Goddess of the Market: Ayn Rand and the American Right.* Also of interest to gain an 'inside perspective' on the neoliberal project is Alan Greenspan's autobiography/economic analysis, *The Age of Turbulence* (2007). Greenspan was part of Rand's 'circle' (acknowledging her as a 'stabilising force' in his life) and gives a detailed account of the economic ideology that forms the foundation of neoliberalism.

Conclusion: thinking, watching, listening and reading sociologically

One of the most influential (and frequently controversial) of contemporary social theorists is without doubt the Slovenian philosopher and cultural thinker, Slavoj Žižek, whose work is primarily based on the psychoanalysis of Jacques Lacan and Marxism. However, a key aspect of Žižek's work is his consistent use of examples from film to express his philosophical analysis of contemporary culture (see his 2001 book *Enjoy Your Symptom: Jacques Lacan in Hollywood and Out*). But while Žižek's work sometimes crosses over into film theory, in books such as *Living In The End Times* (2011), he also illuminates discussions of Lacan, ideology, Plato, Freudianism and Hegel with reference to a series of films that generically ranges from human drama (*Enigma*, 2001, Michael Apted; *Waltz With Bashir*, 2008, Ari Folman), the Western (*3:10 To Yuma*, 2007, James Mangold), superhero adventures (*The Dark Knight*, 2008, Christopher Nolan) and science fiction (*Seconds*, 1966, John Frankenheimer and *I Am Legend*, 2007, Francis Lawrence), to the manic comedy of *The Mask* (1994, Chuck Russell) and the animated antics of *Kung Fu Panda* (2008, Mark Osborne and John Stevenson). What Žižek does here is to express the relevance of highly complex social ideas in the forum of readers' everyday cultural life as these are films that readers are very likely to have seen. Thus, Žižek suggests, while *The Mask* may be viewed as simply a riotous Jim Carrey extravaganza – effectively a classic *Looney Tunes* cartoon presented in live-action form – its central narrative premise of alter egos and unrestrained behaviour evokes Sigmund Freud's pre-Oedipal stage of humans acting without guilt and engaging in unceasing fun: the id let loose without the parental authority of the superego. Therefore, within the context of a film based upon outrageous visuals and an anarchic plot, Žižek deftly weaves in the fundamental thought of the central architect of psychoanalysis.

The point is that theory should not be contained within the pages of books, nor should the analysis of theory always be related to strictly social or political examples. Popular culture is influenced (and frequently inspired) by social 'things' – events and conditions – therefore it is no real surprise that we can discern theoretical ideas and concepts within them. So, while this book has followed Žižek into the realm of film for exemplars of Weber's concept of status, with reference to three very different films – *Mean Girls*, *The Devil Wears Prada*, and *Slumdog Millionaire* – I have extended the scope of cultural examples to include television, popular music, celebrity, sport, fashion, tattooing and fiction. Each of these examples has acted as a means not merely to critically explain theorists such as Marx, Weber, Durkheim, Simmel, Adorno, Ferdinand de Saussaure, Roland Barthes and the broader movements of feminism and neoliberalism, but also critically to illustrate the ways in which these ideas are applicable to contemporary culture and are observable within distinctive texts – be they rap songs, TV talent shows or tattooed human skin. However, while I have chosen eight examples of a particular theory/text matrix, there are of course many more that can be explored, and here are some suggestions that can be developed and extended by the reader beyond those articulated within the book.

Although I refer to ethnicity in Chapter 1 in relation to Marxist-influenced rap music, the issue of ethnic prejudice and conflict could be explored through the approach of one of the major proponents of symbolic interactionism, Herbert Blumer (1900–87) in relation to the graphic novel. Blumer's sociology was based on the view that social reality was the product of individual and collective action, and he emphasized a methodological approach to the study of the social world based on interpretation and participant observation. Therefore, with regard to his analysis of what he called 'race prejudice', Blumer argued that it was a collective social process within a specific group that expressed itself in four distinctive ways: (1) a feeling of superiority; (2) a feeling that the subordinate race or ethnic group is intrinsically different and alien; (3) a feeling of proprietary claim to certain areas of privilege and advantage; and (4) a fear and suspicion that the subordinate group has designs on the rights of the dominant group (1958: 4). While there are numerous films, television series or novels that deal with these factors, a cogent example through which to explore Blumer's classic approach would be the graphic novel, a 'picture novella' or 'comic book that you need a bookmark for' (Fingeroth, 2008: 4). Ranging from superheroes (*The Dark Knight Returns; Watchmen*), Jack the Ripper (*From Hell*) and political allegory (*V For Vendetta*), to tales of female adolescence in differing cultures (*Ghost World; Persepolis*), graphic novels have emerged as a narrative art form that has extended the tropes of the comic book to produce significant works of contemporary literature. Furthermore, graphic novels have also tackled issues of ethnicity and ethnic prejudice, and few as centrally as Art Spiegelman in *Maus* (1986–92). Here, Spiegelman details the (real) story of his parents, Vladek and Anja Spiegelman and their experiences in the Nazi death camp, Auschwitz, during the Holocaust in World War II. With meticulous (and unflinching) detail, the graphic novel conveys the dehumanization of the Jews by the Nazi military and presents the Germans and Jews in the guise of cats and mice to visually convey the rhetoric of racial propaganda employed by the Nazi regime

(Gravett, 2005). *Maus* represents an effective means of critically analysing and illustrating Blumer's sociological conception of prejudice.

Staying with interpretive sociology, but with a social-psychological dimension, readers could also explore the ways in which Erving Goffman's (1922–82) analysis of self and social impression management can be updated in the era of the widespread use of online social network spaces such as Facebook and Twitter, or communal game spaces such as *World of Warcraft*. In *The Presentation of Self in Everyday Life* (1959), Goffman argued that social actors can be interpreted as being manipulative performers always engaged in creating a 'front' in their relations with other social actors. What he means is that in the process of daily social interaction, individuals are continuously communicating self-impressions in all they do. Goffman illustrated such social processes with the metaphor of theatrical performance. On stage, an actor has the task of presenting him- or herself to the audience as a particular character in a play, and they must make it clear exactly what role is being played, an effort assisted through the use of costume, props, scenery and movement, as well as dialogue. When an individual enters a setting or occasion, they are faced with the task of communicating to others who and what they are. Consequently, social actors utilize the resources at their disposal to communicate an impression to a given social 'audience', effectively to put on a show 'for the benefit of other people' (1959: 28). Moreover, social settings can be divided into 'front' and 'back' regions, the front region referring to the place where the performance is given whilst conventionally the backstage area is cut off from public view, often physically, so that the 'audience' is unable to witness what is occurring. Such backstage areas could be private offices, or the kitchen areas of restaurants or hotels (an example Goffman cites), but twenty-first-century culture offers new examples of social interaction that combines these areas – of real-time communication that takes place in backstage areas: online communication in which individuals, as Sherry Turkle expresses it in her book, *Alone Together*, can 'recreate' themselves as online personae and create 'new bodies, homes, jobs, and romances' (2011: 11). In digital spaces it is now seemingly easier than ever to present fronts and express or modify (if not invent) senses of selves online, giving Goffman a new lease of life in the digital world.

Remaining with digital theory/culture connection, Samuel P. Huntington's book *Clash of Civilizations* that posits that the major sources of conflict in the late twentieth century would not be based on the political and economic differences that marked the US/Soviet engagements of the Cold War, but on cultural and religious differences, could be explored with reference to Bungie's globally successful video game series, *Halo*, based as it is on the premise of an intergalactic war between humans and a fundamentalist theocratic alien regime called the Covenant.

The details and contours of these theoretical/cultural connections are for the reader to explore and expand on, but the crucial issue is to be aware of the extent to which the theories and theorists are evident within our culture and can be brought to life through ordinary daily expeerience (you merely have to consider boarding procedure and observe the layout of the jet aeroplane that takes us on our international summer holiday, sub-divided as it is into First Class, Business and Economy, to see just how close the spirit of Weber's conception of status is to everyday life). Therefore, when you close the cover of a classic work of social thought, it is not a work of history, because theory has so much to tell us and it can be found in the most unlikely of places. So, exercise that sociological imagination, often.

References

Abu-Jamal, Mumia (2006) '"A Rap Thing", On Rapping Rap, and Hip Hop or Homeland Security', in Basu, Dipannita and Lemelle, Sidney J. (eds) *The Vinyl Ain't Final: Hip Hop and the Globalization of Black Popular Culture* (London: Pluto Press), pp. 23–27.

Adler, Margot (1986) *Drawing Down the Moon: Witches, Druids, Goddess Worshippers, and Other Pagans in America Today* (London: Penguin Compass).

Adler, Patricia A. and Adler, Peter (1995) 'Dynamics of Inclusion and Exclusion in Preadolescent Cliques', *Social Psychology Quarterly*, Vol. 58, No. 3, pp. 145–62.

Adorno, Theodor W. (1954) 'How to Look at Television', *The Quarterly of Film and Television*, Vol. 8, No. 3, pp. 213–35.

Adorno, Theodor W. (1994) *The Stars Down to Earth* (London and New York: Routledge).

Adorno, Theodor W. (2006) *The Culture Industry* (London and New York: Routledge).

Adriaanse, Johanna A. and Crosswhite, Janice J. (2008) 'David or Mia? The influence of gender on adolescent girls' choice of sport role models', *Women's Studies International Forum*, Vol. 31, Issue 5, pp. 383–89.

Alberoni, Francesco (1972) 'The Powerless "Elite": Theory and Sociological Research on the Phenomenon of the Stars', in Denis McQuail (ed.), *Sociology of Mass Communications* (Harmondsworth: Penguin Books), pp. 75–99.

Alexander, Jeffrey C. (2005) 'The inner development of Durkheim's sociological theory: from early writings to maturity', in Alexander, Jeffrey C. and Smith, Philip (eds) *The Cambridge Companion to Durkheim* (Cambridge: Cambridge University Press), pp. 136–60.

Allen, Kieran (2004) *Max Weber: A Critical Introduction* (London: Pluto Press).

Althusser, Louis (1971) *Lenin and Philosophy and Other Essays* (London: New Left Books).

Andrejevic, Mark (2004) *Reality TV: The Work of Being Watched* (Lanham: Rowman & Littlefield Publishers, INC).

Ang, Ien (1996) *Living Room Wars: Rethinking Media Audiences for a Postmodern World* (London: Routledge).

Armstrong, Edward G. (2001) 'Gangsta Misogyny: A Content Analysis of the Portrayals of Violence Against Women in Rap Music, 1987-1993', *Journal of Criminal Justice and Popular Culture*, Vol. 8, No. 2, pp. 96–126.

Ash, Juliet and Wilson, Elizabeth (eds) (1992) *Chic Thrills: A Fashion Reader* (London: HarperCollins Publishers).

Atkinson, Michael (2003) *Tattooed: The Sociogenesis of a Body Art* (Toronto: University of Toronto Press).

Attali, Jacques (1977) *Noise: The Political Economy of Music* (Manchester: Manchester University Press).

Baker, Geoffrey (2005) 'iHip Hop, Revolución! Nationalizing Rap in Cuba', *Ethnomusicology*, Vol. 49, No. 49, pp. 368–402.

Baker, Jr, Houston A. (1993) *Rap and the Academy* (Chicago and London: University of Chicago Press).

Baker, William and Minogue, Kylie (2002) *Kylie: La La La* (London: Hodder & Stoughton).

Baldaev, Danzig, Vasiliev, Sergei and Plutser-Sarno, Alexei (2009) *Russian Criminal Tattoo Encyclopaedia* (London: Fuel Publishing).

Barnfield, Graham (2002) *Reality TV: How Real is Real?* (London: Hodder & Stoughton).

Barron, Lee (2007) 'The Habitus of Elizabeth Hurley: Celebrity, Fashion and Identity Branding', *Fashion Theory: The Journal of Dress, Body & Culture*, Vol. 11, No. 4, pp. 443–61.

Barron, Lee (2009) 'An Actress Compelled to Act: Angelina Jolie's Notes from My Travels as Celebrity Activist/Travel Narrative', *Postcolonial Studies*, Vol. 12, No. 2, pp 211–28.

Barron, Lee (2010) 'Intergalactic Girlpower: The Gender Politics of Companionship in 21st Century Doctor Who', in Hansen, Chris (ed.) *Ruminations, Peregrinations, and Regenerations: A Critical Approach to Doctor Who* (Cambridge: Scholars Publishing), pp. 130–49.

Barthes, Roland (1993) *Mythologies* (London: Vintage).

Bauman, Zygmunt (1989) *Modernity and the Holocaust* (Cambridge: Polity Press).

Bauman, Zygmunt (2000) *Liquid Modernity* (Cambridge: Polity Press).

Bauman, Zygmunt (2003) *Liquid Love* (Cambridge: Polity Press).

Bauman, Zygmunt (2006) *Liquid Fear* (Cambridge: Polity Press).

Bauman, Zygmunt (2007) *Liquid Times: Living in an Age of Uncertainty* (Cambridge: Polity Press).

Beasley, Chris (1999) *What is Feminism?* (London: Sage).

Bayley, Stephen and Mavity, Roger (2007) *Life's a Pitch* (London: Corgi).

Beeler, Karin and Beeler, Stanley (2007) *Investigating Charmed: The Magic Power of TV* (London: I.B. Tauris).

Bell-Villada, Gene H. (2004) 'Who Was Ayn Rand?', *Salmagundi*, Issue 141/142, pp. 227–42.

Bendix, Reinhard (1966) *Max Weber: An Intellectual Portrait* (London: Methuen).

Benn, Tansin, Pfister, Gertrud and Jawad, Haifaa (eds) (2011) *Muslim Women and Sport* (London and New York: Routledge).

Bennett, Andy (1999) 'Subcultures or Neo-Tribes? Rethinking the Relationship between Youth, Style and Musical Taste', *Sociology*, Vol. 33, pp. 599–617.

Bennett, Andy (2000) *Popular Music and Youth Culture* (Basingstoke: Macmillan Press Ltd).

Bennett, Andy (2004) *After Subculture: Critical Studies in Contemporary Youth Culture* (Basingstoke: Palgrave Macmillan).

Benson, Susan (2000) 'Inscriptions of the Self: Reflections on Tattooing and Piercing in Contemporary Euro-America', in Caplan, Jane (ed.) *Written on the Body* (London: Reaktion Books), pp. 234–54.

Berger, Arthur Asa (2011) 'The Branded Self: On the Semiotics of Identity', *The American Sociologist*, Vol. 42, Issue 2, pp. 232–37.

Bignell, Jonathan (2004) *Media Semiotics* (Manchester and New York: Manchester University Press).

Blumer, Herbert (1958) 'Race Prejudice as a Sense of Group Position', *Pacific Sociological Review*, Vol. 1, No. 1, pp. 3–7.

Boaz, David (ed.) (1998) *The Libertarian Reader* (New York: The Free Press).

Boerma, Lindsey (2011) 'Tea Party Group Pushes Ayn Rand Movie', *The National Journal*, 23 March.

Boorstin, Daniel (1992) *The Image: A Guide to Pseudo-Events in America* (Harmondsworth: Penguin).

Bordo, Susan (1993) '"Material Girl": The Effacement of Postmodern Culture', in Bordo, Susan (ed.) *Unbearable Weight: Feminism, Western Culture and the Body* (Berkeley: University of California Press), pp. 268–75.

Bourdieu, Pierre (1984) *Distinction: A Social Critique of the Judgement of Taste* (Routledge & Kegan Paul).

Bourdieu, Pierre (1998) 'Utopia of Endless Exploitation: The Essence of Neoliberalism', *Le Monde Dipomatique*. http://mondediplo.com/1998/12/08bourdieu (accessed 23/11/2011).

Bowden, Gary (2010) 'Obama, Palin, and Weber: Charisma and Social Change in the 2008 U.S. Election', *Canadian Review of Sociology*, Vol. 47, No. 2, pp. 171–90.

Boyle, Raymond and Haynes, Richard (2000) *Power Play: Sport, the Media and Popular Culture* (Harlow: Pearson Education Limited).

Branston, Gill and Stafford, Roy (2010) *The Media Student's Book*, 5th edn (London and New York: Routledge).

Braudy, Leo (1986) *The Frenzy of Renown: Fame and Its History* (Oxford: Oxford University Press).

Brooker, Will (2002) *Using the Force: Creativity, Community and "Star Wars" Fans* (London: Continuum).

Brooks, Carol (2004) 'What celebrity worship says about us'. USATODAY.com http://www.usatoday.com/news/opinion/editorials/2004-09-13-celebrity-edit_x.htm (accessed 03/06/2011).

Brown, Callum G. (2009) *The Death of Christian Britain: Understanding Secularisation, 1800-2000* (London and New York: Routledge).

Brown, William J., Basil, Michael, D. and Bocarnea, Mihai. C. (2003) 'Social Influence of an International Celebrity: Responses to the Death of Princess Diana', *Journal of Communication*, December.

Buckingham, David (1987) *Public Secrets: EastEnders and its Audience* (London: BFI Books).

Burns, Jennifer (2009) *Goddess of the Market: Ayn Rand and the American Right* (Oxford: Oxford University Press).

Burton Nelson, Mariah (1996) *The Stronger Women Get, The More Men Love Football: Sexism and the Culture of Sport* (London: The Women's Press).

Callinicos, Alex (1989) *Against Postmodernism: A Marxist Critique* (Cambridge: Polity Press).

Callinicos, Alex (2003) *An Anti-Capitalist Manifesto* (Cambridge: Polity Press).

Callinicos, Alex (2007) *Social Theory: A Historical Introduction* (Cambridge: Polity Press).

Carter, Eric M. and Carter, Michael V. (2007) 'A Social Psychological Analysis of Anomie Among National Football League Players', *International Review For The Sociology Of Sport*, Vol. 42, No. 3, pp. 243–70.

Carter, Michael (2003) *Fashion Classics: From Carlyle To Barthes* (Oxford and New York: Berg).

Cashmore, Ellis (2002) *Beckham* (Cambridge: Polity).

Cashmore, Ellis (2010) *Making Sense of Sport* (London and New York: Routledge).

Centellas, Miguel (2010) 'Pop Culture in the Classroom: American Idol, Karl Marx, and Alexis de Tocqueville', *PS: Political Science & Politics*, Vol. 43, pp. 56–65.

Church Gibson, Pamela (2012) *Fashion and Celebrity Culture* (London and New York: Berg).

Coe, Jonathan (1994) *What a Carve Up!* (London: Viking).

Cole, C.L. (2000) 'The Year that Girls Ruled', *Journal of Sport and Social Issues*, Vol. 24, No. 3, pp. 3–7.

Coleman, Mark (2009) 'Ayn Rand's *Atlas Shrugged* climbs up charts during recession', *The Telegraph*, 10 March.

Connell, R.W. (2005) *Masculinities*, Second Edition (Cambridge: Polity).

Connor, Stephen (1989) *Postmodernist Culture: An Introduction to Theories of the Contemporary* (Oxford: Blackwell).

Craik, Jennifer (1994) *The Face of Fashion* (London and New York: Routledge).

Craik, Jennifer (2009) *Fashion: The Key Concepts* (Oxford and New York: Berg).

Crow, David (2010) *Visible Signs: An Introduction to Semiotics in the Visual Arts* (Switzerland: AVA Academia).

Cummings, Dolan, Clark, Bernard, Mapplebeck, Victoria, Dunkley, Christopher and Barnfield, Graham (2002) *Reality TV: How Real Is Real?* (London: Hodder & Stoughton).

Cunningham, Patricia A. and Voso Lab, Susan (1991) *Dress and Popular Culture* (Bowling Green: Bowling Green University Popular Press).

Curry, Patrick (1997) *Defending Middle-Earth: Tolkien: Myth and Modernity* (London: HarperCollinsPublishers).

de Beauvoir, Simone (1988) *The Second Sex* (London: Picador).

de Saussure, Ferdinand (2008) *Course in General Linguistics* (Illinois: Open Court).

Delmar, Rosalind (1986) 'What is Feminism?', in Mitchell, Juliet and Oakley, Ann (eds) *What is Feminism?* (Oxford: Basil Blackwell).

DeMello, Margo (2000) *A Cultural History of the Modern Tattoo Community* (Durham and London: Duke University Press).

Denisoff, Serge R. and Peterson, Richard A. (1972) *The Sounds of Social Change* (Chicago: Rand McNally College Publishing Company).

Derrida, Jacques (trans. Gayatri Chakravorty Spivak) (1997) *Of Grammatology* (Baltimore and London: The Johns Hopkins University Press).

Douglas, J., Uyl, Den and Rasmussen, Douglas B. (1998) 'Ayn Rand on Rights and Capitalism', in Boaz, David (ed.) (1998) *The Libertarian Reader* (New York: The Free Press), pp. 169–81.

Durkheim, Émile (1964) *The Rules of Sociological Method* (New York: The Free Press of Glencoe).

Durkheim, Émile (1976) *The Elementary Forms of the Religious Life* (London: George Allen & Unwin LTD).

Durkheim, Émile (1984) *The Division of Labour in Society* (Basingstoke: MacMillan).

Durkheim, Émile (2002) *Suicide* (London and New York: Routledge).

Dyer, Richard (1982) *Stars* (London: BFI).

Easton Ellis, Bret (1991) *American Psycho* (London: Picador).

Eco, Umberto (1976) *A Theory of Semiotics* (London: Indiana University Press).

Entwistle, Joanne (2000) *The Fashioned Body: Fashion, Dress and Modern Social Theory* (Cambridge: Polity Press).

Evans, Jessica (2004) 'Celebrity, media and history', in Evans, Jessica and Hesmondhalgh, David (eds) *Understanding Media: Inside Celebrity* (Maidenhead: The Open University Press), pp. 11–57.

Eyerman, Ron, and Jamison, Andrew (1998) *Music and Social Movements: Mobilising Traditions in the Twentieth Century* (Cambridge: Cambridge University Press).

Faludi, Susan (1992) *Backlash: The Undeclared War Against Women* (London: Vintage).

Fingeroth, Danny (2008) *The Rough Guide to Graphic Novels* (London: Rough Guides).

Firestone, Shulamith (1971) *The Dialectic of Sex: The Case for Feminist Revolution* (London: Cape).

Fiske, John (1989) *Reading the Popular* (London: Routledge).

Fiske, John (1990) *Introduction to Communication Studies* (London: Routledge).

Forman, Murray (2002) *The Hood Comes First: Race, Space, and Place in Rap and Hip-Hop* (Connecticut: Wesleyan University Press).

Forster, Samantha Vettese (2009) 'Connections between Modern and Postmodern Art and Fashion', *The Design Journal*, Volume 12, No.r 2, pp. 217–41.

Frankel, Susannah (2006) 'Review of the Year: Rise of the Wags', *The Independent*, Friday 29 December.

Friedan, Betty (1963) *The Feminine Mystique* (London: Penguin Books).

Friedman, Milton (1982) *Capitalism and Freedom* (Chicago and London: The University of Chicago Press).

Friedman, Milton and Friedman, Rose (1980) *Free to Choose* (London: Secker & Warburg).

Frisby, David (1985) *Fragments of Modernity* (Cambridge: Polity).

Frisby, David (1992) *Simmel and Since: Essays on Georg Simmel's Social Theory* (London: Routledge).

Frisby, David (2002) *Georg Simmel* (Key Sociologists) (London and New York: Routledge).

Fuller, Simon (2011) 'Simon Fuller on how 'Idol' began', *Variety*: http://www.variety.com/article/VR1118037190?refcatid=14&printerfriendly=true (accessed 01/07/2011).

Gamble, Andrew (1996) *Hayek: The Iron Cage of Liberty* (Cambridge: Polity Press).

Garland, Robert (2010) 'Celebrity Ancient and Modern', *Society*, Vol. 47, No. 6, pp. 484–88.

Gauntlett, David (2004) 'Madonna's Daughters: girl power and the empowered girl-pop breakthrough', in Fouz-Hernandez, Santiago and Jarman-Ivens, Freya (eds) *Madonna's Drowned Worlds: New Approaches to her Cultural Transformations, 1983-2003* (Aldershot: Ashgate), pp. 161–76.

Gerth, H.H. and Mills, C. Wright (1961) *From Max Weber: Essays in Sociology* (London: Routledge & Kegan Paul).

Gibson, Pamela Church (2000) 'Redressing the Balance: Patriarchy, Postmodernism and Feminism', in Bruzzi, Stella and Gibson, Pamela Church (eds) *Fashion Cultures: Theories, Explorations and Analysis* (London and New York: Routledge), pp. 349–63.

Giddens, Anthony (1971) *Capitalism and Modern Social Theory: An Analysis of the Writings of Marx, Durkheim and Max Weber* (Cambridge: Cambridge University Press).

Gilbert, David (2000) 'Urban Outfitting: The City and the Spaces of Fashion Culture', in Bruzzi, Stella and Church Gibson, Pamela (eds) *Fashion Cultures: Theories, Explorations and Analysis* (London and New York: Routledge), pp. 7–25.

Giles, David (2000) *Illusions of Immortality: A Psychology of Fame and Celebrity* (Basingstoke: Macmillan).

Gilman, Charlotte Perkins (1999) *Herland* (Dover Publications).

Gilman, Charlotte Perkins (1998) *Women and Economics* (Berkeley: University of California Press).

Giulianotti, Richard and Robertson, Roland (2009) *Globalization and Football* (Los Angeles and London: Sage).

Goffman, Erving (1959) *The Presentation of Self in Everyday Life* (London: Penguin Books).

Golding, Peter (1974) *The Mass Media* (New York: Longman).

Goodman, Lizzy (2010) *Lady Gaga: Extreme Style* (London: HarperCollins Publishers).

Gorman, Paul (2001) *The Look: Adventures in Pop & Rock Fashion* (London: Sanctuary Publishing Limted).

Gravett, Paul (2005) *Graphic Novels* (London: Collins Designer).

Greenspan, Alan (2007) *The Age of Turbulence: Adventures in a New World* (London: Allen Lane).

Grossberg, Lawrence (1992) 'Is There a Fan in the House? The Affective Sensibility of Fandom', in Lewis, Lisa A. (ed.) *The Adoring audience: fan culture and popular media* (London and New York: Routledge), pp. 50–69

Guins, Raiford and Zaragoza Cruz, Omayra (2005) *Popular Culture: A Reader* (London: Sage).

Gupta-Carlson, Himanee (2010) 'Planet B-Girl: Community Building and Feminism in Hip-Hop', *New Political Science*, Vol. 32, No. 4, pp. 515–29.

Hall, Stuart (1992) 'The Question of Cultural Identity', in Hall, Stuart and McGrew, Tony (eds) *Modernity and its Futures* (Open University Press), pp. 273–27.

Hall, Stuart *et al.* (1978) *Policing The Crisis: Mugging, the State, and Law and Order* (London and Basingstoke: The Macmillan Press LTD).

Hall, Stuart and Jefferson, Tony (eds) (1976) *Resistance Through Rituals: Youth Subcultures in Post-War Britain* (London: Hutchinson).

Hambly, Wilfrid Dyson (2009) *The History of Tattooing* (New York: Dover Publications, Inc).

Hamilton, Peter (1992) 'The Enlightenment and the Birth of Social Science', in Hall, Stuart and Gieben, Bram (eds) *Formations of Modernity* (Cambridge: The Open University), pp. 17–71.

Hargreaves, Jennifer (1994) *Sporting Females: Critical Issues in the History and Sociology of Women's Sports* (London and New York: Routledge).

Harvey, David (2007) *A Brief History of Neoliberalism* (Oxford: Oxford University Press).

Harvey, David (2010) *The Enigma of Capital and the Crises of Capitalism* (London: Profile).

Hawkins, Stan (2002) *Settling the Score: Pop Texts and Identity Politics* (Aldershot: Ashgate).

Hebdige, Dick (1979) *Subculture: The Meaning of Style* (London: Routledge).

Herman, Edward S. and Chomsky, Noam (2002) *Manufacturing Consent: The Political Economy of the Mass Media* (New York: Pantheon Books).

Hill, Annette (2005) *Reality TV: Audiences and Popular Factual Television* (London and New York: Routledge).

Hills, Matt (2002) *Fan Cultures* (London and New York: Routledge).

Himanen, Pekka (2001) *The Hacker Ethic and the Spirit of the Information Age* (London: Vintage).

Hobson, Dorothy (1982) *Crossroads: The Drama of a Soap Opera* (London: Methuen).

Hodkinson, Paul (2002) *Goth: Identity, Style and Subculture* (Oxford and New York: Berg).

Hoe-Lian Goh, Dion, and Sian Lee, Chei (2011) 'An Analysis of Tweets in Response to the Death of Michael Jackson', *New Information Perspectives*, Vol. 63, No. 5, pp. 432–44.

Hollander, Paul (2010) 'Michael Jackson, the Celebrity Cult, and Popular Culture', *Culture and Society*, Vol. 47, pp. 147–52.

Holmes, Su (2004) '"All you've got to worry about is the task, having a cup of tea, and doing a bit of sunbathing": approaching celebrity in *Big Brother'*, in Holmes, Su and Jermyn, Deborah (eds) *Understanding Reality Television* (London and New York: Routledge), pp. 111–36.

hooks, bel (2000) *Feminist Theory: From Margin To Center*, Second Edition (Brooklyn and Boston: South End Press).

Horkheimer, Max and Adorno, Theodor W. (1973) *The Dialectic of Enlightenment* (trans. John Cumming) (London: Allen Lane).

How, Alan (2003) *Critical Theory* (Basingstoke: Palgrave Macmillan).

Huntington, Samuel P. (2002) *The Clash of Civilizations and the Remaking of World Order* (London: Free).

Inglis, Fred (2010) *A Short History of Celebrity* (Princeton: Princeton University Press).

Irving, John (2006) *Until I Find You* (London: Black Swan).

Jenkins, Henry (1992) *Textual Poachers* (New York: Routledge).

Jenkins, Henry (2008) *Convergence Culture: Where Old and New Media Collide* (New York University Press).

Johnson, Richard (2006) 'Exemplary Differences: Mourning (and Not Mourning) A Princess', in Marshall, P. David (ed.) *The Celebrity Culture Reader* (London and New York: Routledge), pp. 510–30.

Jones, Mablen (1987) *Getting It On: The Clothing of Rock 'n' Roll* (New York: Abbeville).

Kaplan, E. Ann (1988) *Rocking Around the Clock: Music Television, Postmodernism and Consumer Culture* (New York and London: Routledge).

Kellner, Douglas (1992) 'Popular Culture and the Construction of Postmodern Identities', in Lash, Scott and Friedman, Jonathan (eds) *Modernity and Identity* (Oxford: Blackwell), pp 141–78.

Kellner, Douglas (1995) *Media Culture: Cultural Studies, Identity and Politics Between the Modern and the Postmodern* (London and New York: Routledge).

Kellner, Douglas (2003) *Media Spectacle* (London and New York: Routledge).

Kendrick, Ames (1999) 'Marxist Overtones in Three Films by James Cameron', *Journal of Popular Film and Television*, Vol. 27, No. 3, pp. 36–44.

King, Anthony (1997) 'The Lads: Masculinity and the New Consumption of Football', *Sociology*, Vol. 31, No. 2, pp. 329–46.

King, Barry (2010) 'Stardom, Celebrity, and the Money Form', *The Velvet Light Trap*, No. 65, pp. 7–19.

Klein, Gabriele (2003) 'Image, Body and Performativity: The Construction of Subcultural Practice in the Globalized World of Pop', in Muggleton, David and Weinzierl, Rupert (eds) *The Post-Subcultures Reader* (Oxford and New York: Berg), pp. 41–51.

Kleinhans, Chuck (2000) 'Marxism and Film', in Hill, John and Church Gibson, Pamela (eds) *Film Studies: Critical Approaches* (Oxford: Oxford University Press), pp. 104–15.

König, Anna (2006) 'Sex and the City: a fashion editor's dream?', in Akass, Kim and McCabe, Janet (eds) *Reading Sex and the City* (London and New York: I.B. Tauris).

Kurzman, Charles et al. (2007) 'Celebrity Status', *Sociological Theory*, Vol. 25, No. 4, pp. 347–67.

Leitch, Vincent B. (1983) *Deconstructive Criticism: An Advanced Introduction* (New York:Columbia University Press).

Lemert, Charles (2006) *Durkheim's Ghosts: Cultural Logics and Social Things* (Cambridge: Cambridge University Press).

Levitt, Linda (2010) 'Death on Display: Reifying Stardom through Hollywood's Dark Tourism', *The Velvet Light Trap*, No. 65, pp. 62–70.

Lister, Linda (2001) 'Divafication: The deification of modern female pop stars', *Popular Music and Society*, Vol. 25, Nos. 3–4, pp. 1–10.

Lockwood, David (1966) *The Blackcoated Worker: A Study in Class Consciousness* (London: Allen & Unwin).

Lombroso, Cesare (2006) (translated by Gibson, Mary and Hahn Rafter, Nicole) *Criminal Man* (Durham and London: Duke University Press).

Longhurst, Brian *et al.* (2008) *Introducing Cultural Studies* (Harlow: Longman).

Lukes, Steven (1973) *Émile Durkheim: His Life and Work* (London: Allen Lane and the Penguin Press).

Lyotard, Jean François (1984) *The Postmodern Condition: A Report on Knowledge* (Manchester: Manchester University Press).

Maher, George Ciccariello (2005) 'Brechtian Hip-Hop: Didactics and Self-Production in Post-Gangsta Political Mixtapes', *Journal of Black Studies*, Vol. 36, No. 1, pp. 129–60.

Marche, Stephen (2010) 'The Glittering Skull: Celebrity Culture as World Religion', *Queen's Quarterly*, Vol. 117, No. 1.

Marcuse, H. (1964) *One-Dimensional Man* (London: Routledge & Kegan Paul).

Marshall, David P. (1997) *Celebrity and Power: Fame in Contemporary Culture* (Minneapolis and London: University of Minneapolis Press).

Marx, Karl (1903) *A Contribution to the Critique of Political Economy* (Forgotten Books).

Marx, Karl (1974) *Capital: Volume 1* (London: Lawrence & Wishart).

Marx, Karl (1990) *Selected Writings in Sociology and Social Philosophy*, edited by Bottomore, T.B. and Rubel, Maximilien (London: Penguin).

Marx, Karl (1991) *Capital: Volume 3* (London: Lawrence & Wishart).

Marx, Karl (1998) *The German Ideology* (New York: Prometheus Books).

Marx, Karl (2007) *Dispatches for the New York Tribune: Selected Journalism of Karl Marx* (London: Penguin).

Marx, Karl and Engels, Friedrich (1985) *The Communist Manifesto* (London: Penguin Books).

McDonald, Chris (2009) *Rush: Rock Music and the Middle Class* (Indianapolis: Indiana University Press).

McDonald, Mary G. (2005) 'Model Behaviours?: Sporting Feminism and Consumer Culture', in Jackson, Steve J. and Andrews, David L. (eds) *Sport, Culture and Advertising: Identities, Commodities and the Politics of Representation* (London and New York: Routledge), pp. 24–39.

McLaughlin, Noel (2000) 'Rock, Fashion and Performativity', in Bruzzi, Stella and Church Gibson, Pamela (eds) *Fashion Cultures: Theories, Explorations and Analysis* (London and New York: Routledge), pp. 264–86.

McRobbie, Angela (1994) *Postmodernism and Popular Culture* (London and New York: Routledge).

McRobbie, Angela (2004) 'Post-Feminism and Popular Culture', *Feminist Media Studies*, Vol. 4, No. 3, pp. 253–64.

McRobbie, Angela (2008) 'Young Women and Consumer Culture', *Cultural Studies*, Vol. 22, No. 5, pp. 531–50.

Melville, C. (2004) 'Beats, Rhymes and Grime', *New Humanist*, Vol. 119, Issue 6. http://newhumanist.org.uk/822/beats-rhymes-and-grime (accessed 12/4/2010).

Mendes, Ana Cristina (2010) 'Showcasing India Unshining: Film Tourism in Danny Boyle's *Slumdog Millionaire*'. *Third Text*, Vol. 24, No. 4, pp. 471–79.

Miliband, Ralph (1973) *The State in Capitalist Society* (London: Quartet Books).

Miller, Janice (2011) *Fashion and Music* (Oxford: Berg).

Mills, C. Wright (1959) *The Sociological Imagination* (London, Oxford and New York: Oxford University Press).

Minogue, Kylie *et al.* (1999) *Kylie* (London: Booth-Clibborn Editions).

Mitrović, Ljubiša (2005) 'Bourdieu's Criticism of the Neoliberal Philosophy of Development, The Myth of *Mondialization* and the New Europe', *Philosophy, Sociology and Psychology*, Vol. 4, No. 1, pp. 37–49.

Miyakawa, Felicia M. (2005) *Five Percenter Rap: God Hop's Music, Message, and Black Muslim Mission* (Bloomington and Indianapolis: Indiana University Press).

Morley, David and Robins, Kevin (1995) *Spaces of Identity: Global Media, Electronic Landscapes and Cultural Boundaries* (London and New York: Routledge).

Napier, Susan J. (2000) *Anime: From Akira to Princess Mononoke* (New York: Palgrave Macmillan).

Negus, Keith (1999) *Music Genres and Corporate Cultures* (London: Routledge).

Nelson, Geoffrey. K. (1969) *Spiritualism and Society* (London: Routledge & Kegan Paul).

Nozick, Robert (1974) *Anarchy, State, and Utopia* (Oxford: Blackwell Publishing).

Ogbar, Jeffrey O.G. (1999) 'Slouching Toward Bork: The Culture Wars and Self-Criticism in Hip-Hop Music', *Journal of Black Studies*, Vol. 30, No. 2, pp. 164–83.

Orend, Angela and Gagné, Patricia (2009) 'Corporate Logo Tattoos and the Commodification of the Body', *Journal of Contemporary Ethnography*, Vol. 38, pp. 493–517.

Ouellette, Laurie and Hay, James (2008) *Better Living Through Reality TV; Television and Post-Welfare Citienship* (Oxford: Blackwell).

Paglia, Camille (2010) 'Lady Gaga and the death of sex', *Sunday Times Magazine*, 12 September http://www.thesundaytimes.co.uk/sto/public/magazine/article389697.ece (accessed 14/10/2011).

Parker, Andrew and Lyle, Samantha (2005) 'Chavs and Metrosexuals: New Men, Masculinities and Popular Culture', *Sociology Review*, Vol. 15, No. 11.

Parkin, Frank (2002) *Max Weber* (London and New York: Routledge).

Parry, Albert (2006) *Tattoo: Secrets of a Strange Art* (New York: Dover Publications, Inc.).

Peters, Georgina (2011) 'Lady Gaga, Guru: More Than Meets The Eye?', *Business Strategy Review*, Issue 2, pp. 69–71.

Phillips, Layli, Reddick-Morgan, Kerri and Stephens, Dionne Patricia (2005) 'Oppositional Consciousness Within An Oppositional Realm: The Case of Feminism and Womanism in Rap and Hip Hop, 1976-2004', *Journal of African American History*, Vol. 90, No. 3, pp. 253–77.

Pierce, Charles (2006) *Moving The Chains: Tom Brady and the Pursuit of Everything* (New York: Farrar, Straus & Giroux).

Pitts, Victoria (2003) *In The Flesh: The Cultural Politics of Body Modification* (New York: Palgrave Macmillan).

Plasketes, George (2005) 'Re-Flections on the Cover Age: A Collage of Continous Coverage in Popular Music', *Popular Music and Society*, Vol. 28, No. 2, pp. 137–61.

Rahmin, Momin (2006) 'Is Straight the New Queer? David Beckham and the Dialectics of Celebrity', in Marshall, P. David (ed.) *The Celebrity Culture Reader* (London and New York: Routledge), pp. 223–29.

Rand, Ayn (1964) *The Virtue of Selfishness* (New York: Signet).

Rand, Ayn (1967) *Capitalism: The Unknown Ideal* (New York: Signet).

Rand, Ayn (1992) *Atlas Shrugged* (New York: Signet).

Rand, Ayn (1994) *The Fountainhead* (London: HarperCollins Publishers).

Rand, Ayn (1995) *Anthem* (New York: Signet).

Rand, Ayn (1996) *We The Living* (New York: Signet).

Redmond, Sean (2010) 'Avatar Obama in the Age of Liquid Celebrity', *Celebrity Studies*, Vol. 1, No. 1, pp. 81–95.

Rief, Silvia (2009) *Club Cultures: Boundaries, Identities, and Otherness* (New York and London: Routledge).

Riley, Boots (2001) 'On Communism, Capitalism and Patriotism', http://www.lyric-stime.com (accessed 14/12/2010).

Ritzer, George. (1996) *The McDonaldization of Society* (California: Pine Forge Press).

Robertson, Pamela (1996) *Guilty Pleasures: Feminist Camp From Mae West To Madonna* (London and New York: I.B. Taurus).

Rogan, Johnny (1988) *Starmakers And Svengalis* (London: Queen Anne Press).

Rojek, Chris (2001) *Celebrity* (London: Reaktion Books).

Rojek, Chris (2007) *Cultural Studies* (Cambridge: Polity).

Roth, Amanda and Baslow, Susan (2004) 'Femininity, Sports, and Feminism: Developing a Theory of Physical Liberation', *Journal of Sport and Social Issue*, Vol. 28, pp. 245–65.

Saliba, John A. (1995) *Perspectives On New Religious Movements* (London: Geoffrey Chapman).

Sanders, Clinton R. (2008) *Customizing The Body: The Art and Culture of Tattooing* (Philadelphia: Temple University Press).

Schroeder, Ralph (1992) *Max Weber and the Sociology of Culture* (London: Sage).

Scambler, Graham (2005) *Sport and Society: History, Power and Culture* (Maidenhead: Open University Press).

Schneir, Miriam (ed.) (1996) *The Vintage Book of Historical Feminism* (London: Vintage).

Sciabarra, Chris Matthew. (2002) 'Rand, Rush, and Rock', *Journal of Ayn Rand Studies*, Vol. 4, No. 1, pp. 161–85.

Sciabarra, Chris Matthew (1995) *Ayn Rand: The Russian Radical* (Pennsylvania State University Press).

Segal, Lynne (1990) *Slow Motion: Changing Masculinities, Changing Men* (London: Virago).

Shermer, Michael (1997) *Why People Believe Weird Things: Pseudoscience, Superstition, and other Confusions of Our Time* (New York: Freeman).

Shuker, Roy (1998) *Key Concepts in Popular Music* (London: Routledge).

Silverstone, Roger (1994) *Television and Everyday Life* (London and New York: Routledge).

Simmel, Georg (1957) 'Fashion', *The American Journal of Sociology*, Vol. LXII, No. 6, pp 541–58.

Simmel, Georg (1971) *On Individuality and Social Forms* (Chicago and London: The University of Chicago Press).

Smart, Barry (2005) *The Sport Star: Modern Sport and the Cultural Economy of Sporting Celebrity* (London: Sage).

Smith, Adam (1999) *The Wealth of Nations: Books I-III* (London: Penguin).

Smitherman, Geneva (1997) '"The Chain Remains the Same": Communicative Practices in the Hip Hop Nation', *Journal of Black Studies*, Vol. 28, No. 1. pp. 3–25.

Snyder-Hall, Claire R. (2010) 'Third-Wave Feminism and the Defense of "Choice"', *Perspectives on Politics*, Vol. 8, No. 1, pp. 255–61.

Sontag, Susan (1994) 'Notes on "Camp"', in *Against Interpretation* (London: Vintage).

Spears, Betty (1978) 'Prologue: The Myth', in Oglesby, Carole. A. (ed.) *Women and Sport: From Myth to Reality* (Philadelphia: Lea & Febiger).

Spiegelman, Art (1996) *Maus: A Survivor's Tale* (London: Penguin Books).

Springhall, John (1998) *Youth, Popular Culture and Moral Panics: Penny Gaffs to Gangsta-Rap, 1830-1996* (Basingstoke: Macmillan).

Stevenson, Nick (2008) 'Living in "X Factor" Britain: Neo-Liberalism and "Educated" Publics', *Soundings: Class and Culture Debate*. http://www.1wbooks.co.uk/journals/soundings/class_and_culture/stevenson.html.

Stiglitz, Joseph (2010) *Freefall: Free Markets and the Sinking of the Global Economy* (London: Allen Lane).

Storey, John (1997) *An Introduction to Cultural Theory and Popular Culture* (Hemel Hempstead: Prentice Hall).

Storey, John (2003) *Cultural Studies and the Study of Popular Culture* (Edinburgh: Edinburgh University Press).

Storey, John (2009) *Cultural Theory and Popular Culture: An Introduction*, 5th edn (Harlow: Pearson).

Straubhaar, Joseph D.and LaRose, Robert (2006) *Media Now: Understanding Media, Culture, and Technolog* (Belmont: Thomson Wadsworth).

Strinati, Dominic (1995) *An Introduction to Theories of Popular Culture* (London and New York: Routledge).

Sullivan, Rachel E. (2003) 'Rap and Race: It's Got a Nice Beat, but What about the Message?', *Journal of Black Studies*, Vol. 33, No. 5, pp. 605–22.

Svendsen, Lars (2006) *Fashion: A Philosophy* (London: Reaktion).

Sweetman, Paul (1999) 'Anchoring the (postmodern) self? Body Modification, Fashion, and Identity', *Body and Society*, Vol. 5, No. 2, pp. 51–76.

Tabb Powell, Catherine (1991) 'Rap Music: An Education with a beat from the Street', *The Journal of Negro Education*, Vol. 60, No. 3, pp. 245–59.

Taylor, Ian, Walton, Paul and Young, Jock (1973) *The New Criminology: For a Social Theory of Deviance* (London and Boston: Routledge).

Tetzlaff, David (1993) 'Metatextual Girl: Patriarchy, Postmodernism, Power, Money, Madonna', in Cathy Schwichtenburg (ed.) The *Madonna Connection: Representational Politics, Subcultural Identites, and Cultural Theory* (New York: Westview).

Thornton, Sarah (1995) *Club Cultures: Music, Media and Subcultural Capital* (Cambridge: Polity Press).

Tincknell, Estella and Raghuram, Parvati (2002) 'Big Brother: reconfiguring the "active" audience of cultural studies?', *European Journal of Cultural Studies,* Vol. 5, No. 2, pp 199–216.

Tiryakian, Edward A. (1972) 'Toward the Sociology of Esoteric Culture', *American Journal of Sociology*, Vol. 78, No. 3, pp. 419–512.

Tong, Rosemarie (2009) *Feminist Thought,* 3rd edn (Boulder: Westview Press).

Toop, David (1984) *The Rap Attack: African Jive to New York Hip Hop* (London: Pluto Press).

Toop, David (1991) *Rap Attack 2: African Rap To Global Hip Hop* (London: Serpent's Tail).

Tumber, Howard (2001) 'Democracy in the information Age: The Role of the Fourth Estate in Cyberspace', *Information, Communication & Society*, Vol. 4, No.1, pp. 95–112.

Tungate, Mark (2008) *Fashion Brands: Branding Style from Armani to Zara* (London and Philadelphia: Kogan Press).

Turkle, Sherry (2011) *Alone Together* (New York: Basic Books).

Turner, Bryan S. (1991) 'Recent Developments in the Theory of the Body', in Featherstone, Mike, Hepworth, Mike and Turner, Bryan S. *The Body: Social Process and Cultural Theory* (London: Sage), pp. 1–36.

Turner, Graeme (2004) *Understanding Celebrity* (London: Sage).

Turnock, Robert (2000) *Interpreting Diana: Television Audiences and the Death of a Princess* (London: British Film Institute).

Vale, Vivian and Juno, Andrea (2010) *Modern Primitives: Modern Primitives: Investigation of Contemporary Adornment Rituals* (San Francisco: RE/Search).

Vale, Vivian and Ryan, Mike (eds) (2004) *J.G. Ballard: Quotes* (San Francisco: RE/Search Publications).

Vincendeau, Ginette (2000) *Stars and Stardom in French Cinema* (London and New York: Continuum).

Vincent, John, Hill, John S. and Lee, Jason W. (2009) 'The Multiple Brand Personalities of David Beckham: A Case Study of the Beckham Brand', *Sport Marketing Quarterly*, Vol. 18, pp. 173–80.

Voloshinov, V. (1973) *Marxism and the Philosophy of Language* (Massachusetts and London: Harvard University Press).

Von Mises, Ludwig (2005) *Liberalism: The Classical Tradition* (Indianapolis: Liberty Press).

Watson, C.W. (1997) 'Born a Lady, Became a Princess, Died a Saint: The Reaction to the Death of Diana, Princess of Wales', *Anthropology Today*, Vol. 13, No. 6, pp. 3–7.

Watson, Molly (2007) 'Wags and Riches', *Spectator*, 23 February.

Weber, Max (1978) *Economy and Class, Vol. 1* (Berkeley and London: University of California Press).

Weber, Max (2000) *The Protestant Ethic and the Spirit of Capitalism* (London and New York: Routledge).

Whannel, Garry (2007) 'Mediating Masculinities: The Production of Media Representations in Sport', in Carmichael Aitchinson, Cara (ed.) *Sport and Gender Identities: Masculinities, Femininities and Sexualities* (London and New York: Routledge).

Whannel, Garry (2010) 'News, Celebrity, and Vortextuality: A Study of the Media Coverage of the Michael Jackson Verdict', *Cultural Politics*, Vol. 6, Issue 1, pp. 65–84.

Wheen, Francis (2004) *How Mumbo-Jumbo Conquered The World* (London: London: Fourth Estate).

Whelehan, Imelda (1995) *Modern Feminist Thought: From the Second Wave to Post-Feminism* (Edinburgh: Edinburgh University Press).

White, Rosie (2007) *Violent Femmes: Women as Spies in Popular Culture* (London: Routledge).

Williams, Raymond (1976) *Keywords* (London: Fontana Press).

Williams, Raymond (1977) *Marxism and Literature* (Oxford: Oxford University Press).

Williams, Raymond (2003) *Television: Technology and Cultural Form* (New York: Routledge).

Wilson, Bryan (ed.) (1999) *New Religious Movements: Challenge and Response* (London: Routledge).

Wilson, Elizabeth (1992) 'Fashion and the Postmodern Body', in Ash, Juliet and Wilson, Elizabeth (eds) *Chic Thrills: A Fashion Reader* (London: HarperCollins), pp. 3–17.

Wilson, Elizabeth (2003) *Adorned in Dreams: Fashion and Modernity* (New Jersey: Rutgers University Press).

Wilson, Ross (2007) *Theodor Adorno* (London and New York: Routledge).

Wilson, Scott (2008) *Great Satan's Rage: American Negativity and Rap/Metal in the Age of Supercapitalism* (Manchester: Manchester University Press).

Wisnewski, J. Jeremy (2007) *Family Guy and Philosophy* (Oxford: Blackwell).

Wolf, Naomi (1991) *The Beauty Myth* (London: Verso).

Wroblewski, Chris (2004) *Skin Shows: The Tattoo Bible* (Hong Kong: Collins & Brown).

Wu, Ping (2009) 'From "Iron Girl" to "Sexy Goddess": An Analysis of the Chinese Media', in Markula, Pirkko (ed.) *Olympic Women and the Media: International Perspectives* (Basingstoke: Palgrave Macmillan), pp. 70–87.

Žižek, Slavoj (2001) *Enjoy Your Symptom: Jacques Lacan in Hollywood and Out* (London and New York: Routledge).

Žižek, Slavoj (2011) *Living in the End Times* (London and New York: Verso).

Index